WORDSWORTH'S
Guide to the Lakes

THE FIFTH EDITION (1835)

With an Introduction, Appendices, and
Notes Textual and Illustrative

BY

ERNEST DE SÉLINCOURT

D1173093

OXFORD   LONDON   NEW YORK
OXFORD UNIVERSITY PRESS
1977

Oxford University Press, Walton Street, Oxford OX2 6DP

OXFORD   LONDON   GLASGOW   NEW YORK
TORONTO   MELBOURNE   WELLINGTON   CAPE TOWN
IBADAN   NAIROBI   DAR ES SALAAM   LUSAKA   ADDIS ABABA
KUALA LUMPUR   SINGAPORE   JAKARTA   HONG KONG   TOKYO
DELHI   BOMBAY   CALCUTTA   MADRAS   KARACHI

ISBN 0 19 281219 X

First published 1906
Reprinted 1930, 1970, 1973
First issued as an Oxford University Press paperback 1977

Publisher's Note to 1970 reprint

In this reprint four illustrations have been added to the eight
in the original edition, facing pp. 166, 169, 171, and 173.
Pocklington's Island (see p. 71) by John Warwick Smith
comes from a set of lakeland engravings of 1795. Joseph
Wilkinson's view of Windermere is representative of the
illustrations to which the *Guide* was first annexed, and
which so angered Wordsworth (see p. iv). Ullswater and
Gatesgarthdale are aquatints from William Gilpin's
Observations relative to Picturesque Beauty (3rd ed. 1792)
(see pp. 194–5).

An index has also been added to this edition.

Printed in Great Britain
at the University Press, Oxford
by Vivian Ridler
Printer to the University

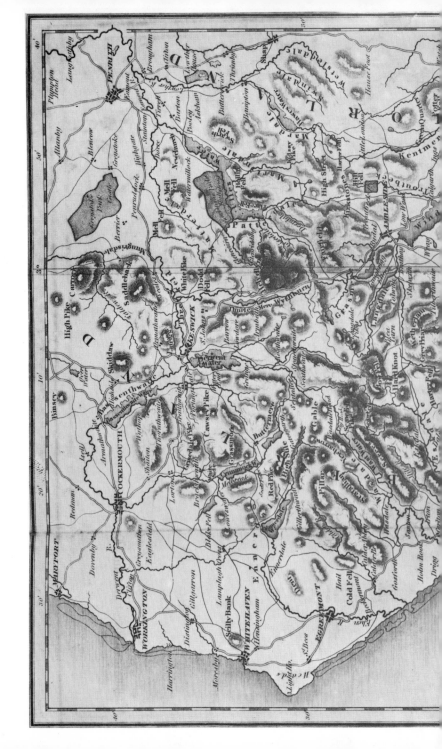

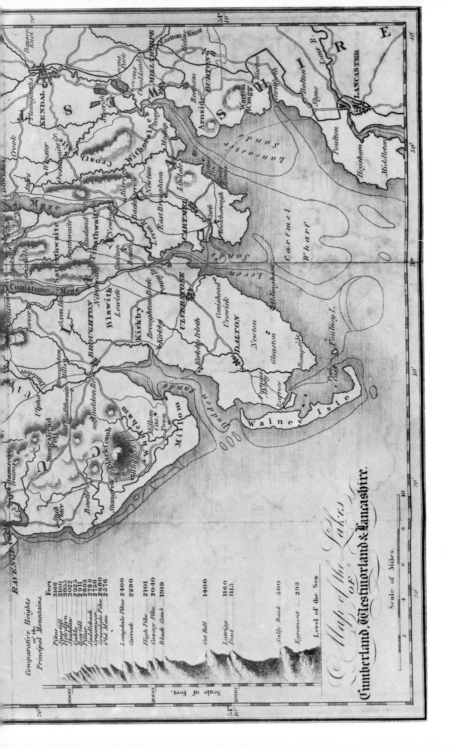

Map of the Lakes
OF
Cumberland, Westmorland & Lancashire.

Scale of Miles.

Comparative Heights
of the
Principal Mountains.

	Feet
Pikes	3166
Sca Fell	3160
Helvellyn	3055
Skiddaw	3022
Gable	2925
Bowfell	2911
Saddleback	2787
Grasmoor	2756
Grisdale Pike	2680
Old Man	2576
Langdale Pikes	2400
Carrock	2290
High Pike	2101
Gowey Pike	2040
Black Comb	1919
Cat Bell	1400
Latrigg	1160
Dent	1115
Selly Bank	500
Egremont	293
Level of the Sea	

Scale of Feet.

Walney Isle

INTRODUCTION

Wordsworth's *Guide to the Lakes* was first published in 1810, as an anonymous introduction to a large folio volume entitled:

Select Views | in | Cumberland, | Westmoreland, | and | Lancashire. | by the Rev. Joseph Wilkinson,[1] | Rector of East and West Wretham, in the county of Norfolk, | and Chaplain to | the Marquis of Huntly. | London : | Published, for the Rev. Joseph Wilkinson, by R. Ackermann, at his | Repository of Arts, 101, Strand. | 1810. |

This work was dedicated, not without pomposity, 'to the Right Honourable Thomas Wallace, M.P. etc. etc. etc. . . . to whose retentive memory and just discrimination' the artist appealed 'with some confidence', believing that his 'sketches have caught not only the general features, but the animation and the spirit . . . of the most picturesque part of the North'. But this confidence was hardly justified ; and the drawings, which are both inaccurate and lifeless,

---

[1] This Mr. Wilkinson, a clergyman, should not be confused with Wordsworth's friend Thomas Wilkinson, the Quaker. Cf. note, p. 184.

need no other comment than that which Wordsworth passed upon them in his letter to Lady Beaumont:—

'The drawings, or etchings, or whatever they may be called, are, I know, such as to you and Sir George must be intolerable. You will receive from them that sort of disgust which I do from bad poetry, a disgust which can never be felt in its full strength but by those who are practised in an art, as well as amateurs of it. I took Sir George's subscription as a kindness done to myself; and Wilkinson, though not superabundant in good sense, told me that he saw it in that light. I do however sincerely hope that the author and his wife may be spared the mortification of having them condemned severely by acknowledged judges. They will please many who in all the arts are most taken with what is worthless.' (*May* 10, 1810.)

Naturally enough, Wordsworth felt that his essay was ill-mated, and desired that it should appear in a form more likely to meet the eyes of sympathetic and intelligent readers. Accordingly, ten years later, it was republished with slight alterations in an octavo volume :

The | River Duddon, | A Series of | Sonnets : | Vaudracour & Julia : | and | Other Poems. | To which is annexed, | A Topographical Description | Of the | Country of the Lakes, | In the North of England. | By William Wordsworth. | London : | Printed for Longman, Hurst, Rees, Orme, and Brown, | Paternoster-Row, | 1820.

Here the essay attracted considerable attention, and two years afterwards made its first independent appearance as a 12mo volume with pp. i–iv of title and contents, 1–156 of text, and a map of the district facing the title-page:

A | Description | of the | Scenery of the Lakes | in | The North of England. | Third Edition, | (now first published separately) | With Additions, | and Illustrative Remarks upon the | Scenery of the Alps. | By William Wordsworth. | London : | Printed for | Longman, Hurst, Rees, Orme, and Brown, | Paternoster-Row. | 1822.

In the next year, 1823, a fourth edition appeared, with the same title as before, but the text in 144 pages, and printed by A. and R. Spottiswoode, New-Street-Square. This is not, as stated by Professor Knight, a mere reprint of the third edition ; apart from many minor alterations of detail, which show a careful revision of the text, it is now considerably enlarged; and several passages noted by Prof. Knight as added in the fifth edition, made their first appearance in the fourth.

In 1835 was issued Wordsworth's final text : A | Guide | Through the | District of the Lakes | in | The North of England, | with | A Description of the Scenery, etc. | For the Use of | Tourists and Residents. | Fifth Edition, | with considerable additions. | By William Wordsworth. Kendal : | Published by Hudson and Nicholson, | and in London by | Longman & Co., Moxon, and Whittaker & Co. | 1835.

This volume is also 12mo ; Title and Contents,

two leaves; Directions and information for the Tourist, pp. i–xxiv; Text, pp. 1–139. A map of the Lakes (reproduced in the present volume) faces the title-page.

The *Guide to the Lakes* had now taken a firm hold upon the popular regard. Mr. Matthew Arnold's story of the naïve ecclesiastic, who inquired of Wordsworth whether he had written anything else, may indeed be interpreted as a satire upon clerical learning, but it is at least a significant corroboration of the general popularity of the book. In 1842 it was incorporated in the *Guide to the Lakes* issued by Messrs. Hudson and Nicholson of Kendal, and edited by them. Its 'Advertisement' states that 'for much of the contents, the Introduction, Description of the Scenery of the Lakes, and a considerable portion of the Directions and Information for the Tourist Mr. Wordsworth is answerable, and he has much satisfaction in having been the means of inducing his friend Professor Sedgwick to contribute Three Letters on the Geology of the District . . . Botanical Notices are furnished by Mr. Gough, the Itineraries and admeasurements of distance having been compiled from Green's excellent *Guide to the Lakes*'. This book was republished in the next year, and reached a fourth edition in 1853, when Professor Sedgwick's three letters were increased to five. Other editions appeared in 1859 and 1864. Later than this, as far as I am aware, the book has had no independent existence; and though it has found its place in the collected Prose Works of Wordsworth, edited in 1876 by Dr. Grosart and in 1896 by Professor Knight, it has not attracted among readers of the poet the attention which is its due. Yet a description from the pen of Wordsworth of the country that none has ever known as he knew it is a rare possession, whilst it supplies a suggestive commentary to much of his greatest and most characteristic work. No apology, therefore, seems necessary for the present volume, an exact reprint of the fifth edition (1835).[1] To the main text have been added, as appendices, part of a letter to Sir George Beaumont *On Building and Gardening and Laying out of Grounds* and the *Letters on the Kendal and Windermere Railway*, which deal with subjects kindred to the theme of the Guide ; the notes contain other illustrative passages, and present a collation of the five editions, which records all but the most trivial alterations that from time to time were introduced into the text.

To the casual reader this somewhat laborious treatment of a guide book may seem unnecessary, even absurd; to the student of Wordsworth it will probably appear in a different light. Wordsworth wrote his book in the desire ' to give a model of the manner in which topographical descriptions ought to be executed, in order to their being either useful or intelligible, by evolving truly and distinctly one appearance from

---

[1] A few misprints of the fifth Edition, however, are corrected in the present issue.

another'; and he thought that in this he 'had not wholly failed'.[1] When he republished it, with the Duddon Sonnets, it was 'from a consciousness of its having been written in the same spirit which dictated several of the poems, and from a belief that it will tend naturally to illustrate them'; and the pains which he took, not only in its original composition, but in its continual improvement, will justify some study of its growth. These changes in the text are often trivial enough—the alteration of a clumsy or ambiguous sentence to one more lucid and shapely, the modification of an over-statement, the more accurate record of memorable phenomena—the importance lying not so much in the change itself as in the author's recognition of its advisability. It is not without amusement that we notice an attack upon the monotony of Scotch scenery, in contrast with the exquisite variety of Lakeland, tempered by the sobriety of advancing years; or a somewhat reckless promise of fine weather in June commuted to an assurance that 'at this time the traveller will be sure of room and comfortable accommodation even in the smaller inns'. But the chief interest of a comparison of successive editions lies in watching the ever growing power to express the heart of the subject, and in noting the supreme touch of colour or imaginative suggestion, added to a picture that a less scrupulous artist would have viewed with entire complacency. Wordsworth, like Milton, may

[1] Letter to Lady Beaumont, May 10, 1821.

have written prose with his left hand, but, like
Milton also, he wrote it far better with his left hand
than many authors with their right. His *Convention
of Cintra* was truly described as the most eloquent
political pamphlet since Burke; his critical essays,
despite their occasional failings in clear and logical
exposition, contain passages of inspired rhetoric
equal to anything, outside Shelley's *Defence of Poesy,*
that has been written upon the poetic art; and so
here, in the *Guide to the Lakes,* is a work instinct
with the genius of a poet, who, though ready for the
occasion to submit to the conditions of prose utterance, is yet unable to abrogate his nature, but continually illumines his subject with gleams of light
that have a rarer source.

Nowadays, alike by tourist and by student, Wordsworth is regarded not merely as the prophet of
Lakeland, but almost as its first discoverer. Yet
at the time of the poet's birth it was already becoming a popular resort, and in the last quarter
of the eighteenth century no part of England was
more often the subject of description and illustration.
As early, indeed, as 1755, one Dalton, an Oxford
Doctor of Divinity of Cumberland origin, published
in quarto his *Descriptive Poem addressed to Two
Ladies at their Return from Viewing The Mines near
Whitehaven,* in which, in fluent octosyllabic verse,
he praises with magnificent impartiality the trium-
phant advance of commercial enterprise and the
natural beauty of Keswick, Skiddaw, and Lodore.

It is probable that his poem attracted no more
attention than it deserved ; yet twenty years later it
gained a place in Pearch's famous collection (1775).
For during those twenty years the literary ideals
of the nation had undergone a gradual change.   The
supremacy of the classical spirit had now been chal-
lenged by a formidable rival, and the public that had
taken its highest pleasure in social satire and the
heroic couplet, now found its looser delight in the
irregular Ode, and showed an ever increasing partiality
for themes remote in time and place from its own
conventional surroundings.   Every one was interested
in the new romantic spirit, many were enthralled by
it ; and just at the time that Macpherson's Ossian
was arousing extravagant enthusiasm for a wilder
scenery, little known to literature, two men, pro-
minent representatives of opposing schools of thought,
came forward to direct attention to the English
Lakes, where the youthful appetite for mountain
and precipice might grow by what it fed on.

Dr. John Brown, the popular divine who ' charmed
the town ' by a lurid picture of its own degeneracy
in the *Estimate of the Manners and Principles
of the Times* (1757), had expressed his allegiance
to Pope in a poetical essay *On Satire* (1745), and he
may be taken as a characteristic representative
of the mid-eighteenth century spirit ; yet he had
a genuine feeling for natural scenery, and addressed
a letter to Lord Lyttelton (published in 1770 as
the work of ' a late popular writer '), in which he

dilated with some eloquence upon the beauties of
the Vale of Keswick. Here, too, in the autumn
of 1769, the poet Gray 'passed six days lap'd in
Elysium', and he recorded in his Journal his own
graceful and sensitive impressions of a memorable tour.

Thus supported by the new spirit and sanctioned
by the old, a feeling for the rugged and the mysterious
in nature became a fashionable affectation. Visitors
flocked to the Lake country in all the spirit of
adventurers, not a little oppressed by their own
hardihood, and furnished forth with all the necessary
emotional equipment. For the rest of the century
there was an immense output of books destined to
guide the path of the willing pilgrim.[1] Judged as
a whole these books are well written, and bear far
more resemblance, both in style and conception, to
the modern book of travel, than to the mere guide-
book. They display some careful observation and are
clearly sincere in their admiration. But they do
not afford invigorating reading. Descriptions of
nature, whether in prose or verse, cannot rank as

[1] The following list, which makes no pretence of complete-
ness will give some idea of the truth of the statement:—
*A Description of the Lake at Keswick (and the adjacent country)
in Cumberland; communicated in a Letter to a Friend, by a late
popular writer* (i. e. Dr. Brown) 1770. *Journal in the Lakes*,
by Thomas Gray, written 1769, published 1775. *Excursion to
the Lakes in Westmoreland and Cumberland*, by W. Hutchinson
(author of a History of Cumberland), published in 1773, 1774,
and 1776. *A Tour in Scotland in 1772*, by Thomas Pennant,
2 vols. 4to, 1774-76; 1790; 12mo, 1798. *A Six Months' Tour
through the North of England* (by Young), 1774. *A Guide to
the Lakes*, 8vo (anon.) 1778. *A Guide to the Lakes*, 8vo (anon.)
1780. *A Guide to the Lakes*, by Thomas West, 1778, 1779, 1784,

literature unless they are presented with so vivid
a sense of the relation of detail to the whole that
they become a picture, or are so vitalized by the
emotion of their author that they become a com-
municable experience. And these writers, in spite of
all their enthusiasm, remain outside their subject.
It is significant that their emotion does not spring
inevitably from the scene they describe, but is
brought into it from without; and they pass with

1789 (10th ed. in 1812). *Observations, relative chiefly to
picturesque beauty, in several parts of England, particularly the
Mountains and Lakes of Cumberland and Westmoreland,* by
William Gilpin, M.A., 2 vols. 8vo, 1786 and 3rd ed. 1792. *A
Survey of the Lakes, &c.,* by James Clarke, folio, 1789. *Remarks
made on a Tour from London to the Lakes* in 1791 by A. Walker,
8vo, 1792. *A fortnight's ramble to the Lakes,* by Joseph Budworth,
1792 (2nd ed. 1795). *A topographical description of Cumberland, Westmoreland, &c.,* by John Housman, 8vo, 1800. *A
descriptive Tour and Guide to the Lakes,* by J. Housman, 8vo,
1800. Green's *Guide to the Lakes* in 2 vols., referred to by
Wordsworth (p. 6, note), as 'a complete Magazine of minute
and accurate information', did not appear till 1818. I have
not been able to see this book.

Among poems attempting to describe the country, besides
those of Dalton (1755), and Richard Cumberland (1775), mentioned above, and those of Brown and Farish quoted by Wordsworth in the *Guide,* are to be mentioned *Netherby: A Poem,* by
Mr. Maurice of University College, Oxford, 4to (1776), and
Windermere: A Poem, by Joseph Budworth, 8vo (1798). But
before this Wordsworth's *Evening Walk* had already been
published. The increasing interest taken in the Lakes from
1770–80 is amusingly illustrated by a quotation in West's *Guide*
(4th ed.) from the *London Magazine* for Oct. 1778.

'Long has been the contention between the gentlemen of
Derbyshire and Cumberland, respecting Dovedale and Keswick,
each claiming the superiority of natural beauties, and Dr. Brown
has by many been thought to carry the dispute in favour of
Keswick. I have carefully surveyed both, without being a
native of either county, and if I might presume to be any
judge of the matter, I should compare Dovedale to the soft and
delicate maiden, and Keswick to the bold and sturdy Briton.'

a palpable uneasiness from the one to the other, relying for poetic effect upon the occasional intrusion of the correct romantic sentiment.[1] Thus William Gilpin, the author of *Observations relative to Picturesque Beauty in Westmoreland, etc.*, stands out from his brother craftsmen as possessed of unusual nicety of judgement, and his 'elegant and correct pen' is often the subject of their eulogy. Yet his final words upon Dunmail Raise betray the characteristic temper of his time. 'The whole view', he writes, 'is entirely of the horrid kind. With a view of adorning such a scene with figures, nothing could suit it better than a group of banditti. Of all the scenes I ever saw this was the most adapted to the perpetration of some dreadful deed.'

But the climax of this 'romantic' sentiment had already been attained in an *Ode to the Sun*, by Richard Cumberland, once a famous dramatist, but now little remembered save as a member of the Johnsonian circle and the victim of an epitaph in Goldsmith's incomparable *Retaliation*. In the au-

---

[1] West, whose Guide-book had by far the greatest vogue, practically acknowledges this difficulty, by drawing for his sentiment upon other authors, and often, naïvely enough, relegating it to a footnote. Thus he writes of Eagle-crag in Borrowdale 'On the front the bird of Jove has his annual nest', and appends this commentary :—' Or in more poetical terms—
Here his dread seat the royal bird hath made,
To awe th' inferior subjects of the shade,
Secure he built it for a length of days
Impervious, but to Phoebus' piercing rays ;
His young he trains to eye the solar light,
And soar beyond the fam'd Icarian flight.'
West was by natural taste an antiquary, but he knew that something of this kind was expected of him in a Guide-book.

tumn of 1775 Cumberland visited the Lakes in the
company of the Earl of Warwick, and commemorated
the event by an irregular ode.   Opening with an
invocation to the Sun, of conventional magnilo-
quence, he proceeds to describe his emotions upon
the ascent of Gowdar, an imposing but not very
lofty crag that rises above Lodore :—

> Trembling now with giddy tread,
> Press the moss on Gowdar's head ;
> But lo, where sits the bird of Jove,
> Couch'd in his eyrie far above ;
> Oh, lend thine eye, thy pinion lend,
> Higher, yet higher let me still ascend :
> 'Tis done ; my forehead smites the skies,
> To the last summit of the cliff I rise ;
> I touch the sacred ground,
> Where step of man was never found ;
> I see all Nature's rude domain around.
>
> .   .   .   .
>
> Press not so fast upon my aching sight,
> Gigantic shapes, nor rear your heads so high,
> As if ye meant to war against the sky,
> Sons of old Chaos and primaeval Night.

From such an eminence the poet can afford to scorn
alike the lowlier aspects of nature and 'the spruce
impertinence of art'; and he is led by an obvious
transition to moralize in the manner of Gray's *Ode to
Spring* :—

> Now downward as I bend my eye,
> What is that atom I espy,

That speck in nature's plan?
Great Heaven ! is that a man ?
And hath that little wretch its cares,
Its freaks, its follies, and its airs ;
And do I hear the insect say
' My lake, my mountain, my domain ' ?
O weak, contemptible, and vain !
  The tenant of a day.
Say to old Skiddaw, ' Change thy place.'
Heave Helvellyn from his base,
Or bid impetuous Derwent stand
At the proud waving of a master's hand.

Then ' with silent step and slow ' he descends from
the dizzy height to lament the death of Gray in
language borrowed at times from the poet himself, at
times from *Lycidas* and *Paradise Lost*. He concludes
with a pious welcome of the sun.

This Ode, Cumberland assures us, ' was literally
struck off upon the spot ', thus testifying to its
immediate inspiration. And there is evidence in
plenty that it was accepted by the age as the ade-
quate expression of the feelings which mountains
evoke in a man of taste and sensibility. Certainly,
even Mrs. Radcliffe, in her prose *Observations during
a Tour to the Lakes*, made no attempt to rival
its intensity ; and though, doubtless, she gained
many a ' horrid ' suggestion from her tour, her
remarks upon it are written with unusual restraint.
Perhaps she judged rightly in concentrating her
powers of romantic description upon the Apennines,
which she had never seen.

On the general character of his predecessors' work Wordsworth might have written an eloquent Appendix to his *Guide*; and it is a sign of grace in him that he said so little where he must have felt so much. Nor is it difficult to conjecture the lines that his indictment of them would have followed. Gray, alone of them all, had brought to his task the susceptibility of a poet's mind, and Wordsworth, not without a thought of the more studied and pretentious efforts of such writers as Gilpin, Young, and West, has a due word of praise for the 'distinctness and unaffected simplicity' of the *Journal*. But even Gray, like the rest of them, wanted that intimacy with his subject which alone could win him success. To call them tourists, bent upon recording a holiday experience, and attracted to the country by reason of its novelty, is a hard saying, but incontrovertible. What wonder then that they saw but its more obvious features and at times misinterpreted even the little that they saw, that when they were accurate they were dull and uninspired, that when they were enthusiastic they tended to become absurd? What wonder that they could not capture the secret of nature's beauty and significance, and remained untouched by those subtler influences which are the silent reward of a life dedicated to her love?

With Wordsworth it was otherwise. Derwent, the fairest of all rivers, had sent forth 'a voice that flowed along' his baby dreams. From his first dawn he was surrounded

> Not with the mean and vulgar works of man,
> But with high objects, and enduring things—
> With life and nature;

and he grew to manhood under the same benignant
tutelage. For all but three years of his life the
Lake Country was his home, and his absence from
it served only to intensify its hold upon him. It
gave him material with which to compare it; and
thereby he gained a fuller understanding of its own
intrinsic quality. Distance had no power to weaken
its fascination, for, wherever he might be, he felt at
his heart 'the spiritual presence of absent things';
and poems written in Somerset and in Germany are
touched alike with intimate reminiscence of his
native hills. Yet not for forty years did he attempt
a systematic delineation of his native country, and
another quarter of a century had passed before he
put the final touches to his picture. During all this
time his study was out of doors, and if the poems
are the first-fruits of his labours, there are few pages
of the *Guide* that do not bear eloquent witness to
the same watchful eye always upon the object, the
same reflective energy and penetrative imagination.
'My book,' said Wordsworth, with quiet truth,
'could not have been written without much experience.'

Wordsworth himself considered that there were
three callings for which nature had endowed him with
qualifications—those of poet, landscape gardener,

and critic of pictures and works of art; and, in point of fact, it is his aptitude for these callings, as he conceived them, that has gained for his *Guide to the Lakes* its unique place in topographical literature. For 'that practice by a strange abuse of terms denominated "ornamental gardening"' Wordsworth had a pious horror. He must have delighted in the satire, in Peacock's *Headlong Hall*, of the ideal and methods of the conventional landscape gardener; and the third section of his book is chiefly devoted to denunciation of the barbarisms that had already begun to desecrate his native region, and to suggestions as to how, in spite of its increasing popularity, it might yet be protected from rash and ignorant assault. His own fundamental principle, that where the traces of man's presence are unavoidable, the 'invisible hand of art should everywhere work in the spirit of Nature' and of 'Antiquity, her sister and co-partner', is fully developed in the *Guide*, and gives him many an opportunity of manifesting the minutest knowledge of every phenomenon characteristic of the country side. His deep-rooted conservatism, entirely noble when it strove to keep inviolate the sanctity of nature rather than to support the ephemeral prejudice of man, resented the intrusion of alien elements. Hence sprung his preference for his native plants, his plea for the sober colouring of buildings, his desire that in the management of grounds the wilder should gradually fade away into the more cultivated, so as 'to leave undisturbed that peaceful harmony of form and colour which has been through long lapse of ages most happily preserved'. Like most principles that have their root in a just instinct, this leads him occasionally into a fine extravagance. The attack upon the larch as a foreigner, when 'the embowering sycamore at the cottage side', admittedly imported from Germany not two hundred years before, is accorded its meed of praise, provokes the inquiry as to how soon the larch itself will be a resident of sufficient standing to be admired; and his relentless onslaught upon its ugliness as an individual tree,— spiky, boughless, a graceless egoist, will tend to raise hostility in the hearts of those who have welcomed in its delicate pink tassels a spring that never comes too soon; and have rejoiced in its early green, at first a mere shimmer upon the branch, but growing daily more vivid with renewed life, though its neighbours are still wrapt in their wintry sleep. Yet where his indictment is directed against the artificial plantation of mathematical shape, its justice is incontestable, and his harshest words fade from the memory before the graceful description of the process by which Nature forms her woods and forests, tolerating no rigid outline nor monotony of colour, but justifying their presence upon the hillside by delicate gradations of tint and form. It is worth our while to notice that Wordsworth's attack upon the poems of Macpherson was based upon this same position. 'In nature everything is distinct, yet nothing defined into absolute independent singleness. In Macpherson's work' (as in the larch plantation) 'everything is defined, insulated . . . yet nothing distinct.' Such a parallelism in his judgements upon the worlds of nature and of art is not without significance; for both, in his eyes, were ultimately referable to the same standard of beauty. Art could never succeed until it had learnt the lessons which nature had to teach, in so far as nature was to him, as to Sir Thomas Browne, the art of God.

And when he spoke of himself as qualified for the calling of critic of painting and the fine arts, he claimed no technical knowledge; rather was he thinking of the continual habit of his mind to reflect upon the principles which underlie all the varied manifestations of loveliness. He was never satisfied with a vague admiration founded upon caprice; his passion for what by instinct he knew to be beautiful was strengthened by his eager search for the grounds of its appeal to his emotions. Here the influence of Coleridge upon his thought is apparent; and the subject must often have been discussed by the two friends in the days of their closest intimacy. The conception of beauty as *Multeity in Unity*, put forward by Coleridge in his *Essay on the Fine Arts*, and of the sense of beauty as 'subsisting in the simultaneous institution of the relation of parts each to each, and of all to the whole', form the basis of much that is illuminating in Wordsworth's criticism of landscape. The margins of the lakes provide him

with an eloquent illustration of the manner in which
'the operations of nature tend to the production
of beauty by a multiplicity of symmetrical parts
uniting in a consistent whole'. And, conversely,
his recognition of this affected the manner in which
he himself studied nature. It exposed to him the
folly of those who go out, notebook in hand, to
make a catalogue of nature's charms, and think
that so her spirit cannot elude them. It became
with him an instinct to judge of a natural scene
in the light of an artistic composition, in which
all irrelevant detail sinks into its proper insignificance, and the main features of the landscape stand
out in bold relief against the sky. Let him but
gather it into 'a heart that watches and receives',
and express it through the medium of intense imaginative feeling, and it is a poem.

There are few pages of the *Guide to the Lakes* which
fail to reveal the poet. Wordsworth had not two ways
of looking at nature, according as his immediate
object was verse or prose. In this he had but one
creed; and in his devotion to it he was entirely
single-hearted. The intensity of his faith might,
indeed, vary with the character of his surroundings
and with the alertness of his vision, but he never
belied it; and if at times, as in the *Excursion*, or some
of the Duddon Sonnets, his spirit flags, so that his
verse sinks to the prosaic, the prose of the *Guide*
is often lit up with passages which not only illustrate the fundamental conceptions of his poetry, but

which, for their beauty of phrase and imaginative suggestion, are worthy of an honourable place beside it.

Wordsworth's attitude to nature as revealed in the *Guide* is in a sense all the more impressive in that it cannot be lightly put aside as due to the excitement of poetic composition,—a pleasing fancy not to be taken too seriously, and deprecated by his more sober judgement. The primary object of the *Guide to the Lakes* is to impart knowledge, and the book would stand above others of its class if it were judged solely by its appeal to the intellect and common sense. But just as a mother may reveal a depth of feeling by the tone of voice in which she tells the barest fact about her child, so Wordsworth cannot divorce his information from that emotion with which he always views its subject.

Of the mountains he can rarely speak except in the figured language of vitalizing love. If he tells us that the crumbling of the rocks is caused by the presence of iron in their composition, he adds that its effect is 'to give to their precipitous sides an inter-mixture of colours like the compound hues of a dove's neck'; if he records, with momentary reluctance, that his mountains are inferior in height to others in the island, he hastens to add that 'in the combinations which they make, towering above each other, or lifting themselves in ridges like the waves of a tumul-tuous sea, they are surpassed by none'. Even the birds whose song, wherever it is heard, goes straight to the poet's heart, have here a profounder beauty. 'Their notes listened to by the side of broad still water, or heard in unison with the murmuring of mountain-brooks, have the compass of their power enlarged accordingly. There is also an imaginative influence in the voice of the cuckoo, when that voice has taken possession of a deep mountain valley, very different from anything which can be excited by the same sound in a flat country.'

Thus the book expresses throughout that intimacy with nature, which springs from the deep joy of a personal devotion, and interprets every sight and sound as a man may read the familiar features of his friend. Such a love was only possible to Wordsworth because he conceived of Nature as herself endowed with life, and capable herself of both inward and responsive joy.

This is not the place to argue the intrinsic value of Wordsworth's faith, but at least it must be recognized that if it was an idle fiction, it was a fiction which haunted him through life, and was not a mere poetic affectation like the 'romantic' sentiment of his predecessors; it is as evident and as fundamental in the *Guide to the Lakes* as in *Hart-leap Well*, or *Yew-Trees*, or *Lines written in Early Spring*. His prose suffers no violent transition of thought or feeling when he speaks of the *mysterious attachments* of the clouds to the mountain tops, and describes them as 'cleaving to their stations or lifting up suddenly their heads from behind rocky barriers, or hurrying out of sight in the speed of the sharpest edge'. This is the habitual frame of mind in which he contemplates the mysterious beauty and the latent power of nature. So the lonely mountain tarn excites in him 'the sense of some *repulsive power strongly put forth,* and thus deepens the melancholy natural to such scenes', a melancholy which irresistibly attracts him, for he, like nature, is a compound of many elements. Similarly, when he deplores the indiscriminate ravages wrought by the axe upon an ancient forest, he is comforted by the thought of how, by Nature's benignity, the scars upon her face will gradually disappear before a *healing spirit.* Long tracts of dreary natural description are incompatible with such a faith; they are transmuted, perforce, into impassioned interpretation. The scene that Wordsworth presents to us is not merely imaged upon our brain, it is 'felt in the blood, and felt along the heart'.

But this sense of life in nature is most fully borne in upon him where a constant change of expression passes over the countenance of immutable loveliness, or where ceaseless motion wages a war with unruffled tranquillity. His watchful eye is continually arrested by scenes which can impart to him

> Authentic tidings of invisible things;
> Of ebb and flow, and ever-during power;
> And central peace, subsisting at the heart
> Of endless agitation.

This is the spell which binds him to the waterfall— 'the contrast maintained between the falling water

and that which is apparently at rest, or rather
settling gradually into quiet in the pool below. The
beauty of such a scene, where there is naturally so
much agitation, is also heightened, in a peculiar
manner, by the *glimmering*, and towards the verge
of the pool, by the *steady* reflection of the surrounding images.' Similarly, in what is perhaps the
subtlest and most finely wrought passage in the book,
he interprets the mysterious significance of the lake:
' Not a breath of air, no restlessness of insects and
not a moving object perceptible—except the clouds
gliding in the depths of the lake, or the traveller
passing along, an inverted image, whose motion
seems governed by the quiet of a time to which its
archetype, the living person, is, perhaps, insensible:—or it may happen, that the figure of one of
the larger birds, a raven or a heron, is crossing
silently among the reflected clouds, while the voice
of the real bird, from the element aloft, gently
awakens in the spectator the recollection of appetites
and instincts, pursuits and occupations, that deform
and agitate the world,—yet have no power to prevent nature from putting on an aspect capable of
satisfying the most intense cravings for the tranquil,
the lovely, and the perfect, to which man, the
noblest of her creatures, is subject.'

Naturally, then, on the climate of the Lake country,
which in the casual visitor is wont to provoke
irritation if not despair, Wordsworth is eloquent;
and upon those ' skiey influences ', that are constant

only in their change, he speaks his most pregnant words. It was so in his poetry. Just as the *Evening Walk*, in its delicate susceptibility to the effects of shifting light and colour, anticipates the distinctive greatness of his maturer work, so when the days of his creative energy were passed and the voice of his song was already enfeebled,

> The gleam—
> The shadow—and the peace supreme

of an evening of extraordinary splendour and beauty had power to kindle within him some of the old imaginative fire. And the same is true of his prose. In the brightness that succeeds a storm, 'when every hill is vocal and every torrent sonorous,' he is exultant; and the showers, upon days of unsettled weather, 'darkening or lightening as they fly from hill to hill,' affect him like finely interwoven passages of sad and gay music. And the heart of the exile in the city or the plain is filled with almost intolerable longing when the pages of Wordsworth unfold before him, as in the pageantry of a dream, visions of mountains 'whose forms and colours are perpetually changed by the clouds and vapours which float around them', of mists 'which brood upon the heights or descend upon the valleys with inaudible motion', of that clear autumn day 'when the atmosphere seems refined and the sky rendered more crystalline as the year abates', so that as the poet gazes upon the lake 'the heavens are brought down to the bosom

of the earth, which is looked at through the medium
of a purer element, and the imagination is carried
into recesses of feeling otherwise impenetrable'.

The full significance of such passages as these in
the history of Wordsworth's soul is only realized as
we recall those fateful discussions with Coleridge,
as together they roamed the Quantock hills, upon
the cardinal points of poetry—'the power of ex-
citing the sympathy of the reader by a faithful
adherence to the truth of nature, and the power
of giving the interest of novelty by the modifying
colours of imagination. The sudden charm which
accidents of light and shade, which moonlight or
sunset diffused over a known and familiar landscape
appeared to represent the practicability of combining
both. *These are the poetry of nature*[1].' Place by
the side of this the chief claim which Wordsworth
advances to the supreme beauty of his home—' I do
not know any tract of country in which, in so narrow
a compass, may be found an equal variety in the
influences of light and shadow upon the sublime and
beautiful features of the landscape,' and we gain
at once a deeper insight into the essential qualties
of his genius. We appreciate the vital relation
between his conceptions of nature and of poetry, and
sympathize with his inability to speak of the one
except in terms of the other.

Yet were I grossly destitute of all
Those human sentiments that make this earth

[1] *Biographia Literaria*, ch. xiv.

So dear, if I should fail with grateful voice
To speak of you, ye mountains, and ye lakes
And sounding cataracts, ye mists and winds
That dwell among the hills where I was born.

In truth, his rich dower of poetry, in no vague sense, was Nature's gift, and the *Guide to the Lakes* is but another token of his gratitude, another act of homage from the disciple.

The illustrations which are to be found among the notes of this volume are reproduced from books which appeared in Wordsworth's lifetime, and before the *Guide to the Lakes*. They will thus convey some idea of the appearance of the country in his day—at least as it was viewed by artists contemporary with him. It only remains to me to express my warmest thanks to Professor Dowden for his kindness in lending original copies of Wordsworth's *Letters on the Kendal and Windermere Railway*, thus enabling me to give a faithful reprint of its text. To my sister Miss T. de Sélincourt and to Miss Margaret Robertson I am indebted for much valuable help in the collation of the five editions of the *Guide*.

ERNEST DE SÉLINCOURT.

A

GUITDE

THROUGH THE

DISTRICT OF THE LAKES

IN

𝕿𝖍𝖊 𝕹𝖔𝖗𝖙𝖍 𝖔𝖋 𝕰𝖓𝖌𝖑𝖆𝖓𝖉,

WITH

A DESCRIPTION OF THE SCENERY, &c.

FOR THE USE OF

TOURISTS AND RESIDENTS.

FIFTH EDITION,
WITH CONSIDERABLE ADDITIONS.

By WILLIAM WORDSWORTH.

KENDAL:
PUBLISHED BY HUDSON AND NICHOLSON,
AND IN LONDON BY
LONGMAN & CO., MOXON, AND WHITTAKER & CO.
1835.

CONTENTS

SECTION THIRD.

CHANGES, AND RULES OF TASTE FOR PREVENTING THEIR BAD EFFECTS.

MISCELLANEOUS OBSERVATIONS.

DIRECTIONS AND INFORMATION

THE TOURIST

In preparing this Manual, it was the Author's principal wish to furnish a Guide or Companion for the *Minds* of Persons of taste, and feeling for Landscape, who might be inclined to explore the District of the Lakes with that degree of attention to which its beauty may fairly lay claim. For the more sure attainment, however, of this primary object, he will begin by undertaking the humble and tedious task of supplying the Tourist with directions how to approach the several scenes in their best, or most convenient, order. But first, supposing the approach to be made from the south, and through Yorkshire, there are certain interesting spots which may be confidently recommended to his notice, if time can be spared before entering upon the Lake District; and the route may be changed in returning.

There are three approaches to the Lakes through Yorkshire; the least advisable is the great north road by Catterick and Greta Bridge, and onwards to Penrith. The Traveller, however, taking this route, might halt at Greta Bridge, and be well recompensed if he can afford to give an hour or two to the banks of the Greta, and of the Tees, at Rokeby. Barnard Castle also, about two miles up the Tees, is a striking object, and the main North Road might be rejoined at Bowes. Every one has heard of the great fall of the Tees above Middleham, interesting for its grandeur, as the avenue of rocks that leads to it is to the geologist. But this place lies so far out of the way as scarcely to be within the compass of our notice. It might, however, be visited by a Traveller on foot, or on horseback, who could rejoin the main road upon Stanemoor.

The second road leads through a more interesting tract of country, beginning at Ripon, from which place see Fountain's Abbey, and thence by Hackfall, and Masham, to Jervaux Abbey, and up the vale of Wensley; turning aside before Askrigg is reached, to see Aysgarth-force, upon the Ure; and again, near Hawes, to Hardraw Scar, of which, with its waterfall, Turner has a fine drawing. Thence over the fells to Sedbergh, and Kendal.

The third approach from Yorkshire is through Leeds. Four miles beyond that town are the ruins of Kirkstall Abbey, should that road to Skipton be chosen; but the other by Otley may be made much more interesting by turning off at Addington to Bolton Bridge, for the sake of visiting the Abbey and grounds. It would be well, however, for a party previously to secure beds, if wanted, at the inn, as there is but one, and it is much resorted to in summer.

The Traveller on foot, or horseback, would do well to follow the banks of the Wharf upwards, to Burnsall, and thence cross over the hills to Gordale—a noble scene, beautifully described in Gray's Tour, and with which no one can be disappointed. Thence to Malham, where there is a respectable village inn, and so on, by Malham Cove, to Settle.

Travellers in carriages must go from Bolton Bridge to Skipton, where they rejoin the main road; and should they be inclined to visit Gordale, a tolerable

road turns off beyond Skipton.   Beyond Settle,
under Giggleswick Scar, the road passes an ebbing
and flowing well, worthy the notice of the Naturalist.
Four miles to the right of Ingleton, is Weathercote
Cave, a fine object, but whoever diverges for this,
must return to Ingleton.   Near Kirkby Lonsdale
observe the view from the bridge over the Lune,
and descend to the channel of the river, and by
no means omit looking at the Vale of Lune from
the Churchyard.

The journey towards the lake country through
Lancashire is, with the exception of the Vale of
the Ribble, at Preston, uninteresting; till you come
near Lancaster, and obtain a view of the fells and
mountains of Lancashire and Westmorland; with
Lancaster Castle, and the Tower of the Church
seeming to make part of the Castle, in the foreground.

They who wish to see the celebrated ruins of
Furness Abbey, and are not afraid of crossing the
Sands, may go from Lancaster to Ulverston; from
which place take the direct road to Dalton; but by
all means return through Urswick, for the sake of
the view from the top of the hill, before descending
into the grounds of Conishead Priory.   From this
quarter the Lakes would be advantageously approached by Coniston; thence to Hawkshead, and
by the Ferry over Windermere, to Bowness: a
much better introduction than by going direct from
Coniston to Ambleside, which ought not to be
done, as that would greatly take off from the effect
of Windermere.

Let us now go back to Lancaster.   The direct
road thence to Kendal is twenty-two miles, but by
making a circuit of eight miles, the Vale of the
Lune to Kirkby Lonsdale will be included.   The

whole tract is pleasing; there is one view mentioned by Gray and Mason especially so.   In West's Guide it is thus pointed out:—'About a quarter of a mile beyond the third mile-stone, where the road makes a turn to the right, there is a gate on the left which leads into a field where the station meant will be found.'   Thus far for those who approach the Lakes from the South.

Travellers from the North would do well to go from Carlisle by Wigton, and proceed along the Lake of Bassenthwaite to Keswick; or, if convenience should take them first to Penrith, it would still be better to cross the country to Keswick, and begin with that vale, rather than with Ullswater.   It is worth while to mention, in this place, that the banks of the river Eden, about Corby, are well worthy of notice, both on account of their natural beauty, and the viaducts which have recently been carried over the bed of the river, and over a neighbouring ravine. In the Church of Wetherby, close by, is a fine piece of monumental sculpture by Nollekins.   The scenes of Nunnery, upon the Eden, or rather that part of them which is upon Croglin, a mountain stream there falling into the Eden, are, in their way, unrivalled. But the nearest road thither, from Corby, is so bad, that no one can be advised to take it in a carriage. Nunnery may be reached from Corby by making a circuit and crossing the Eden at Armathwaite bridge.   A portion of this road, however, is bad enough.

As much the greatest number of Lake Tourists begin by passing from Kendal to Bowness, upon Windermere, our notices shall commence with that Lake.   Bowness is situated upon its eastern side, and at equal distance from each extremity of the Lake of

WINDERMERE.

The lower part of this Lake is rarely visited, but has many interesting points of view especially at Storr's Hall and at Fell-foot, where the Coniston Mountains peer nobly over the western barrier, which elsewhere along the whole Lake is comparatively tame. To one also who has ascended the hill from Grathwaite on the western side, the Promontory called Rawlinson's Nab, Storr's Hall, and the Trout-beck Mountains about sunset make a splendid landscape. The view from the Pleasure-house of the Station near the Ferry has suffered much from Larch plantations; this mischief, however, is gradually dis-appearing, and the Larches, under the management of the proprietor, Mr. Curwen, are giving way to the native wood. Windermere ought to be seen both from its shores and from its surface. None of the other Lakes unfold so many fresh beauties to him who sails upon them. This is owing to its greater size, to the islands, and to its having *two* vales at the head, with their accompanying mountains of nearly equal dignity. Nor can the grandeur of these two terminations be seen at once from any point, except from the bosom of the Lake. The Islands may be explored at any time of the day; but one bright unruffled evening must, if possible, be set apart for the splendour, the stillness, and solemnity of a three hours' voyage upon the higher division of the Lake, not omitting towards the end of the excursion to quit the expanse of water, and peep into the close and calm River at the head; which, in its quiet character, at such a time, appears rather like an overflow of the peaceful Lake itself, than to have any more immediate connexion with the rough mountains whence it has descended, or the turbulent

torrents by which it is supplied. Many persons content
themselves with what they see of Windermere during
their progress in a boat from Bowness to the head
of the Lake, walking thence to Ambleside.   But the
whole road from Bowness is rich in diversity of
pleasing or grand scenery; there is scarcely a field
on the road-side, which, if entered, would not give
to the landscape some additional charm.   Low-wood
Inn, a mile from the head of Windermere, is a most
pleasant halting-place; no inn in the whole district
is so agreeably situated for water views and excursions;
and the fields above it, and the lane that leads to
Troutbeck, present beautiful views towards each extremity of the Lake.   From this place, and from

AMBLESIDE,

Rides may be taken in numerous directions, and the
interesting walks are inexhaustible; [1] a few out of
the main road may be particularized:—the lane that
leads from Ambleside to Skelgill; the ride, or walk
by Rothay Bridge, and up the stream under Loughrigg
Fell, continued on the western side of Rydal Lake,
and along the fell to the foot of Grasmere Lake, and
thence round by the church of Grasmere; or, turning
round Loughrigg Fell by Loughrigg Tarn and the
River Brathay, back to Ambleside.   From Ambleside
is another charming excursion by Clappersgate, where
cross the Brathay, and proceed with the river on the
right to the hamlet of Skelwith-fold; when the
houses are passed, turn, before you descend the hill,
through a gate on the right, and from a rocky
point is a fine view of the Brathay River, Langdale

[1] Mr. Green's Guide to the Lakes, in two vols., contains
a complete Magazine of minute and accurate information of
this kind, with the names of mountains, streams, &c.

Pikes, &c. ; then proceed to Colwith-force and up
Little Langdale to Blea Tarn. The scene in which
this small piece of water lies, suggested to the
Author the following description (given in his Poem
of the Excursion), supposing the spectator to look
down upon it, not from the road, but from one of its
elevated sides.

Behold!
Beneath our feet, a little lowly Vale,
A lowly Vale, and yet uplifted high
Among the mountains ; even as if the spot
Had been, from eldest time by wish of theirs,
So placed, to be shut out from all the world!
Urn-like it was in shape, deep as an Urn ;
With rocks encompassed, save that to the South
Was one small opening, where a heath-clad ridge
Supplied a boundary less abrupt and close ;
A quiet treeless nook,[1] with two green fields,
A liquid pool that glittered in the sun,
And one bare Dwelling ; one Abode, no more!
It seemed the home of poverty and toil,
Though not of want : the little fields, made green
By husbandry of many thrifty years,
Paid cheerful tribute to the moorland House.
—There crows the Cock, single in his domain :
The small birds find in spring no thicket there
To shroud them ; only from the neighbouring Vales
The Cuckoo, straggling up to the hill tops,
Shouteth faint tidings of some gladder place.

From this little Vale return towards Ambleside by
Great Langdale, stopping, if there be time, to see
Dungeon-ghyll waterfall.
The Lake of

[1] No longer strictly applicable, on account of recent plantations.

CONISTON

May be conveniently visited from Ambleside, but is seen to most advantage by entering the country over the Sands from Lancaster. The Stranger, from the moment he sets his foot on those Sands, seems to leave the turmoil and traffic of the world behind him; and, crossing the majestic plain whence the sea has retired, he beholds, rising apparently from its base, the cluster of mountains among which he is going to wander, and towards whose recesses, by the Vale of Coniston, he is gradually and peacefully led. From the Inn at the head of Coniston Lake, a leisurely Traveller might have much pleasure in looking into Yewdale and Tilberthwaite, returning to his Inn from the head of Yewdale by a mountain track which has the farm of Tarn Hows, a little on the right: by this road is seen much the best view of Coniston Lake from the south. At the head of Coniston Water there is an agreeable Inn, from which an enterprising Tourist might go to the Vale of the Duddon, over Walna Scar, down to Seathwaite, Newfield, and to the rocks where the river issues from a narrow pass into the broad Vale. The stream is very interesting for the space of a mile above this point, and below, by Ulpha Kirk, till it enters the Sands, where it is overlooked by the solitary Mountain Black Comb, the summit of which, as that experienced surveyor, Colonel Mudge, declared, commands a more extensive view than any point in Britain. Ireland he saw more than once, but not when the sun was above the horizon.

> Close by the Sea, lone sentinel,
>   Black-Comb his forward station keeps;
> He breaks the sea's tumultuous swell, —
>   And ponders o'er the level deeps.

He listens to the bugle horn,
  Where Eskdale's lovely valley bends;
Eyes Walney's early fields of corn;
  Sea-birds to Holker's woods he sends.

Beneath his feet the sunk ship rests,
In Duddon Sands, its masts all bare:
    *   *   *   *   *

The Minstrels of Windermere, by Chas. Farish, B.D.

The Tourist may either return to the Inn at
Coniston by Broughton, or by turning to the left
before he comes to that town, or, which would be
much better, he may cross from

ULPHA KIRK

Over Birker moor to Birker-force, at the head of
the finest ravine in the country; and thence up the
Vale of the Esk, by Hardknot and Wrynose, back
to Ambleside. Near the road in ascending from
Eskdale, are conspicuous remains of a Roman for-
tress. Details of the Duddon and Donnerdale are
given in the Author's series of Sonnets upon the
Duddon and in the accompanying Notes. In addition to its two Vales at its head, Windermere communicates with two lateral Valleys; that of Troutbeck,
distinguished by the mountains at its head—by
picturesque remains of cottage architecture; and,
towards the lower part, by bold foregrounds formed
by the steep and winding banks of the river. This
Vale, as before mentioned, may be most conveniently
seen from Low Wood. The other lateral Valley,
that of Hawkshead, is visited to most advantage,
and most conveniently, from Bowness; crossing the
Lake by the Ferry—then pass the two villages of
Sawrey, and on quitting the latter you have a fine

view of the Lake of Esthwaite and the cone of one of the Langdale Pikes in the distance.

Before you leave Ambleside give three minutes to looking at a passage of the brook which runs through the town ; it is to be seen from a garden on the right bank of the stream, a few steps above the bridge — the garden at present is rented by Mrs. Airey.— Stockgill-force, upon the same stream, will have been mentioned to you as one of the sights of the neighbourhood. And by a Tourist halting a few days in Ambleside the *Nook* also might be visited ; a spot where there is a bridge over Scandale-beck, which makes a pretty subject for the pencil. Lastly, for residents of a week or so at Ambleside, there are delightful rambles over every part of Loughrigg Fell and among the enclosures on its sides ; particularly about Loughrigg Tarn, and on its eastern side about Fox How and the properties adjoining to the northwards.

ROAD FROM AMBLESIDE TO KESWICK.

The Waterfalls of Rydal are pointed out to every one. But it ought to be observed here, that Rydal-mere is nowhere seen to advantage from the *main road*. Fine views of it may be had from Rydal Park ; but these grounds, as well as those of Rydal Mount and Ivy Cottage, from which also it is viewed to advantage, are private. A foot road passing behind Rydal Mount and under Nab Scar to Gras-mere, is very favourable to views of the Lake and the Vale, looking back towards Ambleside. The horse road also, along the western side of the Lake, under Loughrigg Fell, as before mentioned, does justice to the beauties of this small mere, of which the Traveller who keeps the high road is not at all aware.

GRASMERE.

There are two small Inns in the Vale of Grasmere,
one near the Church, from which it may be conveniently explored in every direction, and a mountain
walk taken up Easedale to Easedale Tarn, one of the
finest tarns in the country, thence to Stickle Tarn,
and to the top of Langdale Pikes. See also the
Vale of Grasmere from Butterlip How. A boat is
kept by the innkeeper, and this circular Vale, in the
solemnity of a fine evening, will ·make, from the
bosom of the Lake, an impression that will be
scarcely ever effaced.

The direct road from Grasmere to Keswick does
not (as has been observed of Rydal Mere) show to
advantage Thirlmere, or Wythburn Lake, with its
surrounding mountains. By a Traveller proceeding
at leisure, a deviation ought to be made from the
main road, when he has advanced a little beyond
the sixth mile-stone short of Keswick, from which
point there is a noble view of the Vale of Legberth-
waite, with Blencathra (commonly called Saddle-
back) in front.   Having previously inquired, at the
Inn near Wythburn Chapel, the best way from this
mile-stone to the bridge that divides the Lake, he
must cross it, and proceed with the Lake on the
right to the hamlet a little beyond its termination,
and rejoin the main road upon Shoulthwaite Moss,
about four miles from Keswick ; or, if on foot, the
Tourist may follow the stream that issues from
Thirlmere down the romantic Vale of St. John's,
and so (inquiring the way at some cottage) to
Keswick, by a circuit of little more than a mile.   A
more interesting tract of country is scarcely anywhere to be seen than the road between Ambleside

and Keswick, with the deviations that have been pointed out. Helvellyn may be conveniently ascended from the Inn at Wythburn.

This Vale stretches, without winding, nearly north and south, from the Head of Derwent-water to the foot of Bassenthwaite Lake. It communicates with Borrowdale on the South ; with the river Greta, and Thirlmere, on the East, with which the Traveller has become acquainted on his way from Ambleside ; and with the Vale of Newlands on the West—which last Vale he may pass through in going to, or returning from, Buttermere. The best views of Keswick Lake are from Crow Park ; Frier's Crag ; the Stable-field, close by ; the Vicarage, and from various points in taking the circuit of the Lake. More distant views, and perhaps full as interesting, are from the side of Latrigg, from Ormathwaite, and Applethwaite ; and thence along the road at the foot of Skiddaw towards Bassenthwaite, for about a quarter of a mile. There are fine bird's-eye views from the Castle-hill ; from Ashness, on the road to Watenlath, and by following the Watenlath stream downwards to the Cataract of Lodore. This Lake also, if the weather be fine, ought to be circumnavigated. There are good views along the western side of Bassenthwaite Lake, and from Armathwaithe at its foot ; but the eastern side from the high road has little to recommend it. The Traveller from Carlisle, approaching by way of Ireby, has, from the old road on the top of Bassenthwaite-hawse, much the most striking view of the Plain and Lake of Bassenthwaite, flanked by Skiddaw, and terminated by Wallowcrag on the south-east of Derwent Lake ; the same point commands an extensive view of Solway Frith and the

Scotch Mountains. They who take the circuit of Derwent Lake, may at the same time include BORROW- DALE, going as far as Bowder-stone, or Rosthwaite. Borrowdale is also conveniently seen on the way to Wastdale over Styhead; or, to Buttermere, by Sea- toller and Honister Crag; or, going over the Stake, through Langdale, to Ambleside. Buttermere may be visited by a shorter way through Newlands, but though the descent upon the Vale of Buttermere, by this approach, is very striking, as it also is to one entering by the head of the Vale, under Honister Crag, yet, after all, the best entrance from Keswick is from the lower part of the Vale, having gone over Whinlater to Scale Hill, where there is a roomy Inn, with very good accommodation. The Mountains of the Vale of

BUTTERMERE AND CRUMMOCK

Are nowhere so impressive as from the bosom of Crummock Water. Scale-force, near it, is a fine chasm, with a lofty, though but slender, fall of water.

From Scale Hill a pleasant walk may be taken to an eminence in Mr. Marshall's woods, and another by crossing the bridge at the foot of the hill, upon which the Inn stands, and turning to the right, after the opposite hill has been ascended a little way, then follow the road for half a mile or so that leads towards Lorton, looking back upon Crummock Water, &c., between the openings of the fences. Turn back and make your way to

LOWES-WATER.

But this small Lake is only approached to advan- tage from the other end; therefore any Traveller going by this road to Wastdale, must look back upon it. This road to Wastdale, after passing the village of Lamplugh Cross, presents suddenly a fine view of the Lake of Ennerdale, with its Mountains; and, six or seven miles beyond, leads down upon Calder Abbey. Little of this ruin is left, but that little is well worthy of notice. At Calder Bridge are two comfortable Inns, and, a few miles beyond, accommodations may be had at the Strands, at the foot of Wastdale. Into

WASTDALE

Are three horse-roads, viz. over the Stye from Borrowdale; a short cut from Eskdale by Burnmoor Tarn, which road descends upon the head of the Lake; and the principal entrance from the open country by the Strands at its foot. This last is much the best approach. Wastdale is well worth the notice of the Traveller who is not afraid of fatigue; no part of the country is more distinguished by sublimity. Wast-water may also be visited from Ambleside; by going up Langdale, over Hardknot and Wrynose—down Eskdale and by Irton Hall to the Strands; but this road can only be taken on foot, or on horseback, or in a cart.

We will conclude with

ULLSWATER,

As being, perhaps, upon the whole, the happiest combination of beauty and grandeur, which any of the Lakes affords. It lies not more than ten miles from Ambleside, and the Pass of Kirkstone and the descent from it are very impressive; but, notwithstanding, this Vale, like the others, loses much of its effect by being entered from the head: so that it is better to go from Keswick through Matterdale, and descend upon Gowbarrow Park; you are thus brought

at once upon a magnificent view of the two higher
reaches of the Lake. Ara-force thunders down the
Ghyll on the left, at a small distance from the road.
If Ullswater be approached from Penrith, a mile and
a half brings you to the winding vale of Eamont,
and the prospects increase in interest till you reach
Patterdale; but the first four miles along Ullswater
by this road are comparatively tame; and in order
to see the lower part of the Lake to advantage, it is
necessary to go round by Pooley Bridge, and to ride
at least three miles along the Westmorland side of
the water, towards Martindale. The views, especially
if you ascend from the road into the fields, are
magnificent; yet this is only mentioned that the
transient Visitant may know what exists; for it
would be inconvenient to go in search of them.
They who take this course of three or four miles
on foot, should have a boat in readiness at the end
of the walk, to carry them across to the Cumberland
side of the Lake, near Old Church, thence to pursue
the road upwards to Patterdale. The Churchyard
Yew-tree still survives at Old Church, but there are
no remains of a Place of Worship, a New Chapel
having been erected in a more central situation,
which Chapel was consecrated by the then Bishop
of Carlisle, when on his way to crown Queen Elizabeth,
he being the only Prelate who would undertake the
office. It may be here mentioned that Bassenthwaite
Chapel yet stands in a bay as sequestered as the Site
of Old Church; such situations having been chosen
in disturbed times to elude marauders.

The Trunk or Body of the Vale of Ullswater
need not be further noticed, as its beauties show
themselves: but the curious Traveller may wish to
know something of its tributary Streams.

At Dalemain, about three miles from Penrith, a

Stream is crossed called the Dacre, or Dacor, which name it bore as early as the time of the Venerable Bede. This stream does not enter the Lake, but joins the Eamont a mile below. It rises in the moorish Country about Penruddock, flows down a soft sequestered Valley, passing by the ancient mansions of Hutton John and Dacre Castle. The former is pleasantly situated, though of a character somewhat gloomy and monastic, and from some of the fields near Dalemain, Dacre Castle, backed by the jagged summit of Saddle-back, with the Valley and Stream in front, forms a grand picture. There is no other stream that conducts to any glen or valley worthy of being mentioned, till we reach that which leads up to Ara-force, and thence into Matterdale, before spoken of. Matterdale, though a wild and interesting spot, has no peculiar features that would make it worth the Stranger's while to go in search of them; but, in Gowbarrow Park, the lover of Nature might linger for hours. Here is a powerful Brook, which dashes among rocks through a deep glen, hung on every side with a rich and happy intermixture of native wood; here are beds of luxuriant fern, aged hawthorns, and hollies decked with honeysuckles; and fallow-deer glancing and bounding over the lawns and through the thickets. These are the attractions of the retired views, or constitute a foreground for ever-varying pictures of the majestic Lake, forced to take a winding course by bold promontories, and environed by mountains of sublime form, towering above each other. At the outlet of Gowbarrow Park, we reach a third stream, which flows through a little recess called Glencoin, where lurks a single house, yet visible from the road. Let the Artist or leisurely Traveller turn aside to it, for the buildings and objects around them are romantic

and picturesque. Having passed under the steeps
of Styebarrow Crag, and the remains of its native
woods, at Glenridding Bridge, a fourth Stream is
crossed.

The opening on the side of Ullswater Vale, down
which this Stream flows, is adorned with fertile fields,
cottages, and natural groves, that agreeably unite
with the transverse views of the Lake; and the
Stream, if followed up after the enclosures are left
behind, will lead along bold water-breaks and waterfalls to a silent Tarn in the recesses of Helvellyn.
This desolate spot was formerly haunted by eagles,
that built in the precipice which forms its western
barrier. These birds used to wheel and hover round
the head of the solitary angler. It also derives a
melancholy interest from the fate of a young man,
a stranger, who perished some years ago, by falling
down the rocks in his attempt to cross over to
Grasmere. His remains were discovered by means
of a faithful dog that had lingered here for the space
of three months, self-supported, and probably retaining to the last an attachment to the skeleton of its
master. But to return to the road in the main Vale
of Ullswater.—At the head of the Lake (being now
in Patterdale) we cross a fifth Stream, Grisdale Beck:
this would conduct through a woody steep, where
may be seen some unusually large ancient hollies, up
to the level area of the Valley of Grisdale; hence
there is a path for foot-travellers, and along which
a horse may be led, to Grasmere. A sublime combination of mountain forms appears in front while
ascending the bed of this valley, and the impression
increases till the path leads almost immediately under
the projecting masses of Helvellyn. Having retraced
the banks of the Stream to Patterdale, and pursued
the road up the main Dale, the next considerable

stream would, if ascended in the same manner, conduct to Deep-dale, the character of which Valley
may be conjectured from its name.   It is terminated
by a cove, a craggy and gloomy abyss, with precipitous sides ; a faithful receptacle of the snows that
are driven into it, by the west wind, from the summit
of Fairfield.   Lastly, having gone along the western
side of Brothers-water and passed Hartsop Hall, a
Stream soon after issues from a cove richly decorated
with native wood.   This spot is, I believe, never
explored by Travellers ; but, from these sylvan and
rocky recesses, whoever looks back on the gleaming
surface of Brothers-water, or forward to the precipitous
sides and lofty ridges of Dove Crag, &c., will be
equally pleased with the beauty, the grandeur, and
the wildness of the scenery.

Seven Glens or Valleys have been noticed, which
branch off from the Cumberland side of the Vale.
The opposite side has only two Streams of any
importance, one of which would lead up from the
point where it crosses the Kirkstone-road, near the
foot of Brothers-water, to the decaying hamlet of
Hartsop, remarkable for its cottage architecture, and
thence to Hayswater, much frequented by anglers.
The other, coming down Martindale, enters Ullswater at Sandwyke, opposite to Gowbarrow Park.
No persons but such as come to Patterdale, merely
to pass through it, should fail to walk as far as
Blowick, the only enclosed land which on this side
borders the higher part of the Lake.   The axe has
here indiscriminately levelled a rich wood of birches
and oaks, that divided this favoured spot into a
hundred pictures.   It has yet its land-locked bays,
and rocky promontories ; but those beautiful woods
are gone, which *perfected* its seclusion ; and scenes,
that might formerly have been compared to an in-

exhaustible volume, are now spread before the eye
in a single sheet,—magnificent indeed, but seemingly
perused in a moment! From Blowick a narrow
track conducts along the craggy side of Place-fell,
richly adorned with juniper, and sprinkled over with
birches, to the village of Sandwyke, a few straggling
houses that, with the small estates attached to them,
occupy an opening opposite to Lyulph's Tower and
Gowbarrow Park. In Martindale,[1] the road loses
sight of the Lake, and leads over a steep hill, bringing you again into view of Ullswater. Its lowest
reach, four miles in length, is before you; and the
view terminated by the long ridge of Cross Fell in
the distance. Immediately under the eye is a deep-
indented bay, with a plot of fertile land, traversed
by a small brook, and rendered cheerful by two or
three substantial houses of a more ornamented and
showy appearance than is usual in those wild spots.

From Pooley Bridge, at the foot of the Lake,
Haweswater may be conveniently visited. Haweswater is a lesser Ullswater, with this advantage, that
it remains undefiled by the intrusion of bad taste.

Lowther Castle is about four miles from Pooley
Bridge, and if during this Tour the Stranger has
complained, as he will have had reason to do, of
a want of majestic trees, he may be abundantly
recompensed for his loss in the far-spreading woods
which surround that mansion. Visitants, for the
most part, see little of the beauty of these magnificent grounds, being content with the view from the
Terrace; but the whole course of the Lowther, from
Askham to the bridge under Brougham Hall, presents almost at every step some new feature of river,
woodland, and rocky landscape. A portion of this

[1] See pp. 122-3.

tract has, from its beauty, acquired the name of the Elysian Fields ;— but the course of the stream can only be followed by the pedestrian.

NOTE.—*Vide* p. 10.—About 200 yards beyond the last house on the Keswick side of Rydal village the road is cut through a low wooded rock, called Thrang Crag. The top of it, which is only a few steps on the south side, affords the best view of the Vale which is to be had by a Traveller who confines himself to the public road.

DESCRIPTION

OF THE

SCENERY OF THE LAKES

SECTION FIRST

VIEW OF THE COUNTRY AS FORMED BY NATURE

At Lucerne, in Switzerland, is shown a Model
of the Alpine country which encompasses the Lake
of the four Cantons.   The Spectator ascends a little
platform, and sees mountains, lakes, glaciers, rivers,
woods, waterfalls, and valleys, with their cottages,
and every other object contained in them, lying at
his feet; all things being represented in their appropriate colours.   It may be easily conceived that this
exhibition affords an exquisite delight to the imagination, tempting it to wander at will from valley to
valley, from mountain to mountain, through the
deepest recesses of the Alps.   But it supplies also
a more substantial pleasure: for the sublime and
beautiful region, with all its hidden treasures, and
their bearings and relations to each other, is thereby
comprehended and understood at once.

Something of this kind, without touching upon
minute details and individualities which would only
confuse and embarrass, will here be attempted, in
respect to the Lakes in the north of England, and
the vales and mountains enclosing and surrounding
them.   The delineation, if tolerably executed, will,

in some instances, communicate to the traveller, who has already seen the objects, new information; and will assist in giving to his recollections a more orderly arrangement than his own opportunities of observing may have permitted him to make; while it will be still more useful to the future traveller, by directing his attention at once to distinctions in things which, without such previous aid, a length of time only could enable him to discover. It is hoped, also, that this Essay may become generally serviceable, by leading to habits of more exact and considerate observation than, as far as the writer knows, have hitherto been applied to local scenery.

To begin, then, with the main outlines of the country;—I know not how to give the reader a distinct image of these more readily, than by requesting him to place himself with me, in imagination, upon some given point; let it be the top of either of the mountains, Great Gavel, or Scawfell; or, rather, let us suppose our station to be a cloud hanging midway between those two mountains, at not more than half a mile's distance from the summit of each, and not many yards above their highest elevation; we shall then see stretched at our feet a number of valleys, not fewer than eight, diverging from the point, on which we are supposed to stand, like spokes from the nave of a wheel. First, we note, lying to the south-east, the vale of Langdale,[1] which will conduct the eye to the long lake of Winandermere, stretched nearly to the sea; or rather to the sands of the vast bay of Morcamb, serving here for the rim of this imaginary wheel;—let us trace it in a direction from the south-east towards

[1] Anciently spelt Langden, and so called by the old inhabitants to this day—*dean*, from which the latter part of the word is derived, being in many parts of England a name for a valley.

the south, and we shall next fix our eyes upon the
vale of Coniston, running up likewise from the sea,
but not (as all the other valleys do) to the nave
of the wheel, and therefore it may be not inaptly
represented as a broken spoke sticking in the rim.
Looking forth again, with an inclination towards
the west, we see immediately at our feet the vale
of Duddon, in which is no lake, but a copious stream
winding among fields, rocks, and mountains, and
terminating its course in the sands of Duddon. The
fourth vale, next to be observed, viz. that of the Esk,
is of the same general character as the last, yet
beautifully discriminated from it by peculiar features.
Its stream passes under the woody steep upon which
stands Muncaster Castle, the ancient seat of the Pen-
ningtons, and after forming a short and narrow estuary
enters the sea below the small town of Ravenglass.
Next, almost due west, look down into, and along
the deep valley of Wastdale, with its little chapel
and half a dozen neat dwellings scattered upon a plain
of meadow and corn-ground intersected with stone
walls apparently innumerable, like a large piece
of lawless patchwork, or an array of mathematical
figures, such as in the ancient schools of geometry
might have been sportively and fantastically traced
out upon sand. Beyond this little fertile plain
lies, within a bed of steep mountains, the long,
narrow, stern, and desolate lake of Wastdale ; and,
beyond this, a dusky tract of level ground conducts
the eye to the Irish Sea. The stream that issues
from Wast-water is named the Irt, and falls into the
estuary of the river Esk. Next comes in view
Ennerdale, with its lake of bold and somewhat
savage shores. Its stream, the Ehen or Enna, flowing
through a soft and fertile country, passes the town
of Egremont, and the ruins of the castle,—then,

seeming, like the other rivers, to break through the barrier of sand thrown up by the winds on this tempestuous coast, enters the Irish Sea. The vale of Buttermere, with the lake and village of that name, and Crummock-water, beyond, next present themselves. We will follow the main stream, the Coker, through the fertile and beautiful vale of Lorton, till it is lost in the Derwent, below the noble ruins of Cockermouth Castle. Lastly, Borrow-dale, of which the vale of Keswick is only a con-tinuation, stretching due north, brings us to a point nearly opposite to the vale of Winandermere with which we began. From this it will appear, that the image of a wheel, thus far exact, is little more than one half complete; but the deficiency on the eastern side may be supplied by the vales of Wytheburn, Ullswater, Haweswater, and the vale of Grasmere and Rydal; none of these, however, run up to the central point between Great Gavel and Scawfell. From this, hitherto our central point, take a flight of not more than four or five miles eastward to the ridge of Helvellyn, and you will look down upon Wytheburn and St. John's Vale, which are a branch of the vale of Keswick; upon Ullswater, stretching due east:— and not far beyond to the south-east (though from this point not visible) lie the vale and lake of Haweswater; and lastly, the vale of Grasmere, Rydal, and Ambleside, brings you back to Winandermere, thus completing, though on the eastern side in a somewhat irregular manner, the representative figure of the wheel.

Such, concisely given, is the general topographical view of the country of the Lakes in the north of England; and it may be observed, that, from the circumference to the centre, that is, from the sea or plain country to the mountain stations specified,

there is—in the several ridges that enclose these
vales, and divide them from each other, I mean in
the forms and surfaces, first of the swelling grounds,
next of the hills and rocks, and lastly of the mountains—an ascent of almost regular gradation, from
elegance and richness, to their highest point of
grandeur and sublimity. It follows therefore from
this, first, that these rocks, hills, and mountains
must present themselves to view in stages rising
above each other, the mountains clustering together
towards the central point; and next, that an ob-
server familiar with the several vales, must, from
their various position in relation to the sun, have
had before his eyes every possible embellishment of
beauty, dignity, and splendour, which light and
shadow can bestow upon objects so diversified. For
example, in the vale of Winandermere, if the spectator looks for gentle and lovely scenes, his eye is
turned towards the south; if for the grand, towards
the north: in the vale of Keswick, which (as hath
been said) lies almost due north of this, it is directly
the reverse. Hence, when the sun is setting in
summer far to the north-west, it is seen, by the
spectator from the shores or breast of Winandermere,
resting among the summits of the loftiest mountains,
some of which will perhaps be half or wholly hidden
by clouds, or by the blaze of light which the orb
diffuses around it; and the surface of the lake will
reflect before the eye correspondent colours through
every variety of beauty, and through all degrees of
splendour. In the vale of Keswick, at the same
period, the sun sets over the humbler regions of the
landscape, and showers down upon *them* the radiance
which at once veils and glorifies,—sending forth,
meanwhile, broad streams of rosy, crimson, purple,
or golden light, towards the grand mountains in the

south and south-east, which, thus illuminated, with all their projections and cavities, and with an inter-mixture of solemn shadows, are seen distinctly through a cool and clear atmosphere. Of course, there is as marked a difference between the *noontide* appearance of these two opposite vales. The be-dimming haze that overspreads the south, and the clear atmosphere and determined shadows of the clouds in the north, at the same time of the day, are each seen in these several vales, with a contrast as striking. The reader will easily conceive in what degree the intermediate vales partake of a kindred variety.

I do not indeed know any tract of country in which, within so narrow a compass, may be found an equal variety in the influences of light and shadow upon the sublime or beautiful features of landscape; and it is owing to the combined circumstances to which the reader's attention has been directed. From a point between Great Gavel and Scawfell, a shep-herd would not require more than an hour to descend into any one of eight of the principal vales by which he would be surrounded; and all the others lie (with the exception of Haweswater) at but a small distance. Yet, though clustered together, every valley has its distinct and separate character; in some instances, as if they had been formed in studied contrast to each other, and in others with the united pleasing differ-ences and resemblances of a sisterly rivalship. This concentration of interest gives to the country a de-cided superiority over the most attractive districts of Scotland and Wales, especially for the pedestrian traveller. In Scotland and Wales are found, un-doubtedly, individual scenes, which, in their several kinds, cannot be excelled. But, in Scotland, par-ticularly, what long tracts of desolate country intervene! so that the traveller, when he reaches a spot deservedly of great celebrity, would find it difficult to determine how much of his pleasure is owing to excellence inherent in the landscape itself; and how much to an instantaneous recovery from an oppression left upon his spirits by the barrenness and desolation through which he has passed.

But to proceed with our survey;—and, first, of the MOUNTAINS. Their *forms* are endlessly diversified, sweeping easily or boldly in simple majesty, abrupt and precipitous, or soft and elegant. In magnitude and grandeur they are individually inferior to the most celebrated of those in some other parts of this island; but, in the combinations which they make, towering above each other, or lifting themselves in ridges like the waves of a tumultuous sea, and in the beauty and variety of their surfaces and colours, they are surpassed by none.

The general *surface* of the mountains is turf, rendered rich and green by the moisture of the climate. Sometimes the turf, as in the neighbourhood of Newlands, is little broken, the whole covering being soft and downy pasturage. In other places rocks predominate; the soil is laid bare by torrents and burstings of water from the sides of the mountains in heavy rains; and not unfrequently their perpendicular sides are seamed by ravines (formed also by rains and torrents) which, meeting in angular points, entrench and scar the surface with numerous figures like the letters W and Y.

In the ridge that divides Eskdale from Wastdale, granite is found; but the MOUNTAINS are for the most part composed of the stone by mineralogists termed schist, which, as you approach the plain country, gives place to lime-stone and free-stone; but schist being the substance of the mountains, the

predominant *colour* of their *rocky* parts is bluish, or
hoary grey—the general tint of the lichens with
which the bare stone is encrusted. With this blue
or grey colour is frequently intermixed a red tinge,
proceeding from the iron that interveins the stone,
and impregnates the soil. The iron is the principle
of decomposition in these rocks; and hence, when
they become pulverized, the elementary particles
crumbling down, overspread in many places the
steep and almost precipitous sides of the mountains
with an intermixture of colours, like the compound
hues of a dove's neck. When in the heat of advancing summer, the fresh green tint of the herbage
has somewhat faded, it is again revived by the
appearance of the fern profusely spread over the
same ground : and, upon this plant, more than upon
anything else, do the changes which the seasons
make in the colouring of the mountains depend.
About the first week in October, the rich green,
which prevailed through the whole summer, is
usually passed away. The brilliant and various
colours of the fern are then in harmony with the
autumnal woods ; bright yellow or lemon colour, at
the base of the mountains, melting gradually, through
orange, to a dark russet brown towards the summits,
where the plant, being more exposed to the weather,
is in a more advanced state of decay. Neither heath
nor furze are *generally* found upon the *sides* of these
mountains, though in many places they are adorned
by those plants, so beautiful when in flower. We
may add, that the mountains are of height sufficient
to have the surface towards the summit softened by
distance, and to imbibe the finest aerial hues. In
common also with other mountains, their apparent
forms and colours are perpetually changed by the
clouds and vapours which float round them : the

effect indeed of mist or haze, in a country of this character, is like that of magic. I have seen six or seven ridges rising above each other, all created in a moment by the vapours upon the side of a mountain, which, in its ordinary appearance, showed not a projecting point to furnish even a hint for such an operation.

I will take this opportunity of observing, that they who have studied the appearances of Nature feel that the superiority, in point of visual interest, of mountainous over other countries—is more strikingly displayed in winter than in summer. This, as must be obvious, is partly owing to the *forms* of the mountains, which, of course, are not affected by the seasons ; but also, in no small degree, to the greater variety that exists in their winter than their summer *colouring*. This variety is such, and so harmoniously preserved, that it leaves little cause of regret when the splendour of autumn is passed away. The oak-coppices, upon the sides of the mountains, retain russet leaves ; the birch stands conspicuous with its silver stem and puce-coloured twigs ; the hollies, with green leaves and scarlet berries, have come forth to view from among the deciduous trees, whose summer foliage had concealed them : the ivy is now plentifully apparent upon the stems and boughs of the trees, and upon the steep rocks. In place of the deep summer-green of the herbage and fern, many rich colours play into each other over the surface of the mountains ; turf (the tints of which are interchangeably tawny-green, olive, and brown), beds of withered fern, and grey rocks, being harmoniously blended together. The mosses and lichens are never so fresh and flourishing as in winter, if it be not a season of frost ; and their minute beauties prodigally adorn the foreground. Wherever we turn, we find these productions of Nature, to which winter is rather favourable than unkindly, scattered over the walls, banks of earth, rocks, and stones, and upon the trunks of trees, with the intermixture of several species of small fern, now green and fresh; and, to the observing passenger, their forms and colours are a source of inexhaustible admiration. Add to this the hoar-frost and snow, with all the varieties they create, and which volumes would not be sufficient to describe. I will content myself with one instance of the colouring produced by snow, which may not be uninteresting to painters. It is extracted from the memorandum-book of a friend; and for its accuracy I can speak, having been an eye-witness of the appearance. ' I observed,' says he, ' the beautiful effect of the drifted snow upon the mountains, and the perfect *tone* of colour. From the top of the mountains downwards a rich olive was produced by the powdery snow and the grass, which olive was warmed with a little brown, and in this way harmoniously combined, by insensible grada-tions, with the white. The drifting took away the monotony of snow; and the whole vale of Grasmere, seen from the terrace walk in Easedale, was as varied, perhaps more so, than even in the pomp of autumn. In the distance was Loughrigg-Fell, the basin-wall of the lake: this, from the summit downward, was a rich orange-olive; then the lake of a bright olive-green, nearly the same tint as the snow-powdered mountain tops and high slopes in Easedale; and lastly, the church, with its firs, forming the centre of the view. Next to the church came nine dis-tinguishable hills, six of them with woody sides turned towards us, all of them oak-copses with their bright red leaves and snow-powdered twigs; these hills—so variously situated in relation to each other, and to the view in general, so variously powdered, some only enough to give the herbage a rich brown tint, one intensely white and lighting up all the others—were yet so placed, as in the most inobtrusive manner to harmonize by contrast with a perfect naked, snowless bleak summit in the far distance.'

Having spoken of the forms, surface, and colour of the mountains, let us descend into the VALES. Though these have been represented under the general image of the spokes of a wheel, they are, for the most part, winding; the windings of many being abrupt and intricate. And, it may be observed, that, in one circumstance, the general shape of them all has been determined by that primitive conformation through which so many became receptacles of lakes. For they are not formed, as are most of the celebrated Welsh valleys, by an approximation of the sloping bases of the opposite mountains towards each other, leaving little more between than a channel for the passage of a hasty river; but the bottom of these valleys is mostly a spacious and gently declining area, apparently level as the floor of a temple, or the surface of a lake, and broken in many cases by rocks and hills, which rise up like islands from the plain. In such of the valleys as make many windings, these level areas open upon the traveller in succession, divided from each other sometimes by a mutual approximation of the hills, leaving only passage for a river, sometimes by correspondent windings, without such approximation; and sometimes by a bold advance of one mountain towards that which is opposite it. It may here be observed with propriety that the several rocks and hills, which have been described as rising up like islands from the level area of the vale, have regulated the choice of the inhabitants in the situation of their dwellings. Where none of these are found, and the inclination of the ground is not sufficiently rapid easily to carry off the waters (as in the higher part of Langdale, for instance), the houses are not sprinkled over the middle of the vales, but confined to their sides, being placed merely so far up the mountain as to be protected from the floods. But where these rocks and hills have been scattered over the plain of the vale (as in Grasmere, Donnerdale, Eskdale, &c.), the beauty which they give to the scene is much heightened by a single cottage, or cluster of cottages, that will be almost always found. under them, or upon their sides; dryness and shelter having tempted the Dalesmen to fix their habitations there.

I shall now speak of the LAKES of this country. The form of the lake is most perfect when, like Derwent-water, and some of the smaller lakes, it least resembles that of a river;—I mean, when being looked at from any given point where the whole may be seen at once, the width of it bears such proportion to the length, that, however the outline may be diversified by far-receding bays, it never assumes the shape of a river, and is contemplated with that placid and quiet feeling which belongs peculiarly to the lake—as a body of still water under the influence of no current; reflecting therefore the clouds, the light, and all the imagery of the sky and surrounding hills; expressing also and making visible the changes of the atmosphere, and motions of the lightest breeze, and subject to agitation only from the winds—

> The visible scene
> Would enter unawares into his mind
> With all its solemn imagery, its rocks,
> Its woods, and that uncertain heaven received
> Into the bosom of the *steady* lake!

It must be noticed, as a favourable characteristic of
the lakes of this country, that, though several of the
largest, such as Winandermere, Ullswater, Haweswater,
do, when the whole length of them is commanded
from an elevated point, lose somewhat of the peculiar
form of the lake, and assume the resemblance of
a magnificent river ; yet, as their shape is winding
(particularly that of Ullswater and Haweswater), when
the view of the whole is obstructed by those barriers
which determine the windings, and the spectator is
confined to one reach, the appropriate feeling is revived ; and one lake may thus in succession present
to the eye the essential characteristic of many. But,
though the forms of the large lakes have this advantage, it is nevertheless favourable to the beauty of the
country that the largest of them are comparatively
small ; and that the same vale generally furnishes
a succession of lakes, instead of being filled with one.
The vales in North Wales, as hath been observed,
are not formed for the reception of lakes ; those of
Switzerland, Scotland, and this part of the North
of England, *are* so formed ; but, in Switzerland and
Scotland, the proportion of diffused water is often
too great, as at the lake of Geneva for instance, and
in most of the Scotch lakes. No doubt it sounds
magnificent and flatters the imagination, to hear at
a distance of expanses of water so many leagues in
length and miles in width ; and such ample room
may be delightful to the fresh-water sailor, scudding
with a lively breeze amid the rapidly-shifting scenery.
But, who ever travelled along the banks of Loch-
Lomond, variegated as the lower part is by islands,
without feeling that a speedier termination of the
long vista of blank water would be acceptable ; and
without wishing for an interposition of green meadows,
trees, and cottages, and a sparkling stream to run by

his side? In fact, a notion of grandeur, as connected with magnitude, has seduced persons of taste into a general mistake upon this subject. It is much more desirable, for the purposes of pleasure, that lakes should be numerous, and small or middle-sized, than large, not only for communication by walks and rides, but for variety, and for recurrence of similar appearances. To illustrate this by one instance:—How pleasing is it to have a ready and frequent opportunity of watching, at the outlet of a lake, the stream pushing its way among the rocks in lively contrast with the stillness from which it has escaped; and how amusing to compare its noisy and turbulent motions with the gentle playfulness of the breezes, that may be starting up or wandering here and there over the faintly-rippled surface of the broad water! I may add, as a general remark, that, in lakes of great width, the shores cannot be distinctly seen at the same time, and therefore contribute little to mutual illustration and ornament; and, if the opposite shores are out of sight of each other, like those of the American and Asiatic lakes, then unfortunately the traveller is reminded of a nobler object; he has the blankness of a sea-prospect without the grandeur and accompanying sense of power.

As the comparatively small size of the lakes in the North of England is favourable to the production of variegated landscape, their *boundary-line* also is for the most part gracefully or boldly indented. That uniformity which prevails in the primitive frame of the lower grounds among all chains or clusters of mountains where large bodies of still water are bedded, is broken by the *secondary* agents of Nature, ever at work to supply the deficiencies of the mould in which things were originally cast. Using the word *deficiencies*, I do not speak with

reference to those stronger emotions which a region
of mountains is peculiarly fitted to excite. The
bases of those huge barriers may run for a long
space in straight lines, and these parallel to each
other; the opposite sides of a profound vale may
ascend as exact counterparts, or in mutual reflection,
like the billows of a troubled sea; and the impression be, from its very simplicity, more awful
and sublime. Sublimity is the result of Nature's first
great dealings with the superficies of the earth; but
the general tendency of her subsequent operations is
towards the production of beauty; by a multiplicity
of symmetrical parts uniting in a consistent whole.
This is everywhere exemplified along the margins
of these lakes. Masses of rock, that have been
precipitated from the heights into the area of waters,
lie in some places like stranded ships; or have
acquired the compact structure of jutting piers; or
project in little peninsulas crested with native wood.
The smallest rivulet—one whose silent influx is
scarcely noticeable in a season of dry weather—so
faint is the dimple made by it on the surface of the
smooth lake—will be found to have been not useless
in shaping, by its deposits of gravel and soil in time
of flood, a curve that would not otherwise have
existed. But the more powerful brooks, encroaching
upon the level of the lake, have, in course of time,
given birth to ample promontories of sweeping outline
that contrasts boldly with the longitudinal base of
the steeps on the opposite shore; while their flat
or gently-sloping surfaces never fail to introduce,
into the midst of desolation and barrenness, the
elements of fertility, even where the habitations
of men may not have been raised. These alluvial
promontories, however, threaten, in some places, to
bisect the waters which they have long adorned;

and, in course of ages, they will cause some of the
lakes to dwindle into numerous and insignificant
pools; which, in their turn, will finally be filled up.
But, checking these intrusive calculations, let us
rather be content with appearances as they are, and
pursue in imagination the meandering shores, whether
rugged steeps, admitting of no cultivation, descend
into the water; or gently-sloping lawns and woods,
or flat and fertile meadows stretch between the
margin of the lake and the mountains. Among
minuter recommendations will be noticed, especially
along bays exposed to the setting-in of strong winds,
the curved rim of fine blue gravel, thrown up in
course of time by the waves, half of it perhaps
gleaming from under the water, and the corresponding half of a lighter hue; and in other parts
bordering the lake, groves, if I may so call them,
of reeds and bulrushes; or plots of water-lilies
lifting up their large target-shaped leaves to the
breeze, while the white flower is heaving upon the
wave.

To these may naturally be added the birds that
enliven the waters. Wild-ducks in spring-time hatch
their young in the islands, and upon reedy shores;—
the sand-piper, flitting along the stony margins, by
its restless note attracts the eye to motions as
restless:—upon some jutting rock, or at the edge
of a smooth meadow, the stately heron may be
descried with folded wings, that might seem to have
caught their delicate hue from the blue waters, by
the side of which she watches for her sustenance.
In winter, the lakes are sometimes resorted to by
wild swans; and in that season habitually by wid-
geons, goldings, and other aquatic fowl of the smaller
species. Let me be allowed the aid of verse to
describe the evolutions which these visitants some-

times perform, on a fine day towards the close of
winter.

> Mark how the feather'd tenants of the flood,
> With grace of motion that might scarcely seem
> Inferior to angelical, prolong
> Their curious pastime! shaping in mid air
> (And sometimes with ambitious wing that soars
> High as the level of the mountain tops,)
> A circuit ampler than the lake beneath,
> Their own domain;—but ever, while intent
> On tracing and retracing that large round,
> Their jubilant activity evolves
> Hundreds of curves and circlets, to and fro,
> Upward and downward, progress intricate
> Yet unperplex'd, as if one spirit swayed
> Their indefatigable flight.—'Tis done—
> Ten times, or more, I fancied it had ceased;
> But lo! the vanish'd company again
> Ascending;—they approach—I hear their wings
> Faint, faint, at first, and then an eager sound
> Past in a moment—and as faint again!
> They tempt the sun to sport amid their plumes;
> They tempt the water or the gleaming ice,
> To show them a fair image;—'tis themselves,
> Their own fair forms, upon the glimmering plain,
> Painted more soft and fair as they descend
> Almost to touch;—then up again aloft,
> Up with a sally and a flash of speed,
> As if they scorn'd both resting-place and rest!

The ISLANDS, dispersed among these lakes, are
neither so numerous nor so beautiful as might be expected from the account that has been given of the
manner in which the level areas of the vales are so
frequently diversified by rocks, hills, and hillocks,
scattered over them; nor are they ornamented (as

are several of the lakes in Scotland and Ireland) by the remains of castles or other places of defence ; nor with the still more interesting ruins of religious edifices. Every one must regret that scarcely a vestige is left of the Oratory, consecrated to the Virgin, which stood upon Chapel-Holm in Windermere, and that the Chauntry has disappeared, where mass used to be sung, upon St. Herbert's Island, Derwent-water. The islands of the last-mentioned lake are neither fortunately placed nor of pleasing shape ; but if the wood upon them were managed with more taste, they might become interesting features in the landscape. There is a beautiful cluster on Winandermere ; a pair pleasingly contrasted upon Rydal ; nor must the solitary green island of Grasmere be forgotten. In the bosom of each of the lakes of Ennerdale and Devockwater is a single rock, which, owing to its neighbourhood to the sea, is—

The haunt of cormorants and sea-mew's clang,

a music well suited to the stern and wild character of the several scenes ! It may be worth while here to mention (not as an object of beauty, but of curiosity) that there occasionally appears above the surface of Derwent-water, and always in the same place, a considerable tract of spongy ground covered with aquatic plants, which is called the Floating, but with more propriety might be named the Buoyant, Island ; and, on one of the pools near the lake of Esthwaite, may sometimes be seen a mossy Islet, with trees upon it, shifting about before the wind, a *lusus naturae* frequent on the great rivers of America, and not unknown in other parts of the world.

Fas habeas invisere Tiburis arva,
Albuneaeque lacum, atque umbras terrasque natantes.[1]

[1] See that admirable Idyllium, the Catillus and Salia, of Landor.

This part of the subject may be concluded with
observing—that, from the multitude of brooks and
torrents that fall into these lakes, and of internal
springs by which they are fed, and which circulate
through them like veins, they are truly living lakes,
vivi lacus; and are thus discriminated from the
stagnant and sullen pools frequent among mountains
that have been formed by volcanoes, and from the
shallow meres found in flat and fenny countries.
The water is also of crystalline purity; so that, if it
were not for the reflections of the incumbent mountains by which it is darkened, a delusion might be
felt, by a person resting quietly in a boat on the
bosom of Winandermere or Derwent-water, similar
to that which Carver so beautifully describes when
he was floating alone in the middle of lake Erie or
Ontario, and could almost have imagined that his
boat was suspended in an element as pure as air, or
rather that the air and water were one.

Having spoken of Lakes I must not omit to
mention, as a kindred feature of this country, those
bodies of still water called TARNS. In the economy
of Nature these are useful, as auxiliars to Lakes; for
if the whole quantity of water which falls upon the
mountains in time of storm were poured down upon
the plains without intervention, in some quarters, of
such receptacles, the habitable grounds would be much
more subject than they are to inundation. But, as
some of the collateral brooks spend their fury, finding
a free course toward and also down the channel of
the main stream of the vale before those that have
to pass through the higher tarns and lakes have
filled their several basins, a gradual distribution is
effected; and the waters thus reserved, instead of
uniting, to spread ravage and deformity, with those
which meet with no such detention, contribute to

support, for a length of time, the vigour of many
streams without a fresh fall of rain. Tarns are
found in some of the vales, and are numerous upon
the mountains. A Tarn, in a *Vale*, implies, for the
most part, that the bed of the vale is not happily
formed; that the water of the brooks can neither
wholly escape, nor diffuse itself over a large area.
Accordingly, in such situations, Tarns are often
surrounded by an unsightly tract of boggy ground;
but this is not always the case, and in the cultivated
parts of the country, when the shores of the Tarn
are determined, it differs only from the Lake in
being smaller, and in belonging mostly to a smaller
valley, or circular recess. Of this class of miniature
lakes, Loughrigg Tarn, near Grasmere, is the most
beautiful example. It has a margin of green firm
meadows, of rocks, and rocky woods, a few reeds
here, a little company of water-lilies there, with beds
of gravel or stone beyond; a tiny stream issuing
neither briskly nor sluggishly out of it; but its
feeding rills, from the shortness of their course, so
small as to be scarcely visible. Five or six cottages
are reflected in its peaceful bosom; rocky and barren
steeps rise up above the hanging enclosures; and the
solemn pikes of Langdale overlook, from a distance,
the low cultivated ridge of land that forms the
northern boundary of this small, quiet, and fertile
domain. The *mountain* Tarns can only be recommended to the notice of the inquisitive traveller who
has time to spare. They are difficult of access and
naked; yet some of them are, in their permanent
forms, very grand; and there are accidents of things
which would make the meanest of them interesting.
At all events, one of these pools is an acceptable
sight to the mountain wanderer; not merely as an
incident that diversifies the prospect, but as forming

in his mind a centre or conspicuous point to which objects, otherwise disconnected or insubordinated, may be referred. Some few have a varied outline, with bold heath-clad promontories; and, as they mostly lie at the foot of a steep precipice, the water, where the sun is not shining upon it, appears black and sullen; and, round the margin, huge stones and masses of rock are scattered; some defying conjecture as to the means by which they came thither; and others obviously fallen from on high—the contribution of ages! A not unpleasing sadness is induced by this perplexity, and these images of decay; while the prospect of a body of pure water unattended with groves and other cheerful rural images by which fresh water is usually accompanied, and unable to give furtherance to the meagre vegetation around it—excites a sense of some repulsive power strongly put forth, and thus deepens the melancholy natural to such scenes. Nor is the feeling of solitude often more forcibly or more solemnly impressed than by the side of one of these mountain pools: though desolate and forbidding, it seems a distinct place to repair to; yet where the visitants must be rare, and there can be no disturbance. Water-fowl flock hither; and the lonely Angler may here be seen; but the imagination, not content with this scanty allowance of society, is tempted to attribute a voluntary power to every change which takes place in such a spot, whether it be the breeze that wanders over the surface of the water, or the splendid lights of evening resting upon it in the midst of awful precipices.

> There, sometimes does a leaping fish
> Send through the tarn a lonely cheer;
> The crags repeat the raven's croak
> In symphony austere:

Thither the rainbow comes, the cloud,
And mists that spread the flying shroud,
And sunbeams, and the sounding blast.

It will be observed that this country is bounded
on the south and east by the sea, which combines
beautifully, from many elevated points, with the
inland scenery; and, from the bay of Morcamb, the
sloping shores and background of distant mountains
are seen, composing pictures equally distinguished
for amenity and grandeur. But the estuaries on
this coast are in a great measure bare at low water;[1]
and there is no instance of the sea running far up
among the mountains, and mingling with the Lakes,
which are such in the strict and usual sense of the
word, being of fresh water. Nor have the streams,
from the shortness of their course, time to acquire
that body of water necessary to confer upon them
much majesty. In fact, the most considerable, while
they continue in the mountain and lake-country, are
rather large brooks than rivers. The water is per-
fectly pellucid, through which in many places are
seen, to a great depth, their beds of rock, or of blue
gravel, which give to the water itself an exquisitely
cerulean colour: this is particularly striking in the
rivers Derwent and Duddon, which may be compared, such and so various are their beauties, to any
two rivers of equal length of course in any country.

---

[1] In fact there is not an instance of a harbour on the Cumberland side of the Solway frith that is not dry at low water; that
of Ravenglass, at the mouth of the Esk, as a natural harbour
is much the best. The Sea appears to have been retiring slowly
for ages from this coast. From Whitehaven to St. Bees ex-
tends a track of level ground, about five miles in length, which
formerly must have been under salt water, so as to have made
an island of the high ground that stretches between it and
the Sea.

The number of the torrents and smaller brooks is infinite, with their water-falls and water-breaks; and they need not here be described. I will only observe that, as many, even of the smallest rills, have either found, or made for themselves, recesses in the sides of the mountains or in the vales, they have tempted the primitive inhabitants to settle near them for shelter; and hence, cottages so placed, by seeming to withdraw from the eye, are the more endeared to the feelings.

The Woods consist chiefly of oak, ash, and birch, and here and there Wych-elm, with underwood of hazel, the white and black thorn, and hollies; in moist places alders and willows abound; and yews among the rocks. Formerly the whole country must have been covered with wood to a great height up the mountains; where native Scotch firs [1] must have grown in great profusion, as they do in the northern part of Scotland to this day. But not one of these old inhabitants has existed, perhaps, for some hundreds of years; the beautiful traces, however, of the universal sylvan [2] appearance the country formerly had, yet survive in the native coppice-woods that have been protected by enclosures, and also in the forest-trees and hollies, which, though disappearing fast, are yet scattered both over the enclosed and unenclosed parts of the mountains. The same is expressed by the beauty and intricacy with which the fields and coppice-woods are often intermingled:

[1] This species of fir is in character much superior to the American which has usurped its place. Where the fir is planted for ornament, let it be by all means of the aboriginal species, which can only be procured from the Scotch nurseries.

[2] A squirrel (so I have heard the old people of Wytheburn say) might have gone from their chapel to Keswick without alighting on the ground.

the plough of the first settlers having followed
naturally the veins of richer, dryer, or less stony
soil; and thus it has shaped out an intermixture of
wood and lawn, with a grace and wildness which it
would have been impossible for the hand of studied
art to produce. Other trees have been introduced
within these last fifty years, such as beeches, larches,
limes, &c., and plantations of firs, seldom with advantage, and often with great injury to the appearance of the country; but the sycamore (which
I believe was brought into this island from Germany,
not more than two hundred years ago) has long been
the favourite of the cottagers; and, with the fir, has
been chosen to screen their dwellings: and is sometimes found in the fields whither the winds or the
waters may have carried its seeds.

The want most felt, however, is that of timber
trees. There are few *magnificent* ones to be found
near any of the lakes; and unless greater care be
taken, there will, in a short time, scarcely be left an
ancient oak that would repay the cost of felling.
The neighbourhood of Rydal, notwithstanding the
havoc which has been made, is yet nobly distinguished. In the woods of Lowther, also, is found
an almost matchless store of ancient trees, and the
majesty and wildness of the native forest.

Among the smaller vegetable ornaments must be
reckoned the bilberry, a ground plant, never so
beautiful as in early spring, when it is seen under
bare or budding trees, that imperfectly intercept the
sunshine, covering the rocky knolls with a pure
mantle of fresh verdure, more lively than the herbage of the open fields;—the broom that spreads
luxuriantly along rough pastures, and in the month
of June interveins the steep copses with its golden
blossoms;—and the juniper, a rich evergreen, that

thrives in spite of cattle, upon the unenclosed parts
of the mountains :—the Dutch myrtle diffuses fra-
grance in moist places; and there is an endless
variety of brilliant flowers in the fields and meadows,
which, if the agriculture of the country were more
carefully attended to, would disappear. Nor can
I omit again to notice the lichens and mosses : their
profusion, beauty, and variety exceed those of any
other country I have seen.

It may now be proper to say a few words respecting climate, and 'skiey influences,' in which this
region, as far as the character of its landscapes is
affected by them, may, upon the whole, be considered fortunate. The country is, indeed, subject
to much bad weather, and it has been ascertained
that twice as much rain falls here as in many parts
of the island; but the number of black drizzling
days, that blot out the face of things, is by no
means *proportionally* great. Nor is a continuance
of thick, flagging, damp air so common as in the
West of England and Ireland. The rain here comes
down heartily, and is frequently succeeded by clear,
bright weather, when every brook is vocal, and every
torrent sonorous; brooks and torrents, which are
never muddy, even in the heaviest floods, except,
after a drought, they happen to be defiled for a
short time by waters that have swept along dusty
roads, or have broken out into ploughed fields.
Days of unsettled weather, with partial showers,
are very frequent; but the showers, darkening, or
brightening, as they fly from hill to hill, are not less
grateful to the eye than finely interwoven passages
of gay and sad music are touching to the ear.
Vapours exhaling from the lakes and meadows after
sunrise, in a hot season, or, in moist weather,
brooding upon the heights, or descending towards

the valleys with inaudible motion, give a visionary character to everything around them; and are in themselves so beautiful, as to dispose us to enter into the feelings of those simple nations (such as the Laplanders of this day) by whom they are taken for guardian deities of the mountains; or to sympathize with others who have fancied these delicate apparitions to be the spirits of their departed ancestors. Akin to these are fleecy clouds resting upon the hill-tops; they are not easily managed in picture, with their accompaniments of blue sky; but how glorious are they in Nature! how pregnant with imagination for the poet! and the height of the Cumbrian mountains is sufficient to exhibit daily and hourly instances of those mysterious attachments. Such clouds, cleaving to their stations, or lifting up suddenly their glittering heads from behind rocky barriers, or hurrying out of sight with speed of the sharpest edge—will often tempt an inhabitant to congratulate himself on belonging to a country of mists and clouds and storms, and make him think of the blank sky of Egypt, and of the cerulean vacancy of Italy, as an unanimated and even a sad spectacle. The atmosphere, however, as in every country subject to much rain, is frequently unfavourable to landscape, especially when keen winds succeed the rain which are apt to produce coldness, spottiness, and an unmeaning or repulsive detail in the distance;—a sunless frost, under a canopy of leaden and shapeless clouds, is, as far as it allows things to be seen, equally disagreeable.

It has been said that in human life there are moments worth ages. In a more subdued tone of sympathy may we affirm, that in the climate of England there are, for the lover of Nature, days which are worth whole months,—I might say—even

years. One of these favoured days sometimes occurs
in spring-time, when that soft air is breathing over
the blossoms and new-born verdure, which inspired
Buchanan with his beautiful Ode to the first of
May; the air, which, in the luxuriance of his fancy,
he likens to that of the golden age,—to that which
gives motion to the funereal cypresses on the banks
of Lethe;—to the air which is to salute beatified
spirits when expiatory fires shall have consumed the
earth with all her habitations. But it is in autumn
that days of such affecting influence most frequently
intervene;—the atmosphere seems refined, and the
sky rendered more crystalline, as the vivifying heat
of the year abates; the lights and shadows are more
delicate; the colouring is richer and more finely
harmonized; and, in this season of stillness, the ear
being unoccupied, or only gently excited, the sense
of vision becomes more susceptible of its appropriate
enjoyments. A resident in a country like this which
we are treating of, will agree with me, that the
presence of a lake is indispensable to exhibit in
perfection the beauty of one of these days; and
he must have experienced, while looking on the
unruffled waters, that the imagination, by their aid,
is carried into recesses of feeling otherwise impenetrable. The reason of this is, that the heavens are
not only brought down into the bosom of the earth,
but that the earth is mainly looked at, and thought
of, through the medium of a purer element. The
happiest time is when the equinoxial gales are departed; but their fury may probably be called to
mind by the sight of a few shattered boughs, whose
leaves do not differ in colour from the faded foliage
of the stately oaks from which these relics of the
storm depend : all else speaks of tranquillity;—not
a breath of air, no restlessness of insects, and not

a moving object perceptible—except the clouds gliding in the depths of the lake, or the traveller passing
along, an inverted image, whose motion seems
governed by the quiet of a time, to which its archetype, the living person, is, perhaps, insensible :—or
it may happen, that the figure of one of the larger
birds, a raven or a heron, is crossing silently among
the reflected clouds, while the voice of the real bird,
from the element aloft, gently awakens in the
spectator the recollection of appetites and instincts,
pursuits and occupations, that deform and agitate
the world,—yet have no power to prevent Nature
from putting on an aspect capable of satisfying the
most intense cravings for the tranquil, the lovely,
and the perfect, to which man, the noblest of her
creatures, is subject.

Thus far, of climate, as influencing the feelings
through its effect on the objects of sense. We may
add, that whatever has been said upon the advantages
derived to these scenes from a changeable atmosphere, would apply, perhaps still more forcibly, to
their appearance under the varied solemnities of
night. Milton, it will be remembered, has given
a *clouded* moon to Paradise itself. In the night-
season also, the narrowness of the vales, and comparative smallness of the lakes, are especially adapted
to bring surrounding objects home to the eye and to
the heart. The stars, taking their stations above
the hill-tops, are contemplated from a spot like the
Abyssinian recess of Rasselas, with much more touching interest than they are likely to excite when
looked at from an open country with ordinary undulations : and it must be obvious, that it is the
bays only of large lakes that can present such contrasts of light and shadow as those of smaller
dimensions display from every quarter. A deep

contracted valley, with diffused waters, such a valley
and plains level and wide as those of Chaldea, are
the two extremes in which the beauty of the heavens
and their connexion with the earth are most sensibly
felt.   Nor do the advantages I have been speaking
of imply here an exclusion of the aerial effects of
distance.   These are ensured by the height of the
mountains, and are found, even in the narrowest
vales, where they lengthen in perspective, or act (if
the expression may be used) as telescopes for the
open country.

The subject would bear to be enlarged upon: but
I will conclude this section with a night-scene
suggested by the Vale of Keswick.   The Fragment
is well known; but it gratifies me to insert it, as
the Writer was one of the first who led the way to
a worthy admiration of this country.

Now sunk the sun, now twilight sunk, and night
Rode in her zenith; not a passing breeze
Sigh'd to the grove, which in the midnight air
Stood motionless, and in the peaceful floods
Inverted hung: for now the billows slept
Along the shore, nor heav'd the deep; but spread
A shining mirror to the moon's pale orb,
Which, dim and waning, o'er the shadowy cliffs,
The solemn woods, and spiry mountain tops,
Her glimmering faintness threw: now every eye,
Oppress'd with toil, was drown'd in deep repose,
Save that the unseen Shepherd in his watch,
Propp'd on his crook, stood listening by the fold,
And gaz'd the starry vault, and pendant moon;
Nor voice, nor sound, broke on the deep serene;
But the soft murmur of swift-gushing rills,
Forth issuing from the mountain's distant steep,
(Unheard till now, and now scarce heard) proclaim'd

All things at rest, and imag'd the still voice
Of quiet, whispering in the ear of night.[1]

[1] Dr. Brown, the author of this fragment, was from his infancy brought up in Cumberland, and should have remembered that the practice of folding sheep by night is unknown among these mountains, and that the image of the Shepherd upon the watch is out of its place, and belongs only to countries, with a warmer climate, that are subject to ravages from beasts ot prey. It is pleasing to notice a dawn of imaginative feeling in these verses. Tickel, a man of no common genius, chose, for the subject of a Poem, Kensington Gardens, in preference to the Banks of the Derwent, within a mile or two of which he was born. But this was in the reign of Queen Anne, or George the First. Progress must have been made in the interval; though the traces of it, except in the works of Thomson and Dyer, are not very obvious.

SECTION SECOND

ASPECT OF THE COUNTRY, AS AFFECTED BY ITS
INHABITANTS

Hitherto I have chiefly spoken of the features by
which Nature has discriminated this country from
others. I will now describe, in general terms, in
what manner it is indebted to the hand of man.
What I have to notice on this subject will emanate
most easily and perspicuously from a description of
the ancient and present inhabitants, their occupations, their condition of life, the distribution of
landed property among them, and the tenure by
which it is holden.

The reader will suffer me here to recall to his
mind the shapes of the valleys, and their position
with respect to each other, and the forms and
substance of the intervening mountains. He will
people the valleys with lakes and rivers ; the coves
and sides of the mountains with pools and torrents ;
and will bound half of the circle which we have
contemplated by the sands of the sea, or by the sea
itself. He will conceive that, from the point upon
which he stood, he looks down upon this scene before
the country had been penetrated by any inhabitants :—to vary his sensations, and to break in upon
their stillness, he will form to himself an image
of the tides visiting and revisiting the friths, the
main sea dashing against the bolder shore, the rivers
pursuing their course to be lost in the mighty mass

of waters. He may see or hear in fancy the winds sweeping over the lakes, or piping with a loud voice among the mountain peaks ; and, lastly, may think of the primaeval woods shedding and renewing their leaves with no human eye to notice, or human heart to regret or welcome the change. 'When the first settlers entered this region (says an animated writer) they found it overspread with wood ; forest trees, the fir, the oak, the ash, and the birch had skirted the fells, tufted the hills, and shaded the valleys, through centuries of silent solitude ; the birds and beasts of prey reigned over the meeker species ; and the *bellum inter omnia* maintained the balance of Nature in the empire of beasts.'

Such was the state and appearance of this region when the aboriginal colonists of the Celtic tribes were first driven or drawn towards it, and became joint tenants with the wolf, the boar, the wild bull, the red deer, and the leigh, a gigantic species of deer which has been long extinct ; while the inaccessible crags were occupied by the falcon, the raven, and the eagle. The inner parts were too secluded, and of too little value, to participate much of the benefit of Roman manners ; and though these conquerors encouraged the Britons to the improvement of their lands in the plain country of Furness and Cumberland, they seem to have had little connexion with the mountains, except for military purposes, or in subservience to the profit they drew from the mines.

When the Romans retired from Great Britain, it is well known that these mountain-fastnesses furnished a protection to some unsubdued Britons, long after the more accessible and more fertile districts had been seized by the Saxon or Danish invader. A few, though distinct, traces of Roman forts or camps, as at Ambleside, and upon Dunmallet, and

a few circles of rude stones attributed to the Druids,[1]
are the only vestiges that remain upon the surface

[1] It is not improbable that these circles were once numerous,
and that many of them may yet endure in a perfect state,
under no very deep covering of soil. A friend of the Author,
while making a trench in a level piece of ground, not far from
the banks of the Eamont, but in no connexion with that river,
met with some stones which seemed to him formally arranged;
this excited his curiosity, and proceeding, he uncovered a perfect circle of stones, from two to three or four feet high, with
a *sanctum sanctorum*,—the whole a complete place of Druidical
worship of small dimensions, having the same sort of relation
to Stonehenge, Long Meg and her Daughters near the river
Eden, and Karl Lofts near Shap (if this last be not Danish),
that a rural chapel bears to a stately church, or to one of our
noble cathedrals. This interesting little monument having
passed, with the field in which it was found, into other hands,
has been destroyed. It is much to be regretted, that the
striking relic of antiquity at Shap has been in a great measure
destroyed also.

The DAUGHTERS of LONG MEG are placed not in an oblong, as
the STONES of SHAP, but in a perfect circle, eighty yards in
diameter, and seventy-two in number, and from above three
yards high, to less than so many feet: a little way out of the
circle stands LONG MEG herself—a single stone eighteen feet
high.

When the Author first saw this monument, he came upon it
by surprise, therefore might overrate its importance as an
object; but he must say, that though it is not to be compared
with Stonehenge, he has not seen any other remains of those
dark ages, which can pretend to rival it in singularity and
dignity of appearance.

A weight of awe not easy to be borne
Fell suddenly upon my spirit, cast
From the dread bosom of the unknown past,
When first I saw that sisterhood forlorn;—
And Her, whose strength and stature seem to scorn
The power of years—pre-eminent, and placed
Apart, to overlook the circle vast.
Speak, Giant-mother! tell it to the Morn,
While she dispels the cumbrous shades of night;
Let the Moon hear, emerging from a cloud,
When, how, and wherefore, rose on British ground
That wondrous Monument, whose mystic round
Forth shadows, some have deemed, to mortal sight
The inviolable God that tames the proud.

of the country, of these ancient occupants; and, as the Saxons and Danes, who succeeded to the possession of the villages and hamlets which had been established by the Britons, seem at first to have confined themselves to the open country,—we may descend at once to times long posterior to the conquest by the Normans, when their feudal polity was regularly established. We may easily conceive that these narrow dales and mountain sides, choked up as they must have been with wood, lying out of the way of communication with other parts of the Island, and upon the edge of a hostile kingdom, could have little attraction for the high-born and powerful; especially as the more open parts of the country furnished positions for castles and houses of defence, sufficient to repel any of those sudden attacks, which, in the then rude state of military knowledge, could be made upon them. Accordingly, the more retired regions (and to such I am now confining myself) must have been neglected or shunned even by the persons whose baronial or signioral rights extended over them, and left, doubtless, partly as a place of refuge for outlaws and robbers, and partly granted out for the more settled habitation of a few vassals following the employment of shepherds or woodlanders. Hence these lakes and inner valleys are unadorned by any remains of ancient grandeur, castles, or monastic edifices, which are only found upon the skirts of the country, as Furness Abbey, Calder Abbey, the Priory of Lannercost, Gleaston Castle,—long ago a residence of the Flemings,—and the numerous ancient castles of the Cliffords, the Lucys, and the Dacres. On the southern side of these mountains (especially in that part known by the name of Furness Fells, which is more remote from the borders), the state of society would necessarily be more settled; though it also was fashioned, not a little, by its neighbourhood to a hostile kingdom. We will, therefore, give a sketch of the economy of the Abbots in the distribution of lands among their tenants, as similar plans were doubtless adopted by other Lords, and as the consequences have affected the face of the country materially to the present day, being, in fact, one of the principal causes which give it such a striking superiority, in beauty and interest, over all other parts of the island.

'When the Abbots of Furness,' says an author before cited, 'enfranchised their villains, and raised them to the dignity of customary tenants, the lands, which they had cultivated for their lord, were divided into whole tenements; each of which, besides the customary annual rent, was charged with the obligation of having in readiness a man completely armed for the king's service on the borders, or elsewhere; each of these whole tenements was again subdivided into four equal parts; each villain had one; and the party tenant contributed his share to the support of the man of arms, and of other burdens. These divisions were not properly distinguished; the land remained mixed; each tenant had a share through all the arable and meadow-land, and common of pasture over all the wastes. These sub-tenements were judged sufficient for the support of so many families; and no further division was permitted. These divisions and subdivisions were convenient at the time for which they were calculated: the land, so parcelled out, was of necessity more attended to, and the industry greater, when more persons were to be supported by the produce of it. The frontier of the kingdom, within which Furness was considered, was in a constant state of attack and defence; more hands, therefore, were

necessary to guard the coast, to repel an invasion
from Scotland, or make reprisals on the hostile
neighbour. The dividing the lands in such manner
as has been shown, increased the number of inhabitants, and kept them at home till called for:
and, the land being mixed, and the several tenants
united in equipping the plough, the absence of the
fourth man was no prejudice to the cultivation of
his land, which was committed to the care of three.

'While the villains of Low Furness were thus distributed over the land, and employed in agriculture;
those of High Furness were charged with the care of
flocks and herds, to protect them from the wolves
which lurked in the thickets, and in winter to browse
them with the tender sprouts of hollies and ash. This
custom was not till lately discontinued in High Furness; and holly-trees were carefully preserved for that
purpose when all other wood was cleared off; large
tracts of common being so covered with these trees,
as to have the appearance of a forest of hollies. At
the Shepherd's call, the flocks surrounded the holly-
bush, and received the croppings at his hand, which
they greedily nibbled up, bleating for more. The
Abbots of Furness enfranchised these pastoral vassals,
and permitted them to enclose *quillets* to their houses,
for which they paid encroachment rent.'—West's
Antiquities of Furness.

However desirable, for the purposes of defence,
a numerous population might be, it was not possible
to make at once the same numerous allotments among
the untilled valleys, and upon the sides of the mountains, as had been made in the cultivated plains. The
enfranchised shepherd, or woodlander, having chosen
there his place of residence, builds it of sods, or of
the mountain-stone, and, with the permission of his
lord, encloses, like Robinson Crusoe, a small croft or

two immediately at his door for such animals as he wishes to protect. Others are happy to imitate his example, and avail themselves of the same privileges: and thus a population, mainly of Danish or Norse origin, as the dialect indicates, crept on towards the more secluded parts of the valleys. Chapels, daughters of some distant mother-church, are first erected in the more open and fertile vales, as those of Bowness and Grasmere, offsets of Kendal: which again, after a period, as the settled population increases, become mother-churches to smaller edifices, planted, at length, in almost every dale throughout the country. The enclosures, formed by the tenantry, are for a long time confined to the homesteads; and the arable and meadow land of the vales is possessed in common field; the several portions being marked out by stones, bushes, or trees: which portions, where the custom has survived, to this day are called *dales*, from the word *deylen*, to distribute; but, while the valley was thus lying open, enclosures seem to have taken place upon the sides of the mountains; because the land there was not intermixed, and was of little comparative value; and, therefore, small opposition would be made to its being appropriated by those to whose habitations it was contiguous. Hence the singular appearance which the sides of many of these mountains exhibit, intersected, as they are, almost to the summit, with stone walls. When first erected, these stone fences must have little disfigured the face of the country; as part of the lines would everywhere be hidden by the quantity of native wood then remaining; and the lines would also be broken (as they still are) by the rocks which interrupt and vary their course. In the meadows, and in those parts of the lower grounds where the soil has not been sufficiently drained, and could not afford a stable foundation,

there, when the increasing value of land, and the
inconvenience suffered from intermixed plots of ground
in common field, had induced each inhabitant to
enclose his own, they were compelled to make the
fences of alders, willows, and other trees. These,
where the native wood had disappeared, have frequently enriched the valleys with a sylvan appearance;
while the intricate intermixture of property has given
to the fences a graceful irregularity, which, where
large properties are prevalent, and large capitals
employed in agriculture, is unknown. This sylvan
appearance is heightened by the number of ash-trees
planted in rows along the quick fences, and along the
walls, for the purpose of browsing the cattle at the
approach of winter. The branches are lopped off and
strewn upon the pastures; and when the cattle have
stripped them of the leaves, they are used for repair-
ing the hedges or for fuel.

We have thus seen a numerous body of Dalesmen
creeping into possession of their homesteads, their
little crofts, their mountain-enclosures; and, finally,
the whole vale is visibly divided; except, perhaps,
here and there some marshy ground, which, till fully
drained, would not repay the trouble of enclosing.
But these last partitions do not seem to have been
general, till long after the pacification of the Borders,
by the union of the two crowns: when the cause,
which had first determined the distribution of land
into such small parcels, had not only ceased,—but
likewise a general improvement had taken place in
the country, with a correspondent rise in the value
of its produce. From the time of the union, it is
certain that this species of feudal population must
rapidly have diminished. That it was formerly much
more numerous than it is at present, is evident from
the multitude of tenements (I do not mean houses,

but small divisions of land) which belonged formerly
each to a several proprietor, and for which separate
fines are paid to the manorial lord at this day. These
are often in the proportion of four to one of the
present occupants. 'Sir Launcelot Threlkeld, who
lived in the reign of Henry VII, was wont to say, he
had three noble houses, one for pleasure, Crosby, in
Westmoreland, where he had a park full of deer; one
for profit and warmth, wherein to reside in winter,
namely, Yanwith, nigh Penrith; and the third,
Threlkeld (on the edge of the vale of Keswick), well
stocked with tenants to go with him to the wars.'
But, as I have said, from the union of the two crowns,
this numerous vassalage (their services not being
wanted) would rapidly diminish; various tenements
would be united in one possessor; and the aboriginal
houses, probably little better than hovels, like the
kraels of savages, or the huts of the Highlanders of
Scotland, would fall into decay, and the places of
many be supplied by substantial and comfortable
buildings, a majority of which remain to this day
scattered over the valleys, and are often the only
dwellings found in them.

From the time of the erection of these houses, till
within the last sixty years, the state of society,
though no doubt slowly and gradually improving,
underwent no material change. Corn was grown in
these vales (through which no carriage-road had yet
been made) sufficient upon each estate to furnish
bread for each family, and no more: notwithstanding the union of several tenements, the possessions
of each inhabitant still being small, in the same field
was seen an intermixture of different crops; and the
plough was interrupted by little rocks, mostly over-
grown with wood, or by spongy places, which the
tillers of the soil had neither leisure nor capital to

convert into firm land. The storms and moisture of the climate induced them to sprinkle their upland property with outhouses of native stone, as places of shelter for their sheep, where, in tempestuous weather, food was distributed to them. Every family spun from its own flock the wool with which it was clothed; a weaver was here and there found among them; and the rest of their wants was supplied by the produce of the yarn, which they carded and spun in their own houses, and carried to market, either under their arms, or more frequently on pack-horses, a small train taking their way weekly down the valley or over the mountains to the most commodious town. They had, as I have said, their rural chapel, and of course their minister, in clothing or in manner of life, in no respect differing from themselves, except on the Sabbath-day; this was the sole distinguished individual among them; everything else, person and possession, exhibited a perfect equality, a community of shepherds and agriculturists, proprietors, for the most part, of the lands which they occupied and cultivated.

While the process above detailed was going on, the native forest must have been everywhere receding; but trees were planted for the sustenance of the flocks in winter,—such was then the rude state of agriculture; and, for the same cause, it was necessary that care should be taken of some part of the growth of the native woods. Accordingly, in Queen Elizabeth's time, this was so strongly felt, that a petition was made to the Crown, praying, 'that the Blomaries in High Furness might be abolished, on account of the quantity of wood which was consumed in them for the use of the mines, to the great detriment of the cattle.' But this same cause, about a hundred years after, produced effects directly contrary to those which had been deprecated. The re-establishment, at that period, of furnaces upon a large scale, made it the interest of the people to convert the steeper and more stony of the enclosures, sprinkled over with remains of the native forest, into close woods, which, when cattle and sheep were excluded, rapidly sowed and thickened themselves. The reader's attention has been directed to the cause by which tufts of wood, pasturage, meadow, and arable land, with its various produce, are intricately intermingled in the same field ; and he will now see, in like manner, how enclosures entirely of wood, and those of cultivated ground, are blended all over the country under a law of similar wildness.

An historic detail has thus been given of the manner in which the hand of man has acted upon the surface of the inner regions of this mountainous country, as incorporated with and subservient to the powers and processes of Nature. We will now take a view of the same agency—acting, within narrower bounds, for the production of the few works of art and accommodations of life which, in so simple a state of society, could be necessary. These are merely habitations of man and coverts for beasts, roads and bridges, and places of worship.

And to begin with the COTTAGES. They are scattered over the valleys, and under the hill-sides, and on the rocks ; and, even to this day, in the more retired dales, without any intrusion of more assuming buildings :

Cluster'd like stars some few, but single most,
And lurking dimly in their shy retreats,
Or glancing on each other cheerful looks,
Like separated stars with clouds between.   MS.

The dwelling-houses, and contiguous outhouses, are, in many instances, of the colour of the native rock, out of which they have been built ; but, frequently the Dwelling or Fire-house, as it is ordinarily called, has been distinguished from the barn or byre by rough-cast and whitewash, which, as the inhabitants are not hasty in renewing it, in a few years acquires, by the influence of weather, a tint at once sober and variegated.   As these houses have been, from father to son, inhabited by persons engaged in the same occupations, yet necessarily with changes in their circumstances, they have received without incongruity additions and accommodations adapted to the needs of each successive occupant, who, being for the most part proprietor, was at liberty to follow his own fancy : so that these humble dwellings remind the contemplative spectator of a production of Nature, and may (using a strong expression) rather be said to have grown than to have been erected ;—to have risen, by an instinct of their own, out of the native rock—so little is there in them of formality, such is their wildness and beauty.   Among the numerous recesses and projections in the walls and in the different stages of their roofs, are seen bold and harmonious effects of contrasted sunshine and shadow. It is a favourable circumstance, that the strong winds, which sweep down the valleys, induced the inhabitants, at a time when the materials for building were easily procured, to furnish many of these dwellings with substantial porches ; and such as have not this defence, are seldom unprovided with a projection of two large slates over their thresholds.   Nor will the singular beauty of the chimneys escape the eye of the attentive traveller.   Sometimes a low chimney, almost upon a level with the roof, is overlaid with a slate, supported upon four slender pillars, to pre-

vent the wind from driving the smoke down the
chimney. Others are of a quadrangular shape, rising
one or two feet above the roof; which low square is
often surmounted by a tall cylinder, giving to the
cottage chimney the most beautiful shape in which
it is ever seen. Nor will it be too fanciful or refined
to remark, that there is a pleasing harmony between
a tall chimney of this circular form, and the living
column of smoke, ascending from it through the still
air. These dwellings, mostly built, as has been said,
of rough unhewn stone, are roofed with slates, which
were rudely taken from the quarry before the present
art of splitting them was understood, and are, therefore, rough and uneven in their surface, so that both
the coverings and sides of the houses have furnished
places of rest for the seeds of lichens, mosses, ferns,
and flowers. Hence buildings, which in their very
form call to mind the processes of Nature, do thus,
clothed in part with a vegetable garb, appear to be
received into the bosom of the living principle of
things, as it acts and exists among the woods and
fields; and, by their colour and their shape, affect-
ingly direct the thoughts to that tranquil course of
Nature and simplicity, along which the humble-
minded inhabitants have, through so many genera-
tions, been led. Add the little garden with its shed
for bee-hives, its small bed of pot-herbs, and its
borders and patches of flowers for Sunday posies,
with sometimes a choice few too much prized to be
plucked; an orchard of proportioned size; a cheese-
press, often supported by some tree near the door;
a cluster of embowering sycamores for summer shade;
with a tall fir, through which the winds sing when
other trees are leafless; the little rill or household
spout murmuring in all seasons;—combine these
incidents and images together, and you have the

representative idea of a mountain-cottage in this
country so beautifully formed in itself, and so richly
adorned by the hand of Nature.

Till within the last sixty years there was no communication between any of these vales by carriage-
roads; all bulky articles were transported on pack-
horses. Owing, however, to the population not being
concentrated in villages, but scattered, the valleys
themselves were intersected as now by innumerable
lanes and pathways leading from house to house
and from field to field. These lanes, where they are
fenced by stone walls, are mostly bordered with
ashes, hazels, wild roses, and beds of tall fern at
their base; while the walls themselves, if old, are
overspread with mosses, small ferns, wild straw-
berries, the geranium, and lichens: and, if the wall
happen to rest against a bank of earth, it is sometimes almost wholly concealed by a rich facing of
stone-fern. It is a great advantage to a traveller
or resident, that these numerous lanes and paths, if
he be a zealous admirer of Nature, will lead him on
into all the recesses of the country, so that the hidden
treasures of its landscapes may, by an ever-ready guide,
be laid open to his eyes.

Likewise to the smallness of the several properties
is owing the great number of bridges over the brooks
and torrents, and the daring and graceful neglect of
danger or accommodation with which so many of
them are constructed, the rudeness of the forms
of some, and their endless variety. But, when
I speak of this rudeness, I must at the same time
add, that many of these structures are in themselves
models of elegance, as if they had been formed upon
principles of the most thoughtful architecture. It is
to be regretted that these monuments of the skill of
our ancestors, and of that happy instinct by which

consummate beauty was produced, are disappearing fast; but sufficient specimens remain [1] to give a high gratification to the man of genuine taste. Travellers who may not have been accustomed to pay attention to things so inobtrusive, will excuse me if I point out the proportion between the span and elevation of the arch, the lightness of the parapet, and the graceful manner in which its curve follows faithfully that of the arch.

Upon this subject I have nothing further to notice, except the PLACES OF WORSHIP, which have mostly a little school-house adjoining.[2] The architecture of these churches and chapels, where they have not been recently rebuilt or modernized, is of

---

[1] Written some time ago. The injury done since is more than could have been calculated upon.

Singula de nobis anni praedantur euntes. This is in the course of things; but why should the genius that directed the ancient architecture of these vales have deserted them? For the bridges, churches, mansions, cottages, and their richly fringed and flat-roofed outhouses, venerable as the grange of some old abbey, have been substituted structures, in which baldness only seems to have been studied, or plans of the most vulgar utility. But some improvement may be looked for in future; the gentry *recently* have copied the old models, and successful instances might be pointed out, if I could take the liberty.

[2] In some places scholars were formerly taught in the church, and at others the school-house was a sort of ante-chapel to the place of worship, being under the same roof; an arrangement which was abandoned as irreverent. It continues, however, to this day in Borrowdale. In the parish register of that chapelry is a notice, that a youth who had quitted the valley, and died in one of the towns on the coast of Cumberland, had requested that his body should be brought and interred at the foot of the pillar by which he had been accustomed to sit while a school-boy. One cannot but regret that parish registers so seldom contain anything but bare names; in a few of this country, especially in that of Lowes-water, I have found interesting notices of unusual natural occurrences—characters of the deceased, and particulars of their lives. There is no good reason why such memorials should not be frequent; these short and simple annals would in future ages become precious.

a style not less appropriate and admirable than that of the dwelling-houses and other structures. How sacred the spirit by which our forefathers were directed ! The *religio loci* is nowhere violated by these unstinted, yet unpretending, works of human hands. They exhibit generally a well-proportioned oblong, with a suitable porch, in some instances a steeple tower, and in others nothing more than a small belfry, in which one or two bells hang visibly. But these objects, though pleasing in their forms, must necessarily, more than others in rural scenery, derive their interest from the sentiments of piety and reverence for the modest virtues and simple manners of humble life with which they may be contemplated. A man must be very insensible who would not be touched with pleasure at the sight of the chapel of Buttermere, so strikingly expressing, by its diminutive size, how small must be the congregation there assembled, as it were, like one family ; and proclaiming at the same time to the passenger, in connexion with the surrounding mountains, the depth of that seclusion in which the people live, that has rendered necessary the building of a separate place of worship for so few. A patriot, calling to mind the images of the stately fabrics of Canterbury, York, or Westminster, will find a heartfelt satisfaction in presence of this lowly pile, as a monument of the wise institutions of our country, and as evidence of the all-pervading and paternal care of that venerable Establishment, of which it is, perhaps, the humblest daughter. The edifice is scarcely larger than many of the single stones or fragments of rock which are scattered near it.

We have thus far confined our observations on this division of the subject, to that part of these Dales which runs up far into the mountains.

As we descend towards the open country, we meet with halls and mansions, many of which have been places of defence against the incursions of the Scottish borderers; and they not unfrequently retain their towers and battlements. To these houses, parks are sometimes attached, and to their successive proprietors we chiefly owe whatever ornament is still left to the country of majestic timber. Through the open parts of the vales are scattered, also, houses of a middle rank between the pastoral cottage and the old hall residence of the knight or esquire. Such houses differ much from the rugged cottages before described, and are generally graced with a little court or garden in front, where may yet be seen specimens of those fantastic and quaint figures which our ancestors were fond of shaping out in yew-tree, holly, or box-wood. The passenger will sometimes smile at such elaborate display of petty art, while the house does not deign to look upon the natural beauty or the sublimity which its situation almost unavoidably commands.

Thus has been given a faithful description, the minuteness of which the reader will pardon, of the face of this country as it was, and had been through centuries, till within the last sixty years. Towards the head of these Dales was found a perfect Republic of Shepherds and Agriculturists, among whom the plough of each man was confined to the maintenance of his own family, or to the occasional accommodation of his neighbour.[1] Two or three cows furnished

[1] One of the most pleasing characteristics of manners in secluded and thinly-peopled districts, is a sense of the degree in which human happiness and comfort are dependent on the contingency of neighbourhood. This is implied by a rhyming adage common here, ' *Friends are far, when neighbours are nar* ' (near). This mutual helpfulness is not confined to out-of-doors work; but is ready upon all occasions. Formerly, if a person

each family with milk and cheese. The chapel was
the only edifice that presided over these dwellings,
the supreme head of this pure Commonwealth; the
members of which existed in the midst of a powerful
empire like an ideal society or an organized community, whose constitution had been imposed and
regulated by the mountains which protected it.
Neither high-born nobleman, knight, nor esquire
was here; but many of these humble sons of the
hills had a consciousness that the land, which they
walked over and tilled, had for more than five
hundred years been possessed by men of their name
and blood; and venerable was the transition, when
a curious traveller, descending from the heart of the
mountains, had come to some ancient manorial
residence in the more open parts of the Vales, which,
through the rights attached to its proprietor, connected the almost visionary mountain republic he
had been contemplating with the substantial frame
of society as existing in the laws and constitution of
a mighty empire.

became sick, especially the mistress of a family, it was usual
for those of the neighbours who were more particularly connected with the party by amicable offices, to visit the house,
carrying a present; this practice, which is by no means
obsolete, is called *owning* the family, and is regarded as a
pledge of a disposition to be otherwise serviceable in a time of
disability and distress.

SECTION THIRD

CHANGES, AND RULES OF TASTE FOR PREVENTING
THEIR BAD EFFECTS

Such, as hath been said, was the appearance of things till within the last sixty years. A practice, denominated Ornamental Gardening, was at that time becoming prevalent over England. In union with an admiration of this art, and in some instances in opposition to it, had been generated a relish for select parts of natural scenery : and Travellers, instead of confining their observations to Towns, Manufactories, or Mines, began (a thing till then unheard of) to wander over the island in search of sequestered spots, distinguished as they might accidently have learned, for the sublimity or beauty of the forms of Nature there to be seen.—Dr. Brown, the celebrated Author of the Estimate of the Manners and Principles of the Times, published a letter to a friend, in which the attractions of the Vale of Keswick were delineated with a powerful pencil, and the feeling of a genuine Enthusiast. Gray, the Poet, followed : he died soon after his forlorn and melancholy pilgrimage to the Vale of Keswick, and the record left behind him of what he had seen and felt in this journey, excited that pensive interest with which the human mind is ever disposed to listen to the farewell words of a man of genius. The journal of Gray feelingly showed how the gloom of ill-health and low spirits had been irradiated by objects, which the Author's powers of mind enabled him to describe with distinctness and unaffected simplicity. Every

reader of this journal must have been impressed with
the words which conclude his notice of the Vale of
Grasmere :—' Not a single red tile, no flaring gentleman's house or garden-wall, breaks in upon the
repose of this little unsuspected paradise ; but all is
peace, rusticity, and happy poverty, in its neatest
and most becoming attire.'

What is here so justly said of Grasmere applied
almost equally to all its sister Vales. It was well
for the undisturbed pleasure of the Poet that he had
no forebodings of the change which was soon to take
place ; and it might have been hoped that these
words, indicating how much the charm of what *was*
depended upon what was *not*, would of themselves
have preserved the ancient franchises of this and
other kindred mountain retirements from trespass ; or
(shall I dare to say ?) would have secured scenes so
consecrated from profanation. The lakes had now
become celebrated ; visitors flocked hither from all
parts of England ; the fancies of some were smitten
so deeply that they became settlers ; and the Islands
of Derwent-water and Winandermere, as they offered
the strongest temptation, were the first places seized
upon, and were instantly defaced by the intrusion.

The venerable wood that had grown for centuries
round the small house called St. Herbert's Hermitage,
had indeed some years before been felled by its
native proprietor, and the whole island planted anew
with Scotch firs, left to spindle up by each other's
side—a melancholy phalanx, defying the power of
the winds, and disregarding the regret of the spectator, who might otherwise have cheated himself into
a belief that some of the decayed remains of those
oaks, the place of which was in this manner usurped,
had been planted by the Hermit's own hand. This
sainted spot, however, suffered comparatively little

injury. At the bidding of an alien improver, the Hind's Cottage, upon Vicar's Island, in the same lake, with its embowering sycamores and cattle-shed, disappeared from the corner where they stood; and right in the middle, and upon the precise point of the island's highest elevation, rose a tall square habitation, with four sides exposed, like an astronomer's observatory, or a warren-house reared upon an eminence for the detection of depredators, or like the temple of Aeolus, where all the winds pay him obeisance. Round this novel structure, but at a respectful distance, platoons of firs were stationed, as if to protect their commander when weather and time should somewhat have shattered his strength. Within the narrow limits of this island were typified also the state and strength of a kingdom, and its religion as it had been, and was,—for neither was the druidical circle uncreated, nor the church of the present establishment; nor the stately pier, emblem of commerce and navigation; nor the fort to deal out thunder upon the approaching invader. The taste of a succeeding proprietor rectified the mistakes as far as was practicable, and has ridded the spot of its puerilities. The church, after having been docked of its steeple, is applied, both ostensibly and really, to the purpose for which the body of the pile was actually erected, namely, a boat-house; the fort is demolished; and, without indignation on the part of the spirits of the ancient Druids who officiated at the circle upon the opposite hill, the mimic arrangement of stones, with its *sanctum sanctorum*, has been swept away.

The present instance has been singled out, extravagant as it is, because, unquestionably, this beautiful country has, in numerous other places, suffered from the same spirit, though not clothed

exactly in the same form, nor active in an equal
degree.   It will be sufficient here to utter a regret
for the changes that have been made upon the
principal Island at Winandermere, and in its neighbourhood.   What could be more unfortunate than
the taste that suggested the paring of the shores,
and surrounding with an embankment this spot of
ground, the natural shape of which was so beautiful!
An artificial appearance has thus been given to the
whole, while infinite varieties of minute beauty have
been destroyed.   Could not the margin of this noble
island be given back to Nature?   Winds and waves
work with a careless and graceful hand: and, should
they in some places carry away a portion of the soil,
the trifling loss would be amply compensated by the
additional spirit, dignity, and loveliness, which these
agents and the other powers of Nature would soon
communicate to what was left behind.   As to the
larch-plantations upon the main shore,—they who
remember the original appearance of the rocky steeps,
scattered over with native hollies and ash-trees, will
be prepared to agree with what I shall have to say
hereafter upon plantations [1] in general.

But, in truth, no one can now travel through the
more frequented tracts, without being offended, at
almost every turn, by an introduction of discordant
objects, disturbing that peaceful harmony of form
and colour, which had been through a long lapse of
ages most happily preserved.

All gross transgressions of this kind originate,
doubtless, in a feeling natural and honourable to the
human mind, viz. the pleasure which it receives from
distinct ideas, and from the perception of order,
regularity, and contrivance.   Now, unpractised minds

---

[1] These are disappearing fast, under the management of the
present Proprietor, and native wood is resuming its place.

receive these impressions only from objects that are divided from each other by strong lines of demarcation; hence the delight with which such minds are smitten by formality and harsh contrast. But I would beg of those who are eager to create the means of such gratification, first carefully to study what already exists; and they will find, in a country so lavishly gifted by Nature, an abundant variety of forms marked out with a precision that will satisfy their desires. Moreover, a new habit of pleasure will be formed opposite to this, arising out of the perception of the fine gradations by which in Nature one thing passes away into another, and the boundaries that constitute individuality disappear in one instance only to be revived elsewhere under a more alluring form. The hill of Dunmallet, at the foot of Ullswater, was once divided into different portions by avenues of fir-trees, with a green and almost perpendicular lane descending down the steep hill through each avenue;—contrast this quaint appearance with the image of the same hill overgrown with self-planted wood,—each tree springing up in the situation best suited to its kind, and with that shape which the situation constrained or suffered it to take. What endless melting and playing into each other of forms and colours does the one offer to a mind at once attentive and active; and how insipid and lifeless, compared with it, appear those parts of the former exhibition with which a child, a peasant perhaps, or a citizen unfamiliar with natural imagery, would have been most delighted!

The disfigurement which this country has undergone has not, however, proceeded wholly from the common feelings of human nature which have been referred to as the primary sources of bad taste in rural imagery; another cause must be added, that has chiefly shown itself in its effect upon buildings. I mean a warping of the natural mind occasioned by a consciousness that, this country being an object of general admiration, every new house would be looked at and commented upon either for approbation or censure. Hence all the deformity and ungracefulness that ever pursue the steps of constraint or affectation. Persons, who in Leicestershire or Northamptonshire would probably have built a modest dwelling like those of their sensible neighbours, have been turned out of their course; and, acting a part, no wonder if, having had little experience, they act it ill. The craving for prospect, also, which is immoderate, particularly in new settlers, has rendered it impossible that buildings, whatever might have been their architecture, should in most instances be ornamental to the landscape; rising as they do from the summits of naked hills in staring contrast to the snugness and privacy of the ancient houses.

No man is to be condemned for a desire to decorate his residence and possessions; feeling a disposition to applaud such an endeavour, I would show how the end may be best attained. The rule is simple; with respect to grounds—work, where you can, in the spirit of Nature, with an invisible hand of art. Planting, and a removal of wood, may thus, and thus only, be carried on with good effect; and the like may be said of building, if Antiquity, who may be styled the co-partner and sister of Nature, be not denied the respect to which she is entitled. I have already spoken of the beautiful forms of the ancient mansions of this country, and of the happy manner in which they harmonize with the forms of Nature. Why cannot such be taken as a model, and modern internal convenience be confined within their external grace and dignity? Expense to be avoided, or difficulties to be overcome, may prevent a close adherence to this model; still, however, it might be followed to a certain degree in the style of architecture and in the choice of situation, if the thirst for prospect were mitigated by those considerations of comfort, shelter, and convenience, which used to be chiefly sought after. But should an aversion to old fashions unfortunately exist, accompanied with a desire to transplant into the cold and stormy North, the elegancies of a villa formed upon a model taken from countries with a milder climate, I will adduce a passage from an English poet, the divine Spenser, which will show in what manner such a plan may be realized without injury to the native beauty of these scenes.

Into that forest farre they thence him led,
Where was their dwelling in a pleasant glade
With MOUNTAINS round about environed,
And MIGHTY WOODS which did the valley shade,
And like a stately theatre it made,
Spreading itself into a spacious plaine;
And in the midst a little river plaide
Emongst the pumy stones which seem'd to plaine
With gentle murmure that his course they did
    restraine.

Beside the same a dainty place there lay,
Planted with mirtle trees and laurels green,
In which the birds sang many a lovely lay
Of God's high praise, and of their sweet loves teene,
As it an earthly paradise had beene;
In whose *enclosed shadow* there was pight
A fair pavilion, *scarcely to be seen,*
The which was all within most richly dight,
That greatest princes living it mote well delight.

Houses or mansions suited to a mountainous

region, should be 'not obvious, not obtrusive, but
retired'; and the reasons for this rule, though they
have been little adverted to, are evident. Mountainous countries, more frequently and forcibly than
others, remind us of the power of the elements, as
manifested in winds, snows, and torrents, and accordingly make the notion of exposure very unpleasing;
while shelter and comfort are in proportion necessary
and acceptable. Far-winding valleys difficult of access, and the feelings of simplicity habitually connected with mountain retirements, prompt us to
turn from ostentation as a thing there eminently
unnatural and out of place. A mansion, amid such
scenes, can never have sufficient dignity or interest
to become principal in the landscape, and to render
the mountains, lakes, or torrents, by which it may
be surrounded, a subordinate part of the view. It
is, I grant, easy to conceive, that an ancient castel-
lated building, hanging over a precipice or raised
upon an island, or the peninsula of a lake, like that
of Kilchurn Castle, upon Loch Awe, may not want,
whether deserted or inhabited, sufficient majesty to
preside for a moment in the spectator's thoughts
over the high mountains among which it is embosomed; but its titles are from antiquity—a power
readily submitted to upon occasion as the vicegerent
of Nature: it is respected, as having owed its existence to the necessities of things, a monument of
security in times of disturbance and danger long
passed away,—as a record of the pomp and violence
of passion, and a symbol of the wisdom of law;—
it bears a countenance of authority, which is not
impaired by decay.

> Child of loud-throated war, the mountain-stream
> Roars in thy hearing; but thy hour of rest
> Is come, and thou art silent in thy age!

To such honours a modern edifice can lay no claim;
and the puny efforts of elegance appear contemptible,
when, in such situations, they are obtruded in rivalship with the sublimities of Nature. But, towards
the verge of a district like this of which we are treating, where the mountains subside into hills of moderate
elevation, or in an undulating or flat country, a gentleman's mansion may, with propriety, become a principal
feature in the landscape; and, itself being a work of
art, works and traces of artificial ornament may, without censure, be extended around it, as they will be
referred to the common centre, the house; the right
of which to impress within certain limits a character
of obvious ornament will not be denied, where no
commanding forms of Nature dispute it, or set it
aside. Now, to a want of the perception of this
difference, and to the causes before assigned, may
chiefly be attributed the disfigurement which the
Country of the Lakes has undergone, from persons
who may have built, demolished, and planted, with
full confidence that every change and addition was or
would become an improvement.

The principle that ought to determine the position,
apparent size, and architecture of a house, viz. that it
should be so constructed, and (if large) so much of
it hidden, as to admit of its being gently incorporated
into the scenery of Nature—should also determine its
colour. Sir Joshua Reynolds used to say, 'If you
would fix upon the best colour for your house, turn
up a stone, or pluck up a handful of grass by the
roots, and see what is the colour of the soil where
the house is to stand, and let that be your choice.'
Of course, this precept given in conversation, could
not have been meant to be taken literally. For
example, in Low Furness, where the soil, from its
strong impregnation with iron, is universally of a deep

red, if this rule were strictly followed, the house also must be of a glaring red; in other places it must be of a sullen black; which would only be adding annoyance to annoyance. The rule, however, as a general guide, is good; and, in agricultural districts, where large tracts of soil are laid bare by the plough, particularly if (the face of the country being undulating) they are held up to view, this rule, though not to be implicitly adhered to, should never be lost sight of;—the colour of the house ought, if possible, to have a cast or shade of the colour of the soil. The principle is, that the house must harmonize with the surrounding landscape: accordingly, in mountainous countries, with still more confidence may it be said, 'Look at the rocks and those parts of the mountains where the soil is visible, and they will furnish a safe direction.' Nevertheless, it will often happen that the rocks may bear so large a proportion to the rest of the landscape, and may be of such a tone of colour, that the rule may not admit, even here, of being implicitly followed. For instance, the chief defect in the colouring of the Country of the Lakes (which is most strongly felt in the summer season) is an overprevalence of a bluish tint, which the green of the herbage, the fern, and the woods, does not sufficiently counteract. If a house, therefore, should stand where this defect prevails, I have no hesitation in saying, that the colour of the neighbouring rocks would not be the best that could be chosen. A tint ought to be introduced approaching nearer to those which, in the technical language of painters, are called *warm*: this, if happily selected, would not disturb but would animate the landscape. How often do we see this exemplified upon a small scale by the native cottages, in cases where the glare of whitewash has been subdued by time and enriched by weather-stains!

No harshness is then seen; but one of these cottages, thus coloured, will often form a central point to a landscape by which the whole shall be connected, and an influence of pleasure diffused over all the objects that compose the picture. But where the cold blue tint of the rocks is enriched by the iron tinge, the colour cannot be too closely imitated; and it will be produced of itself by the stones hewn from the adjoining quarry, and by the mortar, which may be tempered with the most gravelly part of the soil. The pure blue gravel, from the bed of the river, is, however, more suitable to the mason's purpose, who will probably insist also that the house must be covered with rough-cast, otherwise it cannot be kept dry; if this advice be taken, the builder of taste will set about contriving such means as may enable him to come the nearest to the effect aimed at.

The supposed necessity of rough-cast to keep out rain in houses not built of hewn stone or brick, has tended greatly to injure English landscape, and the neighbourhood of these Lakes especially, by furnishing such apt occasion for whitening buildings. That white should be a favourite colour for rural residences is natural for many reasons. The mere aspect of cleanliness and neatness thus given, not only to an individual house, but, where the practice is general, to the whole face of the country, produces moral associations so powerful, that, in many minds, they take place of all others. But what has already been said upon the subject of cottages, must have convinced men of feeling and imagination, that a human dwelling of the humblest class may be rendered more deeply interesting to the affections, and far more pleasing to the eye, by other influences, than a sprightly tone of colour spread over its outside. I do not, however, mean to deny, that a small white

building, embowered in trees, may, in some situations, be a delightful and animating object—in no
way injurious to the landscape; but this only where
it sparkles from the midst of a thick shade, and in
rare and solitary instances; especially if the country
be itself rich and pleasing, and abound with grand
forms.   On the sides of bleak and desolate moors,
we are indeed thankful for the sight of white cottages
and white houses plentifully scattered, where, without
these, perhaps everything would be cheerless: this
is said, however, with hesitation, and with a wilful
sacrifice of some higher enjoyments.   But I have
certainly seen such buildings glittering at sunrise,
and in wandering lights, with no common pleasure.
The continental traveller also will remember, that
the convents hanging from the rocks of the Rhine,
the Rhone, the Danube, or among the Appenines,
or the mountains of Spain, are not looked at with
less complacency when, as is often the case, they
happen to be of a brilliant white.   But this is
perhaps owing, in no small degree, to the contrast
of that lively colour with the gloom of monastic life,
and to the general want of rural residences of smiling
and attractive appearance, in those countries.

The objections to white, as a colour, in large spots
or masses in landscape, especially in a mountainous
country, are insurmountable.   In Nature, pure white
is scarcely ever found but in small objects, such as
flowers; or in those which are transitory, as the
clouds, foam of rivers, and snow.   Mr. Gilpin, who
notices this, has also recorded the just remark of
Mr. Locke, of N——, that white destroys the *gradations* of distance; and, therefore, an object of pure
white can scarcely ever be managed with good effect
in landscape-painting.   Five or six white houses,
scattered over a valley, by their obtrusiveness, dot

the surface, and divide it into triangles, or other mathematical figures, haunting the eye, and disturbing that repose which might otherwise be perfect. I have seen a single white house materially impair the majesty of a mountain; cutting away, by a harsh separation, the whole of its base, below the point on which the house stood. Thus was the apparent size of the mountain reduced, not by the interposition of another object in a manner to call forth the imagination, which will give more than the eye loses; but what had been abstracted in this case was left visible; and the mountain appeared to take its beginning, or to rise, from the line of the house, instead of its own natural base. But, if I may express my own individual feeling, it is after sunset, at the coming on of twilight, that white objects are most to be complained of. The solemnity and quietness of Nature at that time are always marred, and often destroyed by them. When the ground is covered with snow, they are of course inoffensive; and in moonshine they are always pleasing—it is a tone of light with which they accord: and the dimness of the scene is enlivened by an object at once conspicuous and cheerful. I will conclude this subject with noticing that the cold, slaty colour, which many persons, who have heard the white condemned, ·have adopted in its stead, must be disapproved of for the reason already given. The flaring yellow runs into the opposite extreme, and is still more censurable. Upon the whole, the safest colour for general use is something between a cream and a dust-colour, commonly called stone colour;— there are, among the Lakes, examples of this that need not be pointed out.[1]

[1] A proper colouring of houses is now becoming general. It is best that the colouring material should be mixed with the rough-cast, and not laid on as a *wash* afterwards.

The principle taken as our guide, viz. that the house should be so formed, and of such apparent size and colour, as to admit of its being gently incorporated with the works of Nature, should also be applied to the management of the grounds and plantations, and is here more urgently needed; for it is from abuses in this department, far more even than from the introduction of exotics in architecture (if the phrase may be used), that this country has suffered. Larch and fir plantations have been spread, not merely with a view to profit, but in many instances for the sake of ornament. To those who plant for profit, and are thrusting every other tree out of the way, to make room for their favourite, the larch, I would utter first a regret that they should have selected these lovely vales for their vegetable manufactory, when there is so much barren and irreclaimable land in the neighbouring moors, and in other parts of the island, which might have been had for this purpose at a far cheaper rate. And I will also beg leave to represent to them, that they ought not to be carried away by flattering promises from the speedy growth of this tree; because in rich soils and sheltered situations, the wood, though it thrives fast, is full of sap and of little value; and is, likewise, very subject to ravage from the attacks of insects, and from blight. Accordingly, in Scotland, where planting is much better understood, and carried on upon an incomparably larger scale than among us, good soil and sheltered situations are appropriated to the oak, the ash, and other deciduous trees; and the larch is now generally confined to barren and exposed ground. There the plant, which is a hardy one, is of slower growth; much less liable to injury; and the timber is of better quality. But the circumstances of many permit, and their taste leads them, to plant with little regard to profit; and there are others, less wealthy, who have such a lively feeling of the native beauty of these scenes, that they are laudably not unwilling to make some sacrifices to heighten it. Both these classes of persons, I would entreat to inquire of themselves wherein that beauty which they admire consists. They would then see that, after the feeling has been gratified that prompts us to gather round our dwelling a few flowers and shrubs, which from the circumstance of their not being native, may, by their very looks, remind us that they owe their existence to our hands, and their prosperity to our care; they will see that, after this natural desire has been provided for, the course of all beyond has been predetermined by the spirit of the place. Before I proceed, I will remind those who are not satisfied with the restraint thus laid upon them, that they are liable to a charge of inconsistency, when they are so eager to change the face of that country, whose native attractions, by the act of erecting their habitations in it, they have so emphatically acknowledged. And surely there is not a single spot that would not have, if well managed, sufficient dignity to support itself, unaided by the productions of other climates, or by elaborate decorations which might be becoming elsewhere.

Having adverted to the feelings that justify the introduction of a few exotic plants, provided they be confined almost to the doors of the house, we may add that a transition should be contrived, without abruptness, from these foreigners to the rest of the shrubs, which ought to be of the kinds scattered by Nature through the woods—holly, broom, wild-rose, elder, dogberry, white and black thorn, &c.—either these only, or such as are carefully selected in consequence of their being united in form, and harmonizing in colour with them, especially with respect to colour, when the tints are most diversified, as in autumn and spring. The various sorts of fruit-and-blossom-bearing trees usually found in orchards, to which may be added those of the woods—namely, the wilding, black cherry tree, and wild cluster-cherry (here called heck-berry)—may be happily admitted as an intermediate link between the shrubs and the forest trees; which last ought almost entirely to be such as are natives of the country. Of the birch, one of the most beautiful of the native trees, it may be noticed that, in dry and rocky situations, it outstrips even the larch, which many persons are tempted to plant merely on account of the speed of its growth. The Scotch fir is less attractive during its youth than any other plant; but, when full-grown, if it has had room to spread out its arms, it becomes a noble tree; and, by those who are disinterested enough to plant for posterity, it may be placed along with the sycamore near the house; for, from their massiveness, both these trees unite well with buildings, and in some situations with rocks also; having, in their forms and apparent substances, the effect of something intermediate betwixt the immovableness and solidity of stone, and the spray and foliage of the lighter trees. If these general rules be just, what shall we say to whole acres of artificial shrubbery and exotic trees among rocks and dashing torrents, with their own wild wood in sight—where we have the whole contents of the nurseryman's catalogue jumbled together — colour at war with colour, and form with form?—among the most peaceful subjects of Nature's kingdom, everywhere discord, distraction, and bewilderment! But this deformity, bad as it is, is not so obtrusive as the small patches and large tracts of larch-plantations

that are overrunning the hill-sides. To justify our
condemnation of these, let us again recur to Nature.
The process by which she forms woods and forests
is as follows. Seeds are scattered indiscriminately by
winds, brought by waters, and dropped by birds.
They perish, or produce, according as the soil and
situation upon which they fall are suited to them:
and under the same dependence, the seedling or the
sucker, if not cropped by animals (which Nature is
often careful to prevent by fencing it about with
brambles or other prickly shrubs), thrives, and the
tree grows, sometimes single, taking its own shape
without constraint, but for the most part compelled
to conform itself to some law imposed upon it by its
neighbours. From low and sheltered places, vegetation travels upwards to the more exposed; and the
young plants are protected, and to a certain degree
fashioned, by those that have preceded them. The
continuous mass of foliage which would be thus
produced is broken by rocks, or by glades or open
places, where the browsing of animals has prevented
the growth of wood. As vegetation ascends, the
winds begin also to bear their part in moulding the
forms of the trees; but, thus mutually protected,
trees, though not of the hardiest kind, are enabled
to climb high up the mountains. Gradually, however, by the quality of the ground, and by increasing
exposure, a stop is put to their ascent; the hardy
trees only are left: those also, by little and little,
give way—and a wild and irregular boundary is
established, graceful in its outline, and never contemplated without some feeling, more or less distinct,
of the powers of Nature by which it is imposed.

Contrast the liberty that encourages, and the law
that limits, this joint work of Nature and time, with
the disheartening necessities, restrictions, and dis-

advantages, under which the artificial planter must
proceed, even he whom long observation and fine
feeling have best qualified for his task. In the first
place his trees, however well chosen and adapted to
their several situations, must generally start all at
the same time; and this necessity would of itself
prevent that fine connexion of parts, that sympathy
and organization, if I may so express myself, which
pervades the whole of a natural wood, and appears
to the eye in its single trees, its masses of foliage,
and their various colours, when they are held up to
view on the side of a mountain; or when, spread over
a valley, they are looked down upon from an eminence.
It is therefore impossible, under any circumstances,
for the artificial planter to rival the beauty of Nature.
But a moment's thought will show that if ten thousand
of this spiky tree, the larch, are stuck in at once
upon the side of a hill, they can grow up into nothing
but deformity; that while they are suffered to stand,
we shall look in vain for any of those appearances
which are the chief sources of beauty in a natural
wood.

It must be acknowledged that the larch, till it
has outgrown the size of a shrub, shows, when looked
at singly, some elegance in form and appearance,
especially in spring, decorated, as it then is, by the
pink tassels of its blossoms; but, as a tree, it is less
than any other pleasing: its branches (for *boughs* it
has none) have no variety in the youth of the tree,
and little dignity, even when it attains its full growth;
leaves it cannot be said to have, consequently neither
affords shade nor shelter. In spring the larch becomes
green long before the native trees; and its green is
so peculiar and vivid, that finding nothing to harmonize with it, wherever it comes forth, a disagreeable
speck is produced. In summer, when all other trees

are in their pride, it is of a dingy lifeless hue; in autumn of a spiritless unvaried yellow, and in winter it is still more lamentably distinguished from every other deciduous tree of the forest, for they seem only to sleep, but the larch appears absolutely dead. If an attempt be made to mingle thickets, or a certain proportion of other forest-trees, with the larch, its horizontal branches intolerantly cut them down as with a scythe, or force them to spindle up to keep pace with it. The terminating spike renders it impossible that the several trees, where planted in numbers, should ever blend together so as to form a mass or masses of wood. Add thousands to tens of thousands, and the appearance is still the same—a collection of separate individual trees, obstinately presenting themselves as such; and which, from whatever point they are looked at, if but seen, may be counted upon the fingers. Sunshine or shadow has little power to adorn the surface of such a wood; and the trees not carrying up their heads, the wind raises among them no majestic undulations. It is indeed true, that in countries where the larch is a native, and where, without interruption, it may sweep from valley to valley, and from hill to hill, a sublime image may be produced by such a forest, in the same manner as by one composed of any other single tree, to the spreading of which no limits can be assigned. For sublimity will never be wanting, where the sense of innumerable multitude is lost in, and alternates with, that of intense unity; and to the ready perception of this effect, similarity and almost identity of individual form and monotony of colour contribute. But this feeling is confined to the native immeasurable forest; no artificial plantation can give it.

The foregoing observations will, I hope (as nothing

has been condemned or recommended without a substantial reason), have some influence upon those who
plant for ornament merely. To such as plant for
profit, I have already spoken. Let me then entreat
that the native deciduous trees may be left in complete possession of the lower ground; and that
plantations of larch, if introduced at all, may be
confined to the highest and most barren tracts.
Interposition of rocks would there break the dreary
uniformity of which we have been complaining; and
the winds would take hold of the trees, and imprint
upon their shapes a wildness congenial to their
situation.

Having determined what kinds of trees must be
wholly rejected, or at least very sparingly used, by
those who are unwilling to disfigure the country;
and having shown what kinds ought to be chosen;
I should have given, if my limits had not already
been overstepped, a few practical rules for the
manner in which trees ought to be disposed in
planting. But to this subject I should attach little
importance, if I could succeed in banishing such
trees as introduce deformity, and could prevail upon
the proprietor to confine himself, either to those
found in the native woods, or to such as accord with
them. This is, indeed, the main point; for, much
as these scenes have been injured by what has been
taken from them—buildings, trees, and woods, either
through negligence, necessity, avarice, or caprice—
it is not the removals, but the harsh *additions* that
have been made, which are the worst grievance—
a standing and unavoidable annoyance. Often have
I felt this distinction with mingled satisfaction and
regret ; for, if no positive deformity or discordance
be substituted or superinduced, such is the benignity
of Nature, that, take away from her beauty after

beauty, and ornament after ornament, her appearance cannot be marred—the scars, if any be left, will gradually disappear before a healing spirit; and what remains will still be soothing and pleasing.—

                    Many hearts deplored
The fate of those old trees; and oft with pain
The traveller at this day will stop and gaze
On wrongs which Nature scarcely seems to heed:
For sheltered places, bosoms, nooks, and bays,
And the pure mountains, and the gentle Tweed,
And the green silent pastures, yet remain.

There are few ancient woods left in this part of England upon which such indiscriminate ravage as is here 'deplored', could now be committed. But, out of the numerous copses, fine woods might in time be raised, probably without sacrifice of profit, by leaving, at the periodical fellings, a due proportion of the healthiest trees to grow up into timber.— This plan has fortunately, in many instances, been adopted; and they, who have set the example, are entitled to the thanks of all persons of taste. As to the management of planting with reasonable attention to ornament, let the images of Nature be your guide, and the whole secret lurks in a few words; thickets or underwoods—single trees—trees clustered or in groups—groves—unbroken woods, but with varied masses of foliage—glades—invisible or winding boundaries—in rocky districts, a seemly proportion of rock left wholly bare, and other parts half hidden—disagreeable objects concealed, and formal lines broken—trees climbing up to the horizon, and, in some places, ascending from its sharp edge, in which they are rooted, with the whole body of the tree appearing to stand in the clear sky —in other parts, woods surmounted by rocks utterly bare and naked, which add to the sense of height, as if vegetation could not thither be carried, and impress a feeling of duration, power of resistance, and security from change!

The author has been induced to speak thus at length, by a wish to preserve the native beauty of this delightful district, because still further changes in its appearance must inevitably follow, from the change of inhabitants and owners which is rapidly taking place.—About the same time that strangers began to be attracted to the country, and to feel a desire to settle in it, the difficulty that would have stood in the way of their procuring situations was lessened by an unfortunate alteration in the circumstances of the native peasantry, proceeding from a cause which then began to operate, and is now felt in every house.   The family of each man, whether *estatesman* or farmer, formerly had a twofold support; first, the produce of his lands and flocks; and, secondly, the profit drawn from the employment of the women and children, as manufacturers; spinning their own wool in their own houses (work chiefly done in the winter season), and carrying it to market for sale.   Hence, however numerous the children, the income of the family kept pace with its increase.   But, by the invention and universal application of machinery, this second resource has been cut off; the gains being so far reduced as not to be sought after but by a few aged persons disabled from other employment.   Doubtless, the invention of machinery has not been to these people a pure loss; for the profits arising from home-manufactures operated as a strong temptation to choose that mode of labour in neglect of husbandry.   They also participate in the general benefit which the island has derived from the increased value of the produce of land, brought about by the establishment of manufactories, and in the consequent quickening of agricultural industry. But this is far from making them amends; and now that home-manufactures are nearly done away, though the women and children might, at many seasons of the year, employ themselves with advantage in the fields beyond what they are accustomed to do, yet still all possible exertion in this way cannot be rationally expected from persons whose agricultural knowledge is so confined, and, above all, where there must necessarily be so small a capital. The consequence then is—that proprietors and farmers being no longer able to maintain themselves upon small farms, several are united in one, and the buildings go to decay or are destroyed; and that the lands of the *estatesmen* being mortgaged, and the owners constrained to part with them, they fall into the hands of wealthy purchasers, who in like manner unite and consolidate; and, if they wish to become residents, erect new mansions out of the ruins of the ancient cottages, whose little enclosures, with all the wild graces that grew out of them, disappear. The feudal tenure under which the estates are held has indeed done something towards checking this influx of new settlers; but so strong is the inclination, that these galling restraints are endured; and it is probable that in a few years the country on the margin of the Lakes will fall almost entirely into the possession of gentry, either strangers or natives. It is then much to be wished that a better taste should prevail among these new proprietors; and, as they cannot be expected to leave things to themselves, that skill and knowledge should prevent unnecessary deviations from that path of simplicity and beauty along which, without design and unconsciously, their humble predecessors have moved. In this wish the author will be joined by persons of pure taste throughout the whole island, who, by their visits (often repeated) to the Lakes in the North of England, testify that they deem the district a sort of national property, in which every man has a right and interest who has an eye to perceive and a heart to enjoy.

MISCELLANEOUS

OBSERVATIONS

MR. WEST, in his well-known Guide to the Lakes, recommends, as the best season for visiting this country, the interval from the beginning of June to the end of August; and, the two latter months being a time of vacation and leisure, it is almost exclusively in these that strangers resort hither. But that season is by no means the best; the colouring of the mountains and woods, unless where they are diversified by rocks, is of too unvaried a green; and, as a large portion of the valleys is allotted to hay-grass, some want of variety is found there also. The meadows, however, are sufficiently enlivened after hay-making begins, which is much later than in the southern part of the island. A stronger objection is rainy weather, setting in sometimes at this period with a vigour, and continuing with a perseverance, that may remind the disappointed and dejected traveller of those deluges of rain which fall among the Abyssinian mountains, for the annual supply of the Nile. The months of September and October (particularly October) are generally attended with much finer weather; and the scenery is then, beyond comparison, more diversified, more splendid, and beautiful; but, on the other hand, short days prevent long excursions, and sharp and chill gales are unfavourable to parties of pleasure out of doors. Nevertheless, to the sincere admirer of Nature, who is in good health and spirits, and at liberty to make a choice, the six weeks following the first of September may be recommended in preference to July and August. For there is no inconvenience arising from the season which, to such a person, would not be amply compensated by the *autumnal* appearance of any of the more retired valleys, into which discordant plantations and unsuitable buildings have not yet found entrance.—In such spots, at this season, there is an admirable compass and proportion of natural harmony in colour, through the whole scale of objects; in the tender green of the after-grass upon the meadows, interspersed with islands of grey or mossy rock, crowned by shrubs and trees; in the irregular enclosures of standing corn, or stubble-fields, in like manner broken; in the mountain-sides glowing with fern of divers colours; in the calm blue lakes and river-pools; and in the foliage of the trees, through all the tints of autumn,—from the pale and brilliant yellow of the birch and ash, to the deep greens of the unfaded oak and alder, and of the ivy upon the rocks, upon the trees, and the cottages. Yet, as most travellers are either stinted, or stint themselves, for time, the space between the middle or last week in May, and the middle or last week of June, may be pointed out as affording the best combination of long days, fine weather, and variety of impressions. Few of the native trees are then in full leaf; but, for whatever may be wanting in depth of shade, more than an equivalent will be found in the diversity of foliage, in the blossoms of the fruit-and-berry-bearing trees which abound in the woods, and in the golden flowers of the broom and other shrubs, with which many of the copses are interveined. In those woods, also, and on these

mountain-sides which have a northern aspect, and
in the deep dells, many of the spring-flowers still
linger; while the open and sunny places are stocked
with the flowers of the approaching summer. And,
besides, is not an exquisite pleasure still untasted by
him who has not heard the choir of linnets and
thrushes chaunting their love-songs in the copses,
woods, and hedgerows of a mountainous country;
safe from the birds of prey, which build in the
inaccessible crags, and are at all hours seen or heard
wheeling about in the air? The number of these
formidable creatures is probably the cause why, in
the *narrow* valleys, there are no skylarks; as the
destroyer would be enabled to dart upon them from
the near and surrounding crags, before they could
descend to their ground-nests for protection. It is
not often that the nightingale resorts to these vales;
but almost all the other tribes of our English
warblers are numerous; and their notes, when
listened to by the side of broad still waters, or
when heard in unison with the murmuring of mountain-brooks, have the compass of their power enlarged accordingly. There is also an imaginative
influence in the voice of the cuckoo, when that voice
has taken possession of a deep mountain valley, very
different from anything which can be excited by
the same sound in a flat country. Nor must a
circumstance be omitted, which here renders the
close of spring especially interesting; I mean the
practice of bringing down the ewes from the mountains to yean in the valleys and enclosed grounds.
The herbage being thus cropped as it springs, *that*
first tender emerald green of the season, which would
otherwise have lasted little more than a fortnight, is
prolonged in the pastures and meadows for many
weeks: while they are farther enlivened by the

multitude of lambs bleating and skipping about. These sportive creatures, as they gather strength, are turned out upon the open mountains, and with their slender limbs, their snow-white colour, and their wild and light motions, beautifully accord or contrast with the rocks and lawns, upon which they must now begin to seek their food. And last, but not least, at this time the traveller will be sure of room and comfortable accommodation, even in the smaller inns. I am aware that few of those who may be inclined to profit by this recommendation· will be able to do so, as the time and manner of an excursion of this kind are mostly regulated by circumstances which prevent an entire freedom of choice. It will therefore be more pleasant to observe, that though the months of July and August are liable to many objections, yet it often happens that the weather, at this time, is not more wet and stormy than they, who are really capable of enjoying the sublime forms of Nature in their utmost sublimity, would desire. For no traveller, provided he be in good health, and with any command of time, would have a just privilege to visit such scenes, if he could grudge the price of a little confinement among them, or interruption in his journey, for the sight or sound of a storm coming on or clearing away. Insensible must he be who would not congratulate himself upon the bold bursts of sunshine, the descending vapours, wandering lights and shadows, and the invigorated torrents and waterfalls, with which broken weather, in a mountainous region, is accompanied. At such a time there is no cause to complain, either of the monotony of midsummer colouring, or the glaring atmosphere of long, cloudless, and hot days.

Thus far concerning the respective advantages

and disadvantages of the different seasons for visiting this country. As to the order in which objects are best seen—a lake being composed of water flowing from higher grounds, and expanding itself till its receptacle is filled to the brim,—it follows, that it will appear to most advantage when approached from its outlet, especially if the lake be in a mountainous country; for, by this way of approach, the traveller faces the grander features of the scene, and is gradually conducted into its most sublime recesses. Now, every one knows that from amenity and beauty the transition to sublimity is easy and favourable, but the reverse is not so; for, after the faculties have been elevated, they are indisposed to humbler excitement.[1]

It is not likely that a mountain will be ascended without disappointment, if a wide range of prospect be the object, unless either the summit be reached before sunrise, or the visitant remain there until the time of sunset, and afterwards. The precipitous sides of the mountain, and the neighbouring summits, may be seen with effect under any atmosphere which allows them to be seen at all; but *he* is the most fortunate adventurer, who chances to be involved in vapours which open and let in an extent of country

---

[1] The only instances to which the foregoing observations do not apply, are Derwent-water and Lowes-water. Derwent is distinguished from all the other Lakes by being *surrounded* with sublimity: the fantastic mountains of Borrowdale to the south, the solitary majesty of Skiddaw to the north, the bold steeps of Wallow-crag and Lodore to the east, and to the west the clustering mountains of New-lands. Lowes-water is tame at the head, but towards its outlet has a magnificent assemblage of mountains. Yet as far as respects the formation of such receptacles, the general observation holds good: neither Derwent- nor Lowes-water derive any supplies from the streams of those mountains that dignify the landscape towards the outlets.

partially, or, dispersing suddenly, reveal the whole region from centre to circumference.

A stranger to a mountainous country may not be aware that his walk in the early morning ought to be taken on the eastern side of the vale, otherwise he will lose the morning light, first touching the tops and thence creeping down the sides of the opposite hills, as the sun ascends, or he may go to some central eminence, commanding both the shadows from the eastern and the lights upon the western mountains.   But, if the horizon line in the east be low, the western side may be taken for the sake of the reflections, upon the water, of light from the rising sun.   In the evening, for like reasons, the contrary course should be taken.

After all, it is upon the *mind* which a traveller brings along with him that his acquisitions, whether of pleasure or profit, must principally depend.—May I be allowed a few words on this subject?

Nothing is more injurious to genuine feeling than the practice of hastily and ungraciously depreciating the face of one country by comparing it with that of another.   True it is 'Qui *bene* distinguit bene *docet*'; yet fastidiousness is a wretched travelling companion; and the best guide to which in matters of taste we can entrust ourselves, is a disposition to be pleased.   For example, if a traveller be among the Alps, let him surrender up his mind to the fury of the gigantic torrents, and take delight in the contemplation of their almost irresistible violence, without complaining of the monotony of their foaming course, or being disgusted with the muddiness of the water—apparent even where it is violently agitated. In Cumberland and Westmorland, let not the comparative weakness of the streams prevent him from sympathizing with such impetuosity as they possess;

and, making the most of the present objects, let
him, as he justly may do, observe with admiration
the unrivalled brilliancy of the water, and that
variety of motion, mood, and character, that arises
out of the want of those resources by which the
power of the streams in the Alps is supported.—
Again, with respect to the mountains; though these
are comparatively of diminutive size, though there is
little of perpetual snow, and no voice of summer-
avalanches is heard among them; and though traces
left by the ravage of the elements are here comparatively rare and unimpressive, yet out of this very
deficiency proceeds a sense of stability and perma-
nence that is, to many minds, more grateful—

While the coarse rushes to the sweeping breeze
Sigh forth their ancient melodies.

Among the Alps are few places that do not preclude this feeling of tranquil sublimity. Havoc, and
ruin, and desolation, and encroachment, are everywhere more or less obtruded; and it is difficult,
notwithstanding the naked loftiness of the *pikes*, and
the snow-capped summits of the *mounts*, to escape
from the depressing sensation that the whole are in
a rapid process of dissolution; and, were it not that
the destructive agency must abate as the heights
diminish, would, in time to come, be levelled with
the plains. Nevertheless, I would relish to the
utmost the demonstrations of every species of power
at work to effect such changes.

From these general views let us descend a moment
to detail. A stranger to mountain imagery naturally on his first arrival looks out for sublimity in
every object that admits of it; and is almost always
disappointed. For this disappointment there exists,
I believe, no general preventive; nor is it desirable

that there should. But with regard to one class of
objects, there is a point in which injurious ex-
pectations may be easily corrected. It is generally
supposed that waterfalls are scarcely worth being
looked at except after much rain, and that the more
swoln the stream, the more fortunate the spectator;
but this, however, is true only of large cataracts with
sublime accompaniments; and not even of these
without some drawbacks. In other instances, what
becomes, at such a time, of that sense of refreshing
coolness which can only be felt in dry and sunny
weather, when the rocks, herbs, and flowers glisten
with moisture diffused by the breath of the precipitous water? But, considering these things as
objects of sight only, it may be observed that the
principal charm of the smaller waterfalls or cascades
consists in certain proportions of form and affinities
of colour, among the component parts of the scene;
and in the contrast maintained between the falling
water and that which is apparently at rest, or rather
settling gradually into quiet in the pool below. The
beauty of such a scene, where there is naturally so
much agitation, is also heightened, in a peculiar
manner, by the *glimmering*, and, towards the verge
of the pool, by the *steady* reflection of the surrounding images. Now, all those delicate distinctions are
destroyed by heavy floods, and the whole stream
rushes along in foam and tumultuous confusion. A
happy proportion of component parts is indeed
noticeable among the landscapes of the North of
England; and, in this characteristic essential to
a perfect picture, they surpass the scenes of Scotland,
and, in a still greater degree, those of Switzerland.

As a resident among the Lakes, I frequently hear
the scenery of this country compared with that of
the Alps; and therefore a few words shall be

added to what has been incidentally said upon that subject.

If we could recall to this region of lakes the native pine-forests, with which many hundred years ago a large portion of the heights was covered, then, during spring and autumn, it might frequently, with much propriety, be compared to Switzerland—the elements of the landscape would be the same—one country representing the other in miniature. Towns, villages, churches, rural seats, bridges and roads, green meadows and arable grounds, with their various produce, and deciduous woods of diversified foliage which occupy the vales and lower regions of the mountains, would, as in Switzerland, be divided by dark forests from ridges and round-topped heights covered with snow, and from pikes and sharp declivities imperfectly arrayed in the same glittering mantle: and the resemblance would be still more perfect on those days when vapours, resting upon and floating around the summits, leave the elevation of the mountains less dependent upon the eye than on the imagination. But the pine-forests have wholly disappeared; and only during late spring and early autumn is realized here that assemblage of the imagery of different seasons, which is exhibited through the whole summer among the Alps—winter in the distance—and warmth, leafy woods, verdure and fertility at hand, and widely diffused.

Striking, then, from among the permanent materials of the landscape that stage of vegetation which is occupied by pine-forests, and above that the perennial snows, we have mountains, the highest of which little exceed 3,000 feet, while some of the Alps do not fall short of 14,000 or 15,000, and 8,000 or 10,000 is not an uncommon elevation. Our tracts of wood and water are almost as diminutive in comparison;

therefore, as far as sublimity is dependent upon absolute bulk and height, and atmospherical influences in connexion with these, it is obvious that there can be no rivalship. But a short residence among the British Mountains will furnish abundant proof that after a certain point of elevation, viz. that which allows of compact and fleecy clouds settling upon, or sweeping over, the summits, the sense of sublimity depends more upon form and relation of objects to each other than upon their actual magnitude; and that an elevation of 3,000 feet is sufficient to call forth in a most impressive degree the creative, and magnifying, and softening powers of the atmosphere. Hence, on the score even of sublimity, the superiority of the Alps is by no means so great as might hastily be inferred; and, as to the *beauty* of the lower regions of the Swiss Mountains, it is noticeable that, as they are all regularly mown, their surface has nothing of that mellow tone and variety of hues by which mountain turf, that is never touched by the scythe, is distinguished. On the smooth and steep slopes of the Swiss hills these plots of verdure do indeed agreeably unite their colour with that of the deciduous trees, or make a lively contrast with the dark green pine-groves that define them, and among which they run in endless variety of shapes—but this is most pleasing *at first sight*; the permanent gratification of the eye requires finer gradations of tone, and a more delicate blending of hues into each other. Besides, it is only in spring and late autumn that cattle animate by their presence the Swiss lawns; and, though the pastures of the higher regions where they feed during the summer are left in their natural state of flowery herbage, those pastures are so remote, that their texture and colour are of no consequence in the composition of any picture in which a lake of the

Vales is a feature. Yet in those lofty regions, how vegetation is invigorated by the genial climate of that country ! Among the luxuriant flowers there met with, groves, or forests, if I may so call them, of Monkshood are frequently seen ; the plant of deep, rich blue, and as tall as in our gardens ; and this at an elevation where, in Cumberland, Icelandic moss would only be found, or the stony summits be utterly bare.

We have then for the colouring of Switzerland, *principally* a vivid green herbage, black woods, and dazzling snows, presented in masses with a grandeur to which no one can be insensible ; but not often graduated by Nature into soothing harmony, and so ill-suited to the pencil, that though abundance of good subjects may be there found, they are not such as can be deemed *characteristic* of the country ; nor is this unfitness confined to colour : the forms of the mountains, though many of them in some points of view the noblest that can be conceived, are apt to run into spikes and needles, and present a jagged outline which has a mean effect, transferred to canvas. This must have been felt by the ancient masters ; for, if I am not mistaken, they have not left a single landscape, the materials of which are taken from the *peculiar* features of the Alps ; yet Titian passed his life almost in their neighbourhood ; the Poussins and Claude must have been well acquainted with their aspects ; and several admirable painters, as Tibaldi and Luino, were born among the Italian Alps. A few experiments have lately been made by Englishmen, but they only prove that courage, skill, and judgement may surmount any obstacles ; and it may be safely affirmed, that they who have done best in this bold adventure will be the least likely to repeat the attempt. But, though our scenes are better suited to painting than those

of the Alps, I should be sorry to contemplate either
country in reference to that art, further than as its
fitness or unfitness for the pencil renders it more
or less pleasing to the eye of the spectator, who
has learned to observe and feel, chiefly from Nature
herself.

Deeming the points in which Alpine imagery is
superior to British too obvious to be insisted upon,
I will observe that the deciduous woods, though
in many places unapproachable by the axe, and
triumphing in the pomp and prodigality of Nature,
have in general [1] neither the variety nor beauty
which would exist in those of the mountains of
Britain, if left to themselves. Magnificent walnut-
trees grow upon the plains of Switzerland; and fine
trees of that species are found scattered over the
hill-sides : birches also grow here and there in
luxuriant beauty ; but neither these nor oaks are
ever a prevailing tree, nor can even be said to be
common ; and the oaks, as far as I had an opportunity of observing, are greatly inferior to those
of Britain. Among the interior valleys the proportion of beeches and pines is so great that other
trees are scarcely noticeable ; and surely such woods
are at all seasons much less agreeable than that rich
and harmonious distribution of oak, ash, elm, birch,
and alder, that formerly clothed the sides of Snowdon
and Helvellyn ; and of which no mean remains still
survive at the head of Ullswater. On the Italian
side of the Alps, chestnut and walnut-trees grow at
a considerable height on the mountains ; but even
there the foliage is not equal in beauty to the
'natural product' of this climate. In fact the sunshine of the South of Europe, so envied when heard

---

[1] The greatest variety of trees is found in the Valais.

of at a distance, is in many respects injurious to rural
beauty, particularly as it incites to the cultivation
of spots of ground which in colder climates would
be left in the hands of Nature, favouring at the same
time the culture of plants that are more valuable on
account of the fruit they produce to gratify the
palate, than for affording pleasure to the eye as
materials of landscape. Take, for instance, the Promontory of Bellagio, so fortunate in its command
of the three branches of the Lake of Como, yet the
ridge of the Promontory itself, being for the most
part covered with vines interspersed with olive-trees,
accords but ill with the vastness of the green unap-
propriated mountains, and derogates not a little
from the sublimity of those finely contrasted pictures
to which it is a foreground. The vine, when cultivated upon a large scale, notwithstanding all that
may be said of it in poetry,[1] makes but a dull
formal appearance in landscape ; and the olive-tree
(though one is loth to say so) is not more grateful
to the eye than our common willow, which it much
resembles ; but the hoariness of hue, common to
both, has in the aquatic plant an appropriate deli-
cacy, harmonizing with the situation in which it
most delights. The same may no doubt be said
of the olive among the dry rocks of Attica, but I am
speaking of it as found in gardens and vineyards in
the North of Italy. At Bellagio, what Englishman

---

[1] Lucretius has charmingly described a scene of this kind.

Inque dies magis in montem succedere sylvas
Cogebant, infraque locum concedere cultis :
Prata, lacus, rivos, segetes, vinetaque laeta
Collibus et campis ut haberent, atque olearum
Caerula distinguens inter *plaga* currere posset
Per tumulos, et convalleis, camposque profusa :
Ut nunc esse vides vario distincta lepore
Omnia, quae pomis intersita dulcibus ornant,
Arbustisque tenent felicibus obsita circum.

can resist the temptation of substituting, in his fancy, for these formal treasures of cultivation, the natural variety of one of our parks—its pastured lawns, coverts of hawthorn, of wild-rose, and honey-suckle, and the majesty of forest trees?—such wild graces as the banks of Derwent-water showed in the time of the Ratcliffes; and Gowbarrow Park, Lowther, and Rydal do at this day.

As my object is to reconcile a Briton to the scenery of his own country, though not at the expense of truth, I am not afraid of asserting that in many points of view our LAKES, also, are much more interesting than those of the Alps; first, as is implied above, from being more happily pro-portioned to the other features of the landscape; and next, both as being infinitely more pellucid, and less subject to agitation from the winds.[1] Como (which may perhaps be styled the King of Lakes, as Lugano is certainly the Queen) is disturbed by a periodical wind blowing *from* the head in the morning, and *towards* it in the afternoon. The magnificent Lake of the four Cantons, especially its noblest division, called the Lake of Uri, is not only much agitated by winds, but in the night time is disturbed from the bottom, as I was told, and indeed as I witnessed, without any apparent com-

---

[1] It is remarkable that Como (as is probably the case with other Italian Lakes) is more troubled by storms in summer than in winter. Hence the propriety of the following verses.

> Lari! margine ubique confragoso
> Nulli coelicolum negas sacellum
> Picto pariete saxeoque tecto;
> Hinc miracula multa navitarum
> Audis, nec placido refellis ore,
> Sed nova usque paras, Noto vel Euro
> *Aestivas* quatientibus cavernas,
> Vel surgentis ab Adduae cubili
> Caeco grandinis imbre provoluto. LANDOR.

motion in the air; and when at rest, the water is
not pure to the eye, but of a heavy green hue—as
is that of all the other lakes, apparently according
to the degree in which they are fed by melted snows.
If the Lake of Geneva furnish an exception, this
is probably owing to its vast extent, which allows
the water to deposit its impurities. The water of
the English lakes, on the contrary, being of a crystalline clearness, the reflections of the surrounding
hills are frequently so lively, that it is scarcely
possible to distinguish the point where the real
object terminates, and its unsubstantial duplicate
begins. The lower part of the Lake of Geneva,
from its narrowness, must be much less subject to
agitation than the higher divisions, and, as the
water is clearer than that of the other Swiss Lakes,
it will frequently exhibit this appearance, though
it is scarcely possible in an equal degree. During
two comprehensive tours among the Alps, I did
not observe, except on one of the smaller lakes,
between Lugano and Ponte Tresa, a single instance
of those beautiful repetitions of surrounding objects
on the bosom of the water, which are so frequently
seen here: not to speak of the fine dazzling trembling
network, breezy motions, and streaks and circles of
intermingled smooth and rippled water, which makes
the surface of our lakes a field of endless variety.
But among the Alps, where everything tends to the
grand and the sublime, in surfaces as well as in
forms, if the lakes do not court the placid reflections
of land objects those of first-rate magnitude make
compensation, in some degree, by exhibiting those
ever-changing fields of green, blue, and purple shadows
or lights (one scarcely knows which to name them),
that call to mind a sea-prospect contemplated from
a lofty cliff.

The subject of torrents and waterfalls has already been touched upon ; but it may be added that in Switzerland the perpetual accompaniment of snow upon the higher regions takes much from the effect of foaming white streams; while, from their frequency, they obstruct each other's influence upon the mind of the spectator ; and, in all cases, the effect of an individual cataract, excepting the great Fall of the Rhine at Schaffhausen, is diminished by the general fury of the stream of which it is a part.

Recurring to the reflections from still water, I will describe a singular phenomenon of this kind of which I was an eye-witness.

Walking by the side of Ullswater upon a calm September morning, I saw, deep within the bosom of the lake, a magnificent Castle, with towers and battlements, nothing could be more distinct than the whole edifice ;—after gazing with delight upon it for some time, as upon a work of enchantment, I could not but regret that my previous knowledge of the place enabled me to account for the appearance. It was in fact the reflection of a pleasure-house called Lyulph's Tower—the towers and battlements magnified and so much changed in shape as not to be immediately recognized. In the meanwhile, the pleasure-house itself was altogether hidden from my view by a body of vapour stretching over it and along the hill-side on which it stands, but not so as to have intercepted its communication with the lake ; and hence this novel and most impressive object, which, if I had been a stranger to the spot, would from its being inexplicable have long detained the mind in a state of pleasing astonishment.

Appearances of this kind, acting upon the credulity of early ages, may have given birth to, and favoured the belief in, stories of subaqueous palaces, gardens, and pleasure-grounds—the brilliant ornaments of Romance.

With this *inverted* scene I will couple a much more extraordinary phenomenon, which will show how other elegant fancies may have had their origin, less in invention than in the actual processes of Nature.

About eleven o'clock on the forenoon of a winter's day, coming suddenly, in company of a friend, into view of the Lake of Grasmere, we were alarmed by the sight of a newly-created Island ; the transitory thought of the moment was that it had been produced by an earthquake or some other convulsion of Nature. Recovering from the alarm, which was greater than the reader can possibly sympathize with, but which was shared to its full extent by my companion, we proceeded to examine the object before us. The elevation of this new island exceeded considerably that of the old one, its neighbour ; it was likewise larger in circumference, comprehending a space of about five acres ; its surface rocky, speckled with snow, and sprinkled over with birch-trees ; it was divided towards the south from the other island by a narrow frith, and in like manner from the northern shore of the lake ; on the east and west it was separated from the shore by a much larger space of smooth water.

Marvellous was the illusion ! Comparing the new with the old Island, the surface of which is soft, green, and unvaried, I do not scruple to say that, as an object of sight, it was much the more distinct. ' How little faith,' we exclaimed, ' is due to one sense, unless its evidence be confirmed by some of its fellows ! What Stranger could possibly be persuaded that this, which we know to be an unsubstantial mockery, is *really* so ; and that there exists only a single Island

on this beautiful Lake?'   At length the appearance
underwent a gradual transmutation; it lost its
prominence and passed into a glimmering and dim
inversion, and then totally disappeared;—leaving
behind it a clear open area of ice of the same
dimensions.   We now perceived that this bed of ice,
which was thinly suffused with water, had produced
the illusion, by reflecting and refracting (as persons
skilled in optics would no doubt easily explain)
a rocky and woody section of the opposite mountain
named Silver-how.

Having dwelt so much upon the beauty of pure
and still water, and pointed out the advantage which
the Lakes of the North of England have in this
particular over those of the Alps, it would be in-
justice not to advert to the sublimity that must
often be given to Alpine scenes, by the agitations
to which those vast bodies of diffused water are
there subject.   I have witnessed many tremendous
thunder-storms among the Alps, and the most glorious
effects of light and shadow; but I never happened to
be present when any Lake was agitated by those
hurricanes which I imagine must often torment them.
If the commotions be at all proportionable to the
expanse and depth of the waters, and the height
of the surrounding mountains, then if I may judge
from what is frequently seen here, the exhibition
must be awful and astonishing. — On this day,
March 30, 1822, the winds have been acting upon
the small Lake of Rydal, as if they had received
command to carry its waters from their bed into
the sky; the white billows in different quarters
disappeared under clouds, or rather drifts, of spray,
that were whirled along and up into the air by
scouring winds, charging each other in squadrons in
every direction upon the Lake.   The spray, having

been hurried aloft till it lost its consistency and whiteness, was driven along the mountain tops like flying showers that vanish in the distance. Frequently an eddying wind scooped the waters out of the basin, and forced them upwards in the very shape of an Icelandic Geyser, or boiling fountain, to the height of several hundred feet.

This small Mere of Rydal, from its position, is subject in a peculiar degree to these commotions. The present season, however, is unusually stormy;—great numbers of fish, two of them not less than twelve pounds weight, were a few days ago cast on the shores of Derwent-water by the force of the waves.

Lest, in the foregoing comparative estimate, I should be suspected of partiality to my native mountains, I will support my general opinion by the authority of Mr. West, whose Guide to the Lakes has been eminently serviceable to the Tourist for nearly fifty years. The Author, a Roman Catholic clergyman, had passed much time abroad, and was well acquainted with the scenery of the Continent. He thus expresses himself: 'They who intend to make the continental tour should begin here; as it will give, in miniature, an idea of what they are to meet with there, in traversing the Alps and Appenines; to which our northern mountains are not inferior in beauty of line, or variety of summit, number of lakes, and transparency of water; not in colouring of rock, or softness of turf; but in height and extent only. The mountains here are all accessible to the summit, and furnish prospects no less surprising and with more variety than the Alps themselves. The tops of the highest Alps are inaccessible, being covered with everlasting snow, which commencing at regular heights above the cultivated tracts, or wooded and verdant sides, form indeed the highest contrast in Nature. For there may be seen all the variety of climate in one view. To this, however, we oppose the sight of the ocean, from the summits of all the higher mountains, as it appears intersected with promontories, decorated with islands, and animated with navigation.'—West's *Guide*, p. 5.

EXCURSIONS

TO

THE TOP OF SCAWFELL AND ON THE BANKS OF ULLSWATER

It was my intention, several years ago, to describe a regular tour through this country, taking the different scenes in the most favourable order; but after some progress had been made in the work it was abandoned from a conviction that, if well executed, it would lessen the pleasure of the Traveller by anticipation, and, if the contrary, it would mislead him. The Reader may not, however, be displeased with the following extract from a letter to a Friend, giving an account of a visit to a summit of one of the highest of these mountains; of which I am reminded by the observations of Mr. West, and by reviewing what has been said of this district in comparison with the Alps.

Having left Rosthwaite in Borrowdale on a bright morning in the first week of October, we ascended from Seathwaite to the top of the ridge, called Ashcourse, and thence beheld three distinct views;—on

one side, the continuous Vale of Borrowdale, Keswick, and Bassenthwaite,—with Skiddaw, Helvellyn,
Saddle-back, and numerous other mountains,—and,
in the distance, the Solway Frith and the Mountains
of Scotland ;—on the other side, and below us, the
Langdale Pikes—their own vale below *them* ;—
Windermere,—and, far beyond Windermere, Ingle-
borough in Yorkshire.   But how shall I speak of
the deliciousness of the third prospect!   At this
time, *that* was most favoured by sunshine and shade.
The green Vale of Esk—deep and green, with its
glittering serpent stream, lay below us ; and on we
looked to the Mountains near the Sea,—Black Comb
pre-eminent,—and, still beyond, to the Sea itself, in
dazzling brightness.   Turning round we saw the
Mountains of Wastdale in tumult ; to our right,
Great Gavel, the loftiest, a distinct and *huge* form,
though the middle of the mountain was, to our eyes,
as its base.

We had attained the object of this journey ; but
our ambition now mounted higher.   We saw the
summit of Scawfell, apparently very near to us ;
and we shaped our course towards it ; but, dis-
covering that it could not be reached without first
making a considerable descent, we resolved instead
to aim at another point of the same mountain, called
the *Pikes*, which I have since found has been esti-
mated as higher than the summit bearing the name
of Scawfell Head, where the Stone Man is built.

The sun had never once been overshadowed by
a cloud during the whole of our progress from the
centre of Borrowdale.   On the summit of the Pike,
which we gained after much toil, though without
difficulty, there was not a breath of air to stir even
the papers containing our refreshment, as they lay
spread out upon a rock.   The stillness seemed to be

not of this world :—we paused, and kept silence to listen ; and no sound could be heard : the Scawfell Cataracts were voiceless to us ; and there was not an insect to hum in the air. The vales which we had seen from Ash-course lay yet in view ; and side by side with Eskdale we now saw the sister Vale of Donnerdale terminated by the Duddon Sands. But the majesty of the mountains below, and close to us, is not to be conceived. We now beheld the whole mass of Great Gavel from its base,—the Den of Wastdale at our feet—a gulf immeasurable ; Grasmere and the other mountains of Crummock ; Ennerdale and its mountains ; and the Sea beyond ! We sat down to our repast, and gladly would we have tempered our beverage (for there was no spring or well near us) with such a supply of delicious water as we might have procured had we been on the rival summit of Great Gavel ; for on its highest point is a small triangular receptacle in the native rock, which, the shepherds say, is never dry. There we might have slaked our thirst plenteously with a pure and celestial liquid, for the cup or basin, it appears, has no other feeder than the dews of heaven, the showers, the vapours, the hoar frost, and the spotless snow.

While we were gazing around, 'Look,' I exclaimed, 'at yon ship upon the glittering sea !' 'Is it a ship ?' replied our shepherd-guide. 'It can be nothing else,' interposed my companion ; 'I cannot be mistaken, I am so accustomed to the appearance of ships at sea.' The Guide dropped the argument ; but before a minute was gone he quietly said, 'Now look at your ship ; it is changed into a horse.' So indeed it was,—a horse with a gallant neck and head. We laughed heartily ; and, I hope, when again inclined to be positive, I may remember the ship and the

horse upon the glittering sea; and the calm confidence, yet submissiveness, of our wise Man of the
Mountains, who certainly had more knowledge of
clouds than we, whatever might be our knowledge
of ships.

I know not how long we might have remained on
the summit of the Pike, without a thought of
moving, had not our Guide warned us that we must
not linger; for a storm was coming. We looked in
vain to espy the signs of it. Mountains, vales, and
sea were touched with the clear light of the sun.
'It is there,' said he, pointing to the sea beyond
Whitehaven, and there we perceived a light vapour
unnoticeable but by a shepherd accustomed to watch
all mountain bodings. We gazed around again, and
yet again, unwilling to lose the remembrance of what
lay before us in that lofty solitude; and then prepared to depart. Meanwhile the air changed to
cold, and we saw that tiny vapour swelled into
mighty masses of cloud which came boiling over
the mountains. Great Gavel, Helvellyn, and Skiddaw, were wrapped in storm; yet Langdale, and the
mountains in that quarter, remained all bright in
sunshine. Soon the storm reached us; we sheltered
under a crag; and almost as rapidly as it had come
it passed away, and left us free to observe the
struggles of gloom and sunshine in other quarters.
Langdale now had its share, and the Pikes of
Langdale were decorated by two splendid rainbows.
Skiddaw also had his own rainbows. Before we again
reached Ash-course every cloud had vanished from
every summit.

I ought to have mentioned that round the top of
Scawfell-PIKE not a blade of grass is to be seen.
Cushions or tufts of moss, parched and brown,
appear between the huge blocks and stones that

lie in heaps on all sides to a great distance, like skeletons or bones of the earth not needed at the creation, and there left to be covered with never-dying lichens, which the clouds and dews nourish; and adorn with colours of vivid and exquisite beauty. Flowers, the most brilliant feathers, and even gems, scarcely surpass in colouring some of those masses of stone, which no human eye beholds, except the shepherd or traveller be led thither by curiosity: and how seldom must this happen! For the other eminence is the one visited by the adventurous stranger; and the shepherd has no inducement to ascend the PIKE in quest of his sheep; no food being *there* to tempt them.

We certainly were singularly favoured in the weather; for when we were seated on the summit, our conductor, turning his eyes thoughtfully round, said, ' I do not know that in my whole life I was ever, at any season of the year, so high upon the mountains on so *calm* a day.' (It was the seventh of October.) Afterwards we had a spectacle of the grandeur of earth and heaven commingled; yet without terror. We knew that the storm would pass away, for so our prophetic Guide had assured us.

Before we reached Seathwaite in Borrowdale, a few stars had appeared, and we pursued our way down the Vale, to Rosthwaite, by moonlight.

Scawfell and Helvellyn being the two Mountains of this region which will best repay the fatigue of ascending them, the following Verses may be here introduced with propriety. They are from the Author's Miscellaneous Poems.

TO ——

ON HER FIRST ASCENT TO THE SUMMIT OF HELVELLYN

INMATE of a Mountain Dwelling,
Thou hast clomb aloft, and gazed,
From the watch-towers of Helvellyn;
Awed, delighted, and amazed!

Potent was the spell that bound thee
Not unwilling to obey;
For blue Ether's arms, flung round thee,
Stilled the pantings of dismay.

Lo! the dwindled woods and meadows!
What a vast abyss is there!
Lo! the clouds, the solemn shadows,
And the glistenings—heavenly fair!

And a record of commotion
Which a thousand ridges yield;
Ridge, and gulf, and distant ocean
Gleaming like a silver shield!

—Take thy flight;—possess, inherit
Alps or Andes—they are thine!
With the morning's roseate Spirit,
Sweep their length of snowy line;

Or survey the bright dominions
In the gorgeous colours drest
Flung from off the purple pinions,
Evening spreads throughout the west!

Thine are all the coral fountains
Warbling in each sparry vault
Of the untrodden lunar mountains;
Listen to their songs!—or halt,

To Niphate's top invited,
Whither spiteful Satan steered;
Or descend where the ark alighted,
When the green earth re-appeared:

For the power of hills is on thee,
As was witnessed through thine eye
Then, when old Helvellyn won thee
To confess their majesty!

Having said so much of *points of view* to which
few are likely to ascend, I am induced to subjoin an
account of a short excursion through more accessible
parts of the country, made at a *time* when it is
seldom seen but by the inhabitants.   As the journal
was written for one acquainted with the general
features of the country, only those effects and
appearances are dwelt upon, which are produced by
the changeableness of the atmosphere, or belong to
the season when the excursion was made.

A. D. 1805.—On the seventh of November, on a
damp and gloomy morning, we left Grasmere Vale,
intending to pass a few days on the banks of Ullswater.   A mild and dry autumn had been unusually
favourable to the preservation and beauty of foliage;
and, far advanced as the season was, the trees on
the larger Island of Rydal-mere retained a splendour
which did not need the heightening of sunshine.
We noticed, as we passed, that the line of the grey
rocky shore of that island, shaggy with variegated
bushes and shrubs, and spotted and striped with
purplish brown heath, indistinguishably blending
with its image reflected in the still water, produced
a curious resemblance, both in form and colour, to
a richly-coated caterpillar, as it might appear
through a magnifying glass of extraordinary power.
The mists gathered as we went along: but, when we

reached the top of Kirkstone, we were glad we had
not been discouraged by the apprehension of bad
weather. Though not able to see a hundred yards
before us, we were more than contented. At such
a time, and in such a place, every scattered stone the
size of one's head becomes a companion. Near the
top of the Pass is the remnant of an old wall, which
(magnified, though obscured, by the vapour) might
have been taken for a fragment of some monument
of ancient grandeur,—yet that same pile of stones
we had never before even observed. This situation,
it must be allowed, is not favourable to gaiety; but
a pleasing hurry of spirits accompanies the surprise
occasioned by objects transformed, dilated, or dis-
torted, as they are when seen through such a
medium. Many of the fragments of rock on the
top and slopes of Kirkstone, and of similar places,
are fantastic enough in themselves; but the full
effect of such impressions can only be had in a state
of weather when they are not likely to be *sought* for.
It was not till we had descended considerably that
the fields of Hartshope were seen, like a lake tinged
by the reflection of sunny clouds: I mistook them
for Brothers-water, but, soon after, we saw that
Lake gleaming faintly with a steelly brightness,—
then, as we continued to descend, appeared the
brown oaks, and the birches of lively yellow—and
the cottages—and the lowly Hall of Hartshope,
with its long roof and ancient chimneys. During
great part of our way to Patterdale, we had rain, or
rather drizzling vapour; for there was never a drop
upon our hair or clothes larger than the smallest
pearls upon a lady's ring.

   The following morning, incessant rain till eleven
o'clock, when the sky began to clear, and we walked
along the eastern shore of Ullswater towards the

farm of Blowick. The wind blew strong, and drove
the clouds forward, on the side of the mountain
above our heads;—two storm-stiffened black yew-
trees fixed our notice, seen through, or under the
edge of, the flying mists,—four or five goats were
bounding among the rocks;—the sheep moved about
more quietly, or cowered beneath their sheltering
places. This is the only part of the country where
goats are now found;[1] but this morning, before we
had seen these, I was reminded of that picturesque
animal by two rams of mountain breed, both with
Ammonian horns, and with beards majestic as that
which Michael Angelo has given to his statue of
Moses. But to return; when our path had brought
us to that part of the naked common which
overlooks the woods and bush-besprinkled fields of
Blowick, the lake, clouds, and mists were all in
motion to the sound of sweeping winds;—the church
and cottages of Patterdale scarcely visible, or seen
only by fits between the shifting vapours. To the
northward the scene was less visionary;—Place Fell
steady and bold;—the whole lake driving onward
like a great river—waves dancing round the small
islands. The house at Blowick was the boundary of
our walk; and we returned, lamenting to see a
decaying and uncomfortable dwelling in a place
where sublimity and beauty seemed to contend with
each other. But these regrets were dispelled by
a glance on the woods that clothe the opposite
steeps of the lake. How exquisite was the mixture
of sober and splendid hues! The general colouring
of the trees was brown—rather that of ripe hazel
nuts; but towards the water there were yet beds of
green, and in the highest parts of the wood was

[1] A. D. 1805. These also have disappeared.

abundance of yellow foliage, which, gleaming through a vapoury lustre, reminded us of masses of clouds, as you see them gathered together in the west, and touched with the golden light of the setting sun.

After dinner we walked up the Vale: I had never had an idea of its extent and width in passing along the public road on the other side. We followed the path that leads from house to house; two or three times it took us through some of those copses or groves that cover the little hillocks in the middle of the vale, making an intricate and pleasing intermixture of lawn and wood. Our fancies could not resist the temptation; and we fixed upon a spot for a cottage, which we began to build: and finished as easily as castles are raised in the air.—Visited the same spot in the evening. I shall say nothing of the moonlight aspect of the situation which had charmed us so much in the afternoon; but I wish you had been with us when, in returning to our friend's house, we espied his lady's large white dog, lying in the moonshine upon the round knoll under the old yew-tree in the garden, a romantic image— the dark tree and its dark shadow—and the elegant creature, as fair as a spirit! The torrents murmured softly: the mountains down which they were falling did not, to my sight, furnish a background for this Ossianic picture; but I had a consciousness of the depth of the seclusion, and that mountains were embracing us on all sides; 'I saw not, but I *felt* that they were there.'

Friday, November 9.—Rain, as yesterday, till ten o'clock, when we took a boat to row down the lake. The day improved,—clouds and sunny gleams on the mountains. In the large bay under Place Fell, three fishermen were dragging a net,—a picturesque group beneath the high and bare crags! A raven was seen aloft; not hovering like the kite, for that is not the habit of the bird, but passing on with a straight-forward perseverance, and timing the motion of its wings to its own croaking. The waters were agitated; and the iron tone of the raven's voice, which strikes upon the ear at all times as the more dolorous from its regularity, was in fine keeping with the wild scene before our eyes. This carnivorous fowl is a great enemy to the lambs of these solitudes; I recollect frequently seeing, when a boy, bunches of unfledged ravens suspended from the churchyard gates of H——, for which a reward of *so* much a head was given to the adventurous destroyer.— The fishermen drew their net ashore, and hundreds of fish were leaping in their prison. They were all of the kind called skellies, a sort of fresh-water herring, shoals of which may sometimes be seen dimpling or rippling the surface of the lake in calm weather. This species is not found, I believe, in any other of these lakes; nor, as far as I know, is the chevin, that *spiritless* fish (though I am loth to call it so, for it was a prime favourite with Isaac Walton), which must frequent Ullswater, as I have seen a large shoal passing into the lake from the river Eamont. *Here* are no pike, and the char are smaller than those of the other lakes, and of inferior quality; but the grey trout attains a very large size, sometimes weighing above twenty pounds. This lordly creature seems to know that 'retiredness is a piece of majesty'; for it is scarcely ever caught, or even seen, except when it quits the depths of the lake in the spawning season, and runs up into the streams, where it is too often destroyed in disregard of the law of the land and of Nature.

Quitted the boat in the bay of Sandwyke, and pursued our way towards Martindale along a pleasant path—at first through a coppice, bordering the lake, then through green fields—and came to the village (if village it may be called, for the houses are few, and separated from each other), a sequestered spot, shut out from the view of the lake. Crossed the one-arched bridge, below the chapel, with its 'bare ring of mossy wall', and single yew-tree. At the last house in the dale we were greeted by the master, who was sitting at his door, with a flock of sheep collected round him, for the purpose of smearing them with tar (according to the custom of the season) for protection against the winter's cold. He invited us to enter, and view a room built by Mr. Hasell for the accommodation of his friends at the annual chase of red deer in his forests at the head of these dales. The room is fitted up in the sportsman's style, with a cupboard for bottles and glasses, with strong chairs, and a dining-table; and ornamented with the horns of the stags caught at these hunts for a succession of years—the length of the last race each had run being recorded under his spreading antlers. The good woman treated us with oaten cake, new and crisp; and after this welcome refreshment and rest, we proceeded on our return to Patterdale by a short cut over the mountains. On leaving the fields of Sandwyke, while ascending by a gentle slope along the valley of Martindale, we had occasion to observe that in thinly-peopled glens of this character the general want of wood gives a peculiar interest to the scattered cottages embowered in sycamore. Towards its head, this valley splits into two parts; and in one of these (that to the left) there is no house, nor any building to be seen but a cattle-shed on the side of a hill, which is sprinkled over with trees, evidently the remains of an extensive forest. Near the entrance of the other

division stands the house where we were entertained,
and beyond the enclosures of that farm there are no
other.   A few old trees remain, relics of the forest,
a little stream hastens, though with serpentine windings, through the uncultivated hollow, where many
cattle were pasturing.   The cattle of this country
are generally white or light-coloured; but these
were dark brown or black, which heightened the
resemblance this scene bears to many parts of the
Highlands of Scotland.—While we paused to rest
upon the hill-side, though well contented with the
quiet everyday sounds—the lowing of cattle, bleating of sheep, and the very gentle murmuring of the
valley stream, we could not but think what a grand
effect the music of the bugle-horn would have
among these mountains.   It is still heard once every
year, at the chase I have spoken of; a day of
festivity for the inhabitants of this district except
the poor deer, the most ancient of them all.   Our
ascent even to the top was very easy; when it was
accomplished we had exceedingly fine views, some of
the lofty Fells being resplendent with sunshine, and
others partly shrouded by clouds.   Ullswater, bordered by black steeps, was of dazzling brightness;
the plain beyond Penrith smooth and bright, or
rather gleamy, as the sea or sea sands.   Looked
down into Boardale, which, like Styebarrow, has been
named from the wild swine that formerly abounded
here; but it has now no sylvan covert, being smooth
and bare, a long, narrow, deep, cradle-shaped glen,
lying so sheltered that one would be pleased to see
it planted by human hands, there being a sufficiency
of soil; and the trees would be sheltered almost like
shrubs in a greenhouse.—After having walked some
way along the top of the hill, came in view of Glenridding and the mountains at the head of Grisdale.—

Before we began to descend, turned aside to a small ruin, called at this day the chapel, where it is said the inhabitants of Martindale and Patterdale were accustomed to assemble for worship. There are now no traces from which you could infer for what use the building had been erected; the loose stones and the few which yet continue piled up resemble those which lie elsewhere on the mountain; but the shape of the building having been oblong, its remains differ from those of a common sheepfold; and it has stood east and west. Scarcely did the Druids, when they fled to these fastnesses, perform their rites in any situation more exposed to disturbance from the elements. One cannot pass by without being reminded that the rustic psalmody must have had the accompaniment of many a wildly-whistling blast; and what dismal storms must have often drowned the voice of the preacher! As we descend, Patterdale opens upon the eye in grand simplicity, screened by mountains, and proceeding from two heads, Deepdale and Hartshope, where lies the little lake of Brothers-water, named in old maps Broaderwater, and probably rightly so; for Bassenthwaite-mere at this day is familiarly called Broadwater; but the change in the appellation of this small lake or pool (if it be a corruption) may have been assisted by some melancholy accident similar to what happened about twenty years ago, when two brothers were drowned there, having gone out to take their holiday pleasure upon the ice on a new-year's day.

A rough and precipitous peat track brought us down to our friend's house.—Another fine moonlight night; but a thick fog rising from the neighbouring river, enveloped the rocky and wood-crested knoll on which our fancy-cottage had been erected; and, under the damp cast upon my feelings, I consoled myself with moralizing on the folly of hasty decisions in matters of importance, and the necessity of having at least one year's knowledge of a place before you realize airy suggestions in solid stone.

Saturday, November 10.—At the breakfast-table tidings reached us of the death of Lord Nelson, and of the victory at Trafalgar. Sequestered as we were from the sympathy of a crowd, we were shocked to hear that the bells had been ringing joyously at Penrith to celebrate the triumph. In the rebellion of the year 1745, people fled with their valuables from the open country to Patterdale, as a place of refuge secure from the incursions of strangers. At that time, news such as we had heard might have been long in penetrating so far into the recesses of the mountains; but now, as you know, the approach is easy, and the communication, in summer time, almost hourly: nor is this strange, for travellers after pleasure are become not less active, and more numerous than those who formerly left their homes for purposes of gain. The priest on the banks of the remotest stream of Lapland will talk familiarly of Buonaparte's last conquests, and discuss the progress of the French revolution, having acquired much of his information from adventurers impelled by curiosity alone.

The morning was clear and cheerful after a night of sharp frost. At ten o'clock we took our way on foot towards Pooley Bridge, on the same side of the lake we had coasted in a boat the day before.— Looked backwards to the south from our favourite station above Blowick. The dazzling sunbeams striking upon the church and village, while the earth was steaming with exhalations not traceable in other quarters, rendered their forms even more indistinct than the partial and flitting veil of un-

illumined vapour had done two days before. The
grass on which we trod, and the trees in every thicket
were dripping with melted hoar-frost. We observed
the lemon-coloured leaves of the birches, as the
breeze turned them to the sun, sparkle, or rather
flash, like diamonds, and the leafless purple twigs
were tipped with globes of shining crystal.

The day continued delightful, and unclouded to
the end. I will not describe the country which we
slowly travelled through, nor relate our adventures :
and will only add that on the afternoon of the
thirteenth we returned along the banks of Ullswater
by the usual road. The lake lay in deep repose
after the agitations of a wet and stormy morning.
The trees in Gowbarrow Park were in that state
when what is gained by the disclosure of their bark
and branches compensates, almost, for the loss of
foliage, exhibiting the variety which characterizes
the point of time between autumn and winter. The
hawthorns were leafless ; their round heads covered
with rich green berries, and adorned with arches of
green brambles, and eglantines hung with glossy
hips ; and the grey trunks of some of the ancient
oaks, which in the summer season might have been
regarded only for their venerable majesty, now
attracted notice by a pretty embellishment of green
mosses and fern intermixed with russet leaves retained
by those slender outstarting twigs which the veteran
tree would not have tolerated in his strength. The
smooth silver branches of the ashes were bare ; most
of the alders as green as the Devonshire cottage-
myrtle that weathers the snows of Christmas. Will
you accept it as some apology for my having dwelt
so long on the woodland ornaments of these scenes—
that artists speak of the trees on the banks of
Ullswater, and especially along the bays of Styebarrow

Crag, as having a peculiar character of picturesque intricacy in their stems and branches, which their rocky stations and the mountain winds have combined to give them.

At the end of Gowbarrow Park a large herd of deer were either moving slowly or standing still among the fern. I was sorry when a chance companion, who had joined us by the way, startled them with a whistle, disturbing an image of grave simplicity and thoughtful enjoyment; for I could have fancied that those natives of this wild and beautiful region were partaking with us a sensation of the solemnity of the closing day. The sun had been set some time; and we could perceive that the light was fading away from the coves of Helvellyn, but the lake under a luminous sky was more brilliant than before.

After tea at Patterdale, set out again : a fine evening; the seven stars close to the mountain-top; all the stars seemed brighter than usual. The steeps were reflected in Brothers-water, and, above the lake, appeared like enormous black perpendicular walls. The Kirkstone torrents had been swoln by the rains, and now filled the mountain pass with their roaring, which added greatly to the solemnity of our walk. Behind us, when we had climbed to a great height, we saw one light very distinct in the vale, like a large red star—a solitary one in the gloomy region. The cheerfulness of the scene was in the sky above us.

Reached home a little before midnight. The following verses (from the Author's Miscellaneous Poems) after what has just been read may be acceptable to the reader, by way of conclusion to this little Volume.

ODE

THE PASS OF KIRKSTONE

1.

WITHIN the mind strong fancies work,
A deep delight the bosom thrills,
Oft as I pass along the fork
Of these fraternal hills:
Where, save the rugged road, we find
No appanage of human kind;
Nor hint of man, if stone or rock
Seem not his handy-work to mock
By something cognizably shaped;
Mockery—or model roughly hewn,
And left as if by earthquake strewn,
Or from the Flood escaped:
Altars for Druid service fit;
(But where no fire was ever lit,
Unless the glow-worm to the skies
Thence offer nightly sacrifice;)
Wrinkled Egyptian monument;
Green moss-grown tower; or hoary tent;
Tents of a camp that never shall be razed;
On which four thousand years have gazed!

2.

Ye plough-shares sparkling on the slopes!
Ye snow-white lambs that trip
Imprisoned 'mid the formal props
Of restless ownership!
Ye trees, that may to-morrow fall
To feed the insatiate Prodigal!

Lawns, houses, chattels, groves, and fields,
All that the fertile valley shields;
Wages of folly—baits of crime,—
Of life's uneasy game the stake,
Playthings that keep the eyes awake
Of drowsy, dotard Time;
O care! O guilt!—O vales and plains,
Here, 'mid his own unvexed domains,
A Genius dwells, that can subdue
At once all memory of You,—
Most potent when mists veil the sky,
Mists that distort and magnify;
While the coarse rushes, to the sweeping breeze,
Sigh forth their ancient melodies!

3.

List to those shriller notes!—*that* march
Perchance was on the blast,
When through this Height's inverted arch,
Rome's earliest legion passed!
—They saw, adventurously impelled,
And older eyes than theirs beheld,
This block—and yon, whose Church-like frame
Gives to the savage Pass its name.
Aspiring Road! that lov'st to hide
Thy daring in a vapoury bourn,
Not seldom may the hour return
When thou shalt be my Guide:
And I (as often we find cause,
When life is at a weary pause,
And we have panted up the hill
Of duty with reluctant will)
Be thankful, even though tired and faint,
For the rich bounties of Constraint;
Whence oft invigorating transports flow
That Choice lacked courage to bestow!

4.

My Soul was grateful for delight
That wore a threatening brow;
A veil is lifted—can she slight
The scene that opens now?
Though habitation none appear,
The greenness tells, man must be there;
The shelter—that the perspective
Is of the clime in which we live;
Where Toil pursues his daily round;
Where Pity sheds sweet tears, and Love,
In woodbine bower or birchen grove,
Inflicts his tender wound.
—Who comes not hither ne'er shall know
How beautiful the world below;
Nor can he guess how lightly leaps
The brook adown the rocky steeps.
Farewell, thou desolate Domain!
Hope, pointing to the cultured Plain,
Carols like a shepherd boy;
And who is she?—Can that be Joy!
Who, with a sun-beam for her guide,
Smoothly skims the meadows wide;
While Faith, from yonder opening cloud,
To hill and vale proclaims aloud,
'Whate'er the weak may dread, the wicked dare,
Thy lot, O man, is good, thy portion fair!

The Publishers, with permission of the Author,
have added the following

ITINERARY OF THE LAKES

FOR THE USE OF TOURISTS

STAGES			Miles
Lancaster to Kendal, by Kirkby Lonsdale . . .	30
Lancaster to Kendal, by Burton	22
Lancaster to Kendal, by Milnthorpe	21
Lancaster to Ulverston, over Sands	21
Lancaster to Ulverston, by Levens Bridge . . .	35½
Ulverston to Hawkshead, by Coniston Water-Head .	19
Ulverston to Bowness, by Newby Bridge . . .	17
Hawkshead to Ambleside	5
Hawkshead to Bowness	6
Kendal to Ambleside	14
Kendal to Ambleside, by Bowness	15
From and back to Ambleside round the two Langdales .	18
Ambleside to Ullswater	10
Ambleside to Keswick	16¼
Keswick to Borrowdale, and round the Lake .	12
Keswick to Borrowdale and Buttermere . . .	23
Keswick to Wastdale and Calder Bridge . . .	27
Calder Bridge to Buttermere and Keswick . . .	29
Keswick, round Bassenthwaite Lake	18
Keswick to Patterdale, Pooley Bridge, and Penrith .	38
Keswick to Pooley Bridge and Penrith . . .	24
Keswick to Penrith	17½
Whitehaven to Keswick	27
Workington to Keswick . . . . , . .	21
Excursion from Penrith to Haweswater . . .	27
Carlisle to Penrith	18
Penrith to Kendal	26

Inns and Public Houses, when not mentioned,
are marked thus *.

LANCASTER to KENDAL, by KIRKBY LONSDALE, 30 m.

Miles		Miles	Miles		Miles
5	Caton . . .	5	2	Tunstall . .	13
2	Claughton . .	7	2	Burrow . .	15
2	Hornby* . .	9	2	Kirkby Lonsdale .	17
2	Melling . .	11	13	Kendal . .	30

INNS.—*Lancaster*, King's Arms, Commercial Inn, Royal Oak.
INNS.—*Kirkby Lonsdale*, Rose and Crown, Green Dragon.

LANCASTER to KENDAL, by BURTON, 21¾ m.

10¾	Burton . .	10¾	½	End Moor* . .	16
4¾	Crooklands* .	15½	5¾	Kendal . .	21¾

INNS.—*Kendal*, King's Arms, Commercial Inn. *Burton*, Royal
Oak, King's Arms.

LANCASTER to KENDAL, by MILNTHORPE, 21¼ m.

2¾	Slyne* . .	2¾	4	Hale* . . .	12
1¼	Bolton-le-Sands* .	4	½	Beethom* . .	12½
2	Carnforth* . .	6	1¼	Milnthorpe . .	13¾
2	Junction of the		1¼	Heversham* .	15
	Milnthorpe and		1½	Levens Bridge .	16½
	Burton roads .	8	4¾	Kendal . .	21¼

INN.—*Milnthorpe*, Cross Keys.

LANCASTER to ULVERSTON, OVER SANDS, 21 m.

3½	Hest Bank* . .	3½	1¼	Flookburgh* .	15
¼	Lancaster Sands .	3¾	¾	Cark . . .	15¾
9	Kent's Bank	12¾	¼	Leven Sands .	16
1	Lower Allithwaite	13¾	5	Ulverston . .	21

INNS.—*Ulverston*, Sun Inn, Bradyll's Arms.

LANCASTER to ULVERSTON, by LEVENS BRIDGE, 35½ m.

12	Hale* . . .	12	3	Lindal* . .	23½
½	Beethom* .	12½	2	Newton* . .	25½
1¼	Milnthorpe .	13¾	2	Newby Bridge* .	27½
1¼	Heversham* .	15	2	Low Wood . .	29½
1½	Levens Bridge .	16½	3	Greenodd . .	32½
4	Witherslack* .	20½	3	Ulverston . .	35½

ULVERSTON to HAWKSHEAD, by Coniston Water-Head, 19 m.

6	Lowick Bridge	6	8	Coniston Water-Head*	16
2	Nibthwaite	8	3	Hawkshead	19

Inn.—*Hawkshead*, Red Lion.

ULVERSTON to BOWNESS, by Newby Bridge, 16 m.

3	Green Odd	3	2	Newby Bridge	8
3	Low Wood	6	8	Bowness	16

Inns.—*Bowness*, White Lion, Crown Inn.

HAWKSHEAD to AMBLESIDE, 5 m.

HAWKSHEAD to BOWNESS, 5½ m.

2	Sawrey	2	1½	Bowness	5½
2	Windermere Ferry*	4			

KENDAL to AMBLESIDE, 13½ m.

5	Staveley*	5	1½	Troutbeck Bridge*	10
1½	Ings Chapel	6½	2	Low Wood Inn	12
2	Orrest-head	8½	1½	Ambleside	13½

Inns.—*Ambleside*, Salutation Hotel, Commercial Inn.

KENDAL to AMBLESIDE, by Bowness, 15 m.

4	Crook*	4	2½	Troutbeck Bridge	11½
2	Gilpin Bridge*	6	2	Low Wood Inn	13½
3	Bowness	9	1½	Ambleside	15

A CIRCUIT from and back to AMBLESIDE by LITTLE and GREAT LANGDALE, 18 m.

3	Skelwith Bridge*	3	2	Langdale Chapel Stile*	13
2	Colwith Cascade	5			
3	Blea Tarn	8	5	By High Close and Rydal to Ambleside	18
3	Dungeon Ghyll	11			

AMBLESIDE to ULLSWATER, 10 m.

	Top of Kirkstone .	4		3	Inn at Patterdale .	10
3	Kirkstone Foot .	7				

AMBLESIDE to KESWICK, 16¼ m.

1½	Rydal . . .	1½		4	Smalthwaite Bridge	12¼
3½	Swan, Grasmere*	5		3	Castlerigg . .	15¼
2	Dunmail Raise .	7		1	Keswick . .	16¼
1¼	Nag's Head, Wyth-					
	burn . .	8¼				

EXCURSIONS FROM KESWICK

INNS.—*Keswick*, Royal Oak, Queen's Head.

To BORROWDALE, and ROUND THE LAKE, 12 m.

2	Barrow-house .	2		1	Return to Grange .	6
1	Lodore . .	3		4½	Portinscale . .	10½
1	Grange . .	4		1½	Keswick . .	12
1	Bowder Stone .	5				

To BORROWDALE and BUTTERMERE

5	Bowder Stone .	5		2	Buttermere* .	14
1	Rosthwaite . .	6		9	Keswick, by New-	
2	Seatoller . .	8			lands . .	23
4	Gatesgarth . .	12				

TWO DAYS' EXCURSION TO WASTDALE, ENNER-DALE, and LOWES-WATER

FIRST DAY

6	Rosthwaite . .	6		6	Strands*, Nether	
2	Seatoller . .	8			Wastdale . .	20
1	Seathwaite . .	9		4	Gosforth* . .	24
3	Sty-head . .	12		3	Calder Bridge* .	27
2	Wastdale-head .	14				

SECOND DAY

7	Ennerdale Bridge .	7		2	Scale-hill* . .	16
3	Lamplugh Cross .	10		4	Buttermere* .	20
4	Lowes-water .	14		9	Keswick . .	29

KESWICK ROUND BASSENTHWAITE WATER

8	Peel Wyke* .	.	8	3	Bassenthwaite Sand-		
1	Ouse Bridge	.	9		bed .	.	. 13
1	Castle Inn .	.	10	5	Keswick	.	. 18

KESWICK to PATTERDALE, and by POOLEY BRIDGE to PENRITH

10	Springfield* .	.	10	10	Pooley Bridge *	
7	Gowbarrow Park .		17		through Gow-	
5	Patterdale* .	.	22		barrow Park	. 32
				6	Penrith	. . 38

INNS. — *Penrith*, Crown Inn, The George.

KESWICK to POOLEY BRIDGE and PENRITH

| 12 | Penruddock* | . | 12 | 3 | Pooley Bridge | . 18 |
| 3 | Dacre* . | . | . 15 | 6 | Penrith | . . 24 |

KESWICK to PENRITH, 17½ m.

| 4 | Threlkeld* . | . | 4 | 3½ | Stainton* | . | . 15 |
| 7½ | Penruddock . | . | 11½ | 2½ | Penrith | . | . 17½ |

WHITEHAVEN to KESWICK, 27 m.

2	Moresby	.	. 2	5	Cockermouth	. 14
2	Distington .	.	4	2½	Embleton .	. 16½
2	Winscales .	.	6	6½	Thornthwaite	. 23
3	Little Clifton	.	9	4	Keswick .	. 27

INNS. — *Whitehaven*, Black Lion, Golden Lion, The Globe.
INNS. — *Cockermouth*, The Globe, The Sun.

WORKINGTON to KESWICK, 21 m.

The road joins that from Whitehaven to Keswick 4 miles from Workington.

INNS. — *Workington*, Green Dragon, New Crown, King's Arms.

EXCURSION from PENRITH to HAWESWATER

5	Lowther, or Ask-ham* .	5	
7	By Bampton* to Haweswater .	12	
4	Return by Butters-wick . .	16	
5	Over Moor Dovack to Pooley . .	21	
6	By Dalemain to Penrith . .	27	

CARLISLE to PENRITH, 18 m.

2½	Carlton* .	2½	
7	Low Hesket* .	9½	
1½	High Hesket* .	11	
2	Plumpton* . .	13	
5	Penrith . .	18	

INNS.—*Carlisle*, The Bush, Coffee House, King's Arms.

PENRITH to KENDAL, 26 m.

1	Eamont Bridge* .	1	
1½	Clifton* . .	2½	
2	Hackthorpe* .	4½	
5¾	Shap . . .	10¼	
6¾	Hawse Foot* .	17	
4	Plough Inn* .	21	
2½	Skelsmergh Stocks*	23½	
2½	Kendal . .	26	

INNS.—*Shap*, Greyhound, King's Arms.

HERE ENDS THE FIFTH EDITION OF THE GUIDE.

APPENDIX I

OF BUILDING AND GARDENING AND LAYING OUT OF GROUNDS

From a Letter to Sir George H. Beaumont, Bart.

GRASMERE, October 17, 1805.

MY DEAR SIR GEORGE,
    I was very glad to learn that you had room for me at Coleorton, and far more so, that your health was so much mended.   Lady Beaumont's last letter to my sister has made us wish that you were fairly through your present engagements with workmen and builders, and, as to improvements, had smoothed over the first difficulties, and gotten things into a way of improving themselves.   I do not suppose that any man ever built a house, without finding in the progress of it obstacles that were unforeseen, and something that might have been better planned ; things teazing and vexatious when they come, however the mind may have been made up at the outset to a general expectation of the kind.
    With respect to the grounds, you have there the advantage of being in good hands, namely, those of Nature ; and, assuredly, whatever petty crosses from contrariety of opinion or any other cause you may now meet with, these will soon disappear, and leave nothing behind but satisfaction and harmony.   Setting out from the distinction made by Coleridge which you mentioned, that your house will belong to the country, and not the country be an appendage to your house, you cannot be wrong.   Indeed, in the present state of society, I see nothing interesting either to the imagination or the heart, and, of course, nothing which true taste can approve, in any interference with Nature, grounded upon

any other principle.   In times when the feudal system
was in its vigor, and the personal importance of every
chieftain might be said to depend entirely upon the
extent of his landed property and rights of seignory;
when the king, in the habits of people's minds, was
considered as the primary and true proprietor of the
soil, which was granted out by him to different lords,
and again by them to their several tenants under them,
for the joint defence of all; there might have been
something imposing to the imagination in the whole
face of a district, testifying, obtrusively even, its dependence upon its chief.   Such an image would have been
in the spirit of the society, implying power, grandeur,
military state, and security; and, less directly, in the
person of the chief, high birth, and knightly education
and accomplishments; in short, the most of what was
then deemed interesting or affecting.   Yet, with the
exception of large parks and forests, nothing of this kind
was known at that time, and these were left in their wild
state, so that such display of ownership, so far from
taking from the beauty of Nature, was itself a chief
cause of that beauty being left unspoiled and unimpaired.
The *improvements*, when the place was sufficiently tranquil
to admit of any, though absurd and monstrous in themselves, were confined (as our present Laureate has
observed, I remember, in one of his essays) to an acre
or two about the house in the shape of garden with
terraces, &c.   So that Nature had greatly the advantage
in those days, when what has been called English
gardening was unheard of.   This is now beginning to
be perceived, and we are setting out to travel backwards.
Painters and poets have had the credit of being reckoned
the fathers of English gardening; they will also have,
hereafter, the better praise of being fathers of a better
taste.   Error is in general nothing more than getting
hold of good things, as everything has two handles, by
the wrong one.   It was a misconception of the meaning
and principles of poets and painters which gave countenance to the modern system of gardening, which is now,

I hope, on the decline; in other words, we are submitting to the rule which you at present are guided by, that of having our houses belong to the country, which will of course lead us back to the simplicity of Nature. And leaving your own individual sentiments and present work out of the question, what good can come of any other guide, under any circumstances? We have, indeed, distinctions of rank, hereditary legislators, and large landed proprietors; but from numberless causes the state of society is so much altered, that nothing of that lofty or imposing interest, formerly attached to large property in land, can now exist; none of the poetic pride, and pomp, and circumstance; nor anything that can be considered as making amends for violation done to the holiness of Nature. Let us take an extreme case, such as a residence of a Duke of Norfolk, or Northumberland: of course you would expect a mansion, in some degree answerable to their consequence, with all conveniences. The names of Howard and Percy will always stand high in the regards of Englishmen; but it is degrading, not only to such families as these, but to every really interesting one, to suppose that their importance will be most felt where most displayed, particularly in the way I am now alluding to. This is contracting a general feeling into a local one. Besides, were it not so, as to what concerns the Past, a man would be sadly astray, who should go, for example, to modernize Alnwick and its dependencies, with his head full of the ancient Percies: he would find nothing there which would remind him of them, except by contrast; and of that kind of admonition he would, indeed, have enough. But this by the by, for it is against the principle itself I am contending, and not the misapplication of it. After what was said above, I may ask, if anything connected with the families of Howard and Percy, and their rank and influence, and thus with the state of government and society, could, in the present age, be deemed a recompence for their thrusting themselves in between us and Nature. Surely it is a substitution of little things for great when we would put a whole country into a nobleman's livery. I know nothing which to me would be so pleasing or affecting, as to be able to say when I am in the midst of a large estate—This man is not the victim of his condition; he is not the spoiled child of worldly grandeur; the thought of himself does not take the lead in his enjoyments; he is, where he ought to be, lowly-minded, and has human feelings; he has a true relish of simplicity, and therefore stands the best chance of being happy; at least, without it there is no happiness, because there can be no true sense of the bounty and beauty of the creation, or insight into the constitution of the human mind.   Let a man of wealth and influence show, by the appearance of the country in his neighbourhood, that he treads in the steps of the good sense of the age, and occasionally goes foremost; let him give countenance to improvements in agriculture, steering clear of the pedantry of it, and showing that its grossest utilities will connect themselves harmoniously with the more intellectual arts, and even thrive the best under such connexion; let him do his utmost to be surrounded with tenants living comfortably, which will bring always with it the best of all graces which a country can have— flourishing fields and happy-looking houses; and, in that part of his estate devoted to park and pleasure-ground, let him keep himself as much out of sight as possible; let Nature be all in all, taking care that everything done by man shall be in the way of being adopted by her.   If people choose that a great mansion should be the chief figure in a country, let this kind of keeping prevail through the picture, and true taste will find no fault.

I am writing now rather for writing's sake than anything else, for I have many remembrances beating about in my head which you would little suspect. I have been thinking of you, and Coleridge, and our Scotch Tour, and Lord Lowther's grounds, and Heaven knows what. I have had before me the tremendously

long ell-wide gravel walks of the Duke of Athol, among
the wild glens of Blair, Brunar Water, and Dunkeld,
brushed neatly, without a blade of grass or weed upon
them, or anything that bore traces of a human footstep;
much indeed of human hands, but wear or tear of foot
was none. Thence I passed to our neighbour, Lord
Lowther. You know that his predecessor, greatly,
without doubt, to the advantage of the place, left it to
take care of itself. The present lord seems disposed to
do something, but not much. He has a neighbour,
a Quaker, an amiable, inoffensive man[1], and a little
of a poet too, who has amused himself, upon his own
small estate upon the Emont, in twining pathways
along the banks of the river, making little cells and
bowers with inscriptions of his own writing, all very
pretty as not spreading far. This man is at present
Arbiter Elegantiarum, or master of the grounds, at
Lowther, and what he has done hitherto is very well,
as it is little more than making accessible what could
not before be got at. You know something of Lowther.
I believe a more delightful spot is not under the sun.
Last summer I had a charming walk along the river, for
which I was indebted to this man, whose intention is
to carry the walk along the river-side till it joins the
great road at Lowther Bridge, which you will recollect,
just under Brougham, about a mile from Penrith.   This
to my great sorrow ! for the manufactured walk, which
was absolutely necessary in many places, will in one
place pass through a few hundred yards of forest
ground, and will there efface the most beautiful
specimen of a forest pathway ever seen by human eyes,
and which I have paced many an hour, when I was
a youth, with some of those I best love. This path
winds on under the trees with the wantonness of a river
or a living creature ; and even if I may say so with the
subtlety of a spirit, contracting or enlarging itself,
visible or invisible as it likes. There is a continued
opening between the trees, a narrow slip of green turf

[1] Mr. Thomas Wilkinson. See poem, 'To his Spade.'

besprinkled with flowers, chiefly daisies, and here it is, if I may use the same kind of language, that this pretty path plays its pranks, wearing away the turf and flowers at its pleasure.   When I took the walk I was speaking of, last summer, it was Sunday.   I met several of the people of the country posting to and from church, in different parts; and in a retired spot by the river-side were two musicians (belonging probably to some corps of volunteers) playing upon the hautboy and clarionet. You may guess I was not a little delighted; and as you had been a visitor at Lowther, I could not help wishing you were with me.   And now I am brought to the sentiment which occasioned this detail; I may say, brought back to my subject, which is this,—that all just and solid pleasure in natural objects rests upon two pillars, God and Man.   Laying out grounds, as it is called, may be considered as a liberal art, in some sort like poetry and painting; and its object, like that of all the liberal arts, is, or ought to be, to move the affections under the control of good sense; that is, those of the best and wisest : but, speaking with more precision, it is to assist Nature in moving the affections, and, surely, as I have said, the affections of those who have the deepest perception of the beauty of Nature; who have the most valuable feelings, that is, the most permanent, the most independent, the most ennobling, connected with Nature and human life.   No liberal art aims merely at the gratification of an individual or a class : the painter or poet is degraded in proportion as he does so; the true servants of the Arts pay homage to the human kind as impersonated in unwarped and enlightened minds.   If this be so when we are merely putting together words or colours, how much more ought the feeling to prevail when we are in the midst of the realities of things; of the beauty and harmony, of the joy and happiness of living creatures; of men and children, of birds and beasts, of hills and streams, and trees and flowers; with the changes of night and day. evening and morning, summer and winter; and all their unwearied actions and energies, as benign in the spirit that animates them as they are beautiful and grand in that form and clothing which is given to them for the delight of our senses! But I must stop, for you feel these things as deeply as I; more deeply, if it were only for this, that you have lived longer. What then shall we say of many great mansions with their un-qualified expulsion of human creatures from their neighbourhood, happy or not; houses, which do what is fabled of the upas tree, that they breathe out death and desolation! I know you will feel with me here, both as a man and a lover and professor of the arts. I was glad to hear from Lady Beaumont that you did not think of removing your village. Of course much here will depend upon circumstances, above all, with what kind of inhabitants, from the nature of the employments in that district, the village is likely to be stocked. But, for my part, strip my neighbourhood of human beings, and I should think it one of the greatest privations I could undergo. You have all the poverty of solitude, nothing of its elevation. In a word, if I were disposed to write a sermon (and this is something like one) upon the subject of taste in natural beauty, I should take for my text the little pathway in Lowther Woods, and all which I had to say would begin and end in the human heart, as under the direction of the Divine Nature, conferring value on the objects of the senses, and pointing out what is valuable in them.

I began this subject with Coleorton in my thoughts, and a confidence, that whatever difficulties or crosses (as of many good things it is not easy to choose the best) you might meet with in the practical application of your principles of Taste, yet, being what they are, you will soon be pleased and satisfied. Only (if I may take the freedom to say so) do not give way too much to others: considering what your studies and pursuits have been, your own judgement must be the best: professional men may suggest hints, but I would keep the decision to myself.

APPENDIX II

KENDAL AND WINDERMERE RAILWAY
TWO LETTERS
RE-PRINTED FROM THE MORNING POST
REVISED, WITH ADDITIONS

KENDAL :

PRINTED BY R. BRANTHWAITE AND SON
[1844]

SONNET ON THE PROJECTED KENDAL AND WINDERMERE RAILWAY

Is then no nook of English ground secure
From rash assault ?   Schemes of retirement sown
In youth, and 'mid the busy world kept pure
As when their earliest flowers of hope were blown,
Must perish ;—how can they this blight endure ?
And must he too the ruthless change bemoan
Who scorns a false utilitarian lure
'Mid his paternal fields at random thrown ?
Baffle the threat, bright Scene, from Orrest-head
Given to the pausing traveller's rapturous glance :
Plead for thy peace, thou beautiful romance
Of nature ; and, if human hearts be dead,
Speak, passing winds ; ye torrents, with your strong
And constant voice, protest against the wrong.

RYDAL MOUNT,   WILLIAM WORDSWORTH.
    October 12th, 1844.

The degree and kind of attachment which many ot
the yeomanry feel to their small inheritances can
scarcely be overrated.   Near the house of one of them
stands a magnificent tree, which a neighbour of the
owner advised him to fell for profit's sake.   ' Fell it,'
exclaimed the yeoman, ' I had rather fall on my knees
and worship it.'   It happens, I believe, that the intended railway would pass through this little property,
and I hope that an apology for the answer will not be
thought necessary by one who enters into the strength
of the feeling.   W. W.

KENDAL AND WINDERMERE RAILWAY

No. I.

To the Editor of the Morning Post.

Sir—

Some little time ago you did me the favour of inserting a sonnet expressive of the regret and indignation which, in common with others all over these Islands, I felt at the proposal of a railway to extend from Kendal to Low Wood, near the head of Windermere. The project was so offensive to a large majority of the proprietors through whose lands the line, after it came in view of the lake, was to pass, that, for this reason, and the avowed one of the heavy expense without which the difficulties in the way could not be overcome, it has been partially abandoned, and the terminus is now announced to be at a spot within a mile of Bowness. But as no guarantee can be given that the project will not hereafter be revived, and an attempt made to carry the line forward through the vales of Ambleside and Grasmere, and as in one main particular the case remains essentially the same, allow me to address you upon certain points which merit more consideration than the favourers of the scheme have yet given them. The matter, though seemingly local, is really one in which all persons of taste must be interested, and, therefore, I hope to be excused if I venture to treat it at some length.

I shall barely touch upon the statistics of the question, leaving these to the two adverse parties, who will lay their several statements before the Board of Trade, which may possibly be induced to refer the matter to the House of Commons; and, contemplating that possibility, I hope that the observations I have to make may not be altogether without influence upon the public, and upon individuals whose duty it may be to decide in their place whether the proposed measure shall be referred to a Committee of the House. Were the case before us an ordinary one, I should reject such an attempt as presumptuous and futile; but it is not only different from all others, but, in truth, peculiar.

In this district the manufactures are trifling; mines it has none, and its quarries are either wrought out or superseded; the soil is light, and the cultivateable parts of the country are very limited; so that it has little to send out, and little has it also to receive. Summer Tourists (and the very word precludes the notion of a railway) it has in abundance; but the inhabitants are so few and their intercourse with other places so infrequent, that one daily coach, which could not be kept going but through its connection with the Post-office, suffices for three-fourths of the year along the line of country as far as Keswick. The staple of the district is, in fact, its beauty and its character of seclusion and retirement; and to these topics and to others connected with them my remarks shall be confined.

The projectors have induced many to favour their schemes by declaring that one of their main objects is to place the beauties of the Lake district within easier reach of those who cannot afford to pay for ordinary conveyances. Look at the facts. Railways are completed, which, joined with others in rapid progress, will bring travellers who prefer approaching by Ullswater to within four miles of that lake. The Lancaster and Carlisle Railway will approach the town of Kendal, about eight or nine miles from eminences that command the whole vale of Windermere. The lakes are therefore at present of very easy access for *all* persons; but if they be not made still more so, the poor, it is said, will be

wronged.   Before this be admitted let the question be
fairly looked into, and its different bearings examined.
No one can assert that, if this intended mode of approach be not effected, anything will be taken away
that is actually possessed.   The wrong, if any, must lie
in the unwarrantable obstruction of an attainable benefit.   First, then, let us consider the probable amount of
that benefit.

Elaborate gardens, with topiary works, were in high
request, even among our remote ancestors, but the
relish for choice and picturesque natural *scenery* (a poor
and mean word which requires an apology, but will be
generally understood) is quite of recent origin.   Our
earlier travellers—Ray, the naturalist, one of the first
men of his age—Bishop Burnet, and others who had
crossed the Alps, or lived some time in Switzerland, are
silent upon the sublimity and beauty of those regions ;
and Burnet even uses these words, speaking of the
Grisons—' When they have made up estates elsewhere
they are glad to leave Italy and the best parts of Germany, and to come and live among those mountains of
which the very sight is enough to fill a man with horror.'
The accomplished Evelyn, giving an account of his
journey from Italy through the Alps, dilates upon the
terrible, the melancholy, and the uncomfortable ; but,
till he comes to the fruitful country in the neighbourhood of Geneva, not a syllable of delight or praise.
In the *Sacra Telluris Theoria* of the other Burnet there
is a passage—omitted, however, in his own English
translation of the work—in which he gives utterance to
his sensations, when, from a particular spot he beheld
a tract of the Alps rising before him on the one hand,
and on the other the Mediterranean Sea spread beneath
him.   Nothing can be worthier of the magnificent
appearances he describes than his language.   In a noble
strain also does the Poet Gray address, in a Latin Ode,
the *Religio loci* at the Grande Chartruise.   But before
his time, with the exception of the passage from Thomas
Burnet just alluded to, there is not, I believe, a single

English traveller whose published writings would dis-
prove the assertion, that, where precipitous rocks and
mountains are mentioned at all, they are spoken of as
objects of dislike and fear, and not of admiration. Even
Gray himself, describing, in his Journal, the steeps at
the entrance of Borrowdale, expresses his terror in the
language of Dante :—' Let us not speak of them, but
look and pass on.' In my youth, I lived some time in
the vale of Keswick, under the roof of a shrewd and
sensible woman, who more than once exclaimed in my
hearing, ' Bless me ! folk are always talking about
prospects : when I was young there was never sic a
thing neamed.' In fact, our ancestors, as everywhere
appears, in choosing the site of their houses, looked
only at shelter and convenience, especially of water,
and often would place a barn or any other out-house
directly in front of their habitations, however beautiful
the landscape which their windows might otherwise
have commanded. The first house that was built in the
Lake district for the sake of the beauty of the country
was the work of a Mr. English, who had travelled in
Italy, and chose for his site, some eighty years ago, the
great island of Windermere ; but it was sold before his
building was finished, and he showed how little he was
capable of appreciating the character of the situation by
setting up a length of high garden-wall, as exclusive as
it was ugly, almost close to the house. The nuisance
was swept away when the late Mr. Curwen became the
owner of this favoured spot. Mr. English was followed
by Mr. Pocklington, a native of Nottinghamshire, who
played strange pranks by his buildings and plantations
upon Vicar's Island, in Derwentwater, which his admiration, such as it was, of the country, and probably a wish
to be a leader in a new fashion, had tempted him to
purchase. But what has all this to do with the subject ?—Why, to show that a vivid perception of romantic
scenery is neither inherent in mankind, nor a necessary
consequence of even a comprehensive education. It is
benignly ordained that green fields, clear blue skies,

running streams of pure water, rich groves and woods, orchards, and all the ordinary varieties of rural nature, should find an easy way to the affections of all men, and more or less so from early childhood till the senses are impaired by old age and the sources of mere earthly enjoyment have in a great measure failed. But a taste beyond this, however desirable it may be that every one should possess it, is not to be implanted at once; it must be gradually developed both in nations and individuals. Rocks and mountains, torrents and wide-spread waters, and all those features of nature which go to the composition of such scenes as this part of England is distinguished for, cannot, in their finer relations to the human mind, be comprehended, or even very imperfectly conceived, without processes of culture or opportunities of observation in some degree habitual. In the eye of thousands and tens of thousands, a rich meadow, with fat cattle grazing upon it, or the sight of what they would call a heavy crop of corn, is worth all that the Alps and Pyrenees in their utmost grandeur and beauty could show to them ; and, notwithstanding the grateful influence, as we have observed, of ordinary nature and the productions of the fields, it is noticeable what trifling conventional prepossessions will, in common minds, not only preclude pleasure from the sight of natural beauty, but will even turn it into an object of disgust. ' If I had to do with this garden,' said a respectable person, one of my neighbours, ' I would sweep away all the black and dirty stuff from that wall.' The wall was backed by a bank of earth, and was exquisitely decorated with ivy, flowers, moss, and ferns, such as grow of themselves in like places ; but the mere notion of fitness associated with a trim garden-wall prevented, in this instance, all sense of the spontaneous bounty and delicate care of nature. In the midst of a small pleasure-ground, immediately below my house, rises a detached rock, equally remarkable for the beauty of its form, the ancient oaks that grow out of it, and the flowers and shrubs which adorn it. ' What a nice place would this be,' said a Manchester tradesman, pointing to the rock, 'if that ugly lump were but out of the way.'　Men as little advanced in the pleasure which such objects give to others are so far from being rare, that they may be said fairly to represent a large majority of mankind. This is a fact, and none but the deceiver and the willingly deceived can be offended by its being stated.　But as a more susceptible taste is undoubtedly a great acquisition, and has been spreading among us for some years, the question is, what means are most likely to be beneficial in extending its operation?　Surely that good is not to be obtained by transferring at once uneducated persons in large bodies to particular spots, where the combinations of natural objects are such as would afford the greatest pleasure to those who have been in the habit of observing and studying the peculiar character of such scenes, and how they differ one from another. Instead of tempting artisans and labourers, and the humbler classes of shopkeepers, to ramble to a distance, let us rather look with lively sympathy upon persons in that condition, when, upon a holiday, or on the Sunday, after having attended divine worship, they make little excursions with their wives and children among neighbouring fields, whither the whole of each family might stroll, or be conveyed at much less cost than would be required to take a single individual of the number to the shores of Windermere by the cheapest conveyance. It is in some such way as this only, that persons who must labour daily with their hands for bread in large towns, or are subject to confinement through the week, can be trained to a profitable intercourse with nature where she is the most distinguished by the majesty and sublimity of her forms.

For further illustration of the subject, turn to what we know of a man of extraordinary genius, who was bred to hard labour in agricultural employments, Burns, the poet.　When he had become distinguished by the publication of a volume of verses, and was enabled to travel by the profit his poems brought him, he made a tour, in the course of which, as his companion, Dr. Adair, tells us, he visited scenes inferior to none in Scotland in beauty, sublimity, and romantic interest; and the Doctor having noticed, with other companions, that he seemed little moved upon one occasion by the sight of such a scene, says—'I doubt if he had much taste for the picturesque.' The personal testimony, however, upon this point is conflicting; but when Dr. Currie refers to certain local poems as decisive proofs that Burns' fellow-traveller was mistaken, the biographer is surely unfortunate. How vague and tame are the poet's expressions in those few local poems, compared with his language when he is describing objects with which his position in life allowed him to be familiar! It appears, both from what his works contain, and from what is not to be found in them, that, sensitive as they abundantly prove his mind to have been in its intercourse with common rural images, and with the general powers of nature exhibited in storm and in stillness, in light or darkness, and in the various aspects of the seasons, he was little affected by the sight of one spot in preference to another, unless where it derived an interest from history, tradition, or local associations. He lived many years in Nithsdale, where he was in daily sight of Skiddaw, yet he never crossed the Solway for a better acquaintance with that mountain; and I am persuaded that, if he had been induced to ramble among our lakes, by that time sufficiently celebrated, he would have seldom been more excited than by some ordinary Scottish stream or hill with a tradition attached to it, or which had been the scene of a favourite ballad or love song. If all this be truly said of such a man, and the like cannot be denied of the eminent individuals before named, who to great natural talents added the accomplishments of scholarship or science, then what ground is there for maintaining that the poor are treated with disrespect, or wrong done to them or any class of visitants, if we be reluctant to introduce a railway into this country for the sake of lessening, by eight or nine miles only, the fatigue or expense of their journey to Windermere?—And wherever any one among the labouring classes has made even an approach to the sensibility which drew a lamentation from Burns when he had uprooted a daisy with his plough, and caused him to turn the 'weeder-clips aside' from the thistle, and spare 'the symbol dear' of his country, then surely such a one, could he afford by any means to travel as far as Kendal, would not grudge a two hours' walk across the skirts of the beautiful country that he was desirous of visiting.

The wide-spread waters of these regions are in their nature peaceful; so are the steep mountains and the rocky glens; nor can they be profitably enjoyed but by a mind disposed to peace. Go to a pantomime, a farce, or a puppet-show, if you want noisy pleasure—the crowd of spectators who partake your enjoyment will, by their presence and acclamations, enhance it; but may those who have given proof that they prefer other gratifications continue to be safe from the molestation of cheap trains pouring out their hundreds at a time along the margin of Windermere; nor let any one be liable to the charge of being selfishly disregardful of the poor, and their innocent and salutary enjoyments, if he does not congratulate himself upon the especial benefit which would thus be conferred on such a concourse.

> O, Nature, a' thy shows an' forms,
> To feeling pensive hearts hae charms!

So exclaimed the Ayrshire ploughman, speaking of ordinary rural nature under the varying influences of the seasons, and the sentiment has found an echo in the bosoms of thousands in as humble a condition as he himself was when he gave vent to it. But then they were feeling, pensive hearts; men who would be among the first to lament the facility with which they had approached this region, by a sacrifice of so much of its quiet and beauty, as, from the intrusion of a railway, would be inseparable. What can, in truth, be more absurd than that either rich or poor should be spared the trouble of travelling by the high roads over so short a space, according to their respective means, if the unavoidable consequence must be a great disturbance of the retirement, and in many places a destruction of the beauty of the country, which the parties are come in search of? Would not this be pretty much like the child's cutting up his drum to learn where the sound came from?

Having, I trust, given sufficient reason for the belief that the imperfectly educated classes are not likely to draw much good from rare visits to the lakes performed in this way, and surely on their own account it is not desirable that the visits should be frequent, let us glance at the mischief which such facilities would certainly produce. The directors of railway companies are always ready to devise or encourage entertainments for tempting the humbler classes to leave their homes. Accordingly, for the profit of the shareholders and that of the lower class of inn-keepers, we should have wrestling matches, horse and boat races without number, and pot-houses and beer-shops would keep pace with these excitements and recreations, most of which might too easily be had elsewhere. The injury which would thus be done to morals, both among this influx of strangers and the lower class of inhabitants, is obvious; and, supposing such extraordinary temptations not to be held out, there cannot be a doubt that the Sabbath day in the towns of Bowness and Ambleside, and other parts of the district, would be subject to much additional desecration.

Whatever comes of the scheme which we have endeavoured to discountenance, the charge against its opponents of being selfishly regardless of the poor, ought to cease. The cry has been raised and kept up by three classes of persons—they who wish to bring into discredit all such as stand in the way of their gains or gambling speculations; they who are dazzled by the application of physical science to the useful arts, and indiscriminately applaud what they call the spirit of the age as manifested in this way ; and, lastly, those persons who are ever ready to step forward in what appears to them to be the cause of the poor, but not always with becoming attention to particulars. I am well aware that upon the first class what has been said will be of no avail, but upon the two latter some impression will, I trust, be made.

To conclude. The railway power, we know well, will not admit of being materially counteracted by sentiment; and who would wish it where large towns are connected, and the interests of trade and agriculture are substantially promoted, by such mode of intercommunication ? But be it remembered, that this case is, as has been said before, a peculiar one, and that the staple of the country is its beauty and its character of retirement. Let then the beauty be undisfigured and the retirement unviolated, unless there be reason for believing that rights and interests of a higher kind and more apparent than those which have been urged in behalf of the projected intrusion will compensate the sacrifice. Thanking you for the judicious observations that have appeared in your paper upon the subject of railways,

I remain, Sir,
Your obliged,
Wm. Wordsworth.

Rydal Mount, Dec. 9, 1844.

Note.—To the instances named in this letter of the indifference even of men of genius to the sublime forms of nature in mountainous districts, the author of the interesting Essays, in the Morning Post, entitled Table Talk, has justly added Goldsmith, and I give the passage in his own words.

' The simple and gentle-hearted Goldsmith, who had an exquisite sense of rural beauty in the familiar forms of hill and dale, and meadows with their hawthorn-scented hedges, does not seem to have dreamt of any such thing as beauty in the Swiss Alps, though he traversed them on foot, and had therefore the best opportunities of observing them. In his poem "The Traveller," he describes the Swiss as loving their mountain homes, not by reason of the romantic beauty of the situation, but in spite of the miserable character of the soil, and the stormy horrors of their mountain steeps —

Turn we to survey
Where rougher climes a nobler race display,
Where the bleak Swiss their stormy mansion tread,
And force a churlish soil for scanty bread.
No produce here the barren hills afford,
But man and steel, the soldier and his sword:
No vernal blooms their torpid rocks array,
But winter lingering chills the lap of May;
No Zephyr fondly sues the mountain's breast,
But meteors glare and stormy glooms invest.
Yet still, *even here*, content can spread a charm,
Redress the clime, and all its rage disarm.'

In the same Essay (December 18th, 1844) are many observations judiciously bearing upon the true character of this and similar projects.

No. II.

To the Editor of the Morning Post.

SIR,

As you obligingly found space in your journal for observations of mine upon the intended Kendal and Windermere Railway, I venture to send you some further remarks upon the same subject. The scope of the main argument, it will be recollected, was to prove that the perception of what has acquired the name of picturesque and romantic scenery is so far from being intuitive, that it can be produced only by a slow and gradual process of culture; and to show, as a consequence, that the humbler ranks of society are not, and cannot be, in a state to gain material benefit from a more speedy access than they now have to this beautiful region. Some of our opponents dissent from this latter proposition, though the most judicious of them readily admit the former; but then, overlooking not only positive assertions, but reasons carefully given, they say, 'As you allow that a more comprehensive taste is desirable, you ought to side with us'; and they illustrate their position, by reference to the British Museum and National Picture Gallery. 'There,' they add, 'thanks to the easy entrance now granted, numbers are seen, indicating by their dress and appearance their humble condition, who, when admitted for the first time, stare vacantly around them, so that one is inclined to ask what brought them hither? But an impression is made, something gained which may induce them to repeat the visit until light breaks in upon them, and they take an intelligent interest in what they behold.' Persons who talk thus forget that, to produce such an improvement, frequent access at small cost of time and labour is indispensable. Manchester lies, perhaps, within eight hours' railway distance of London; but surely no one would advise that Manchester operatives should contract a habit of running to and fro between that town and London, for the sake of forming an intimacy with the British Museum and National Gallery? No, no; little would all but a very few gain from the opportunities which, consistently with common sense, could be afforded them for such expeditions. Nor would it fare better with them in respect of trips to the Lake district; an assertion, the truth of which no one can doubt, who has learned by experience how many men of the same or higher rank, living from their birth in this very region, are indifferent to those objects around them in which a cultivated taste takes so much pleasure. I should not have detained the reader so long upon this point, had I not heard (glad tidings for the directors and traffickers in shares!) that among the affluent and benevolent manufacturers of Yorkshire and Lancashire are some who already entertain the thought of sending, at their own expense, large bodies of their workmen, by railway, to the banks of Windermere. Surely those gentlemen will think a little more before they put such a scheme into practice. The rich man cannot benefit the poor, nor the superior the inferior, by anything that degrades him. Packing off men after this fashion, for holiday entertainment, is, in fact, treating them like children. They go at the will of their master, and must return at the same, or they will be dealt with as transgressors.

A poor man, speaking of his son, whose time of service in the army was expired, once said to me (the reader will be startled at the expression, and I, indeed, was greatly shocked by it), 'I am glad he has done with that *mean* way of life.' But I soon gathered what was at the bottom of the feeling. The father overlooked all the glory that attaches to the character of a British soldier, in the consciousness that his son's will must have been in so great a degree subject to that of others. The poor man felt where the true dignity of his species lay, namely, in a just proportion between actions governed by a man's own inclinations and those of other men; but, according to the father's notion, that proportion did not exist in the course of life from which his son had been released. Had the old man known from experience the degree of liberty allowed to the common soldier, and the moral effect of the obedience required, he would have thought differently, and had he been capable of extending his views, he would have felt how much of the best and noblest part of our civic spirit was owing to our military and naval institutions, and that perhaps our very existence as a free people had by them been maintained. This extreme instance has been adduced to show how deeply seated in the minds of Englishmen is their sense of personal independence. Master-manufacturers ought never to lose sight of this truth. Let them consent to a Ten Hours' Bill, with little or, if possible, no diminution of wages, and the necessaries of life being more easily procured, the mind will develope itself accordingly, and each individual would be more at liberty to make at his own cost excursions in any direction which might be most inviting to him. There would then be no need for their masters sending them in droves scores of miles from their homes and families to the borders of Windermere, or anywhere else.   Consider also the state of the Lake district; and look, in the first place, at the little town of Bowness, in the event of such railway inundations. What would become of it in this, not the Retreat, but the Advance, of the Ten Thousand? Leeds, I am told, has sent as many at once to Scarborough. We should have the whole of Lancashire, and no small part of Yorkshire, pouring in upon us to meet the men of Durham, and the borderers from Cumberland and Northumberland. Alas, alas, if the lakes are to pay this penalty for their own attractions!

—Vane could tell what ills from beauty spring,
And Sedley cursed the form that pleased a king.

The fear of adding to the length of my last long letter prevented me from entering into details upon private and personal feelings among the residents, who have cause to lament the threatened intrusion. These are not matters to be brought before a Board of Trade, though I trust there will always be of that board members who know well that as we do 'not live by bread alone,' so neither do we live by political economy alone. Of the present board I would gladly believe there is not one who, if his duty allowed it, would not be influenced by considerations of what may be felt by a gallant officer now serving on the coast of South America, when he shall learn that the nuisance, though not intended actually to enter his property, will send its omnibuses, as fast as they can drive, within a few yards of his modest abode, which he built upon a small domain purchased at a price greatly enhanced by the privacy and beauty of the situation. Professor Wilson (him I take the liberty to name), though a native of Scotland, and familiar with the grandeur of his own country, could not resist the temptation of settling long ago among our mountains. The place which his public duties have compelled him to quit as a residence, and may compel him to part with, is probably dearer to him than any spot upon earth. The reader should be informed with what respect he has been treated. Engineer agents, to his astonishment, came and intruded with their measuring instruments, upon his garden. He saw them; and who will not admire the patience that kept his hands from their shoulders? I must stop.

But with the fear before me of the line being carried, at a day not distant, through the whole breadth of the district, I could dwell, with much concern for other residents, upon the condition which they would be in if that outrage should be committed; nor ought it to be deemed impertinent were I to recommend this point to the especial regard of Members of Parliament who may have to decide upon the question. The two Houses of Legislature have frequently shown themselves not unmindful of private feeling in these matters. They have, in some cases, been induced to spare parks and pleasure grounds. But along the great railway lines these are of rare occurrence. They are but a part, and a small part; here it is far otherwise. Among the ancient inheritances of the yeomen, surely worthy of high respect, are interspersed through the entire district villas, most of them with such small domains attached that the occupants would be hardly less annoyed by a railway passing through their neighbour's ground than through their own. And it would be unpardonable not to advert to the effect of this measure on the interests of the very poor in this locality. With the town of Bowness I have no *minute* acquaintance; but of Ambleside, Grasmere, and the neighbourhood, I can testify from long experience, that they have been favoured by the residence of a gentry whose love of retirement has been a blessing to these vales; for their families have ministered, and still minister, to the temporal and spiritual necessities of the poor, and have personally superintended the education of the children in a degree which does those benefactors the highest honour, and which is, I trust, gratefully acknowledged in the hearts of all whom they have relieved, employed, and taught. Many of those friends of our poor would quit this country if the apprehended change were realized, and would be succeeded by strangers not linked to the neighbourhood, but flitting to and fro between their fancy-villas and the homes where their wealth was accumulated and accumulating by trade and manufactures. It is obvious that persons, so unsettled, whatever might be their good wishes and readiness to part with money for charitable purposes, would ill supply the loss of the inhabitants who had been driven away.

It will be felt by those who think with me upon this occasion that I have been writing on behalf of a social condition which no one who is competent to judge of it will be willing to subvert, and that I have been endeavouring to support moral sentiments and intellectual pleasures of a high order against an enmity which seems growing more and more formidable every day; I mean 'Utilitarianism,' serving as a mask for cupidity and gambling speculations. My business with this evil lies in its reckless mode of action by Railways, now its favourite instruments. Upon good authority I have been told that there was lately an intention of driving one of these pests, as they are likely too often to prove, through a part of the magnificent ruins of Furness Abbey—an outrage which was prevented by some one pointing out how easily a deviation might be made; and the hint produced its due effect upon the engineer.

Sacred as that relic of the devotion of our ancestors deserves to be kept, there are temples of Nature, temples built by the Almighty, which have a still higher claim to be left unviolated. Almost every reach of the winding vales in this district might once have presented itself to a man of imagination and feeling under that aspect, or as the Vale of Grasmere appeared to the Poet Gray more than seventy years ago. 'No flaring gentleman's-house,' says he, 'nor garden-walls break in upon the repose of this little unsuspected *paradise*, but all is peace,' &c., &c. Were the Poet now living, how would he have lamented the probable intrusion of a railway with its scarifications, its intersections, its noisy machinery, its smoke, and swarms of pleasure-hunters, most of them thinking that they do not fly fast enough through the country which they have come to see. Even a broad highway may in some places greatly impair the characteristic beauty of the country, as will be readily acknowledged by those who remember what the Lake of Grasmere was before the new road that runs along its eastern margin had been constructed.

> Quanto praestantius esset
> Numen aquae viridi si margine clauderet undas
> Herba—

As it once was, and fringed with wood, instead of the breastwork of bare wall that now confines it. In the same manner has the beauty, and still more the sublimity of many Passes in the Alps been injuriously affected. Will the reader excuse a quotation from a MS. poem in which I attempted to describe the impression made upon my mind by the descent towards Italy along the Simplon before the new military road had taken the place of the old muleteer track with its primitive simplicities ?

> Brook and road
> Were fellow-travellers in this gloomy pass,
> And with them did we journey several hours
> At a slow step. The immeasurable height
> Of woods decaying, never to be decayed,
> The stationary blasts of waterfalls,
> And in the narrow rent, at every turn,
> Winds thwarting winds bewildered and forlorn,
> The torrents shooting from the clear blue sky,
> The rocks that muttered close upon our ears,
> Black drizzling crags that spake by the way-side
> As if a voice were in them, the sick sight
> And giddy prospect of the raving stream,
> The unfettered clouds and region of the heavens,
> Tumult and peace, the darkness and the light,
> Were all like workings of one mind, the features

Of the same face, blossoms upon one tree,
Characters of the great Apocalypse,
The types and symbols of Eternity,
Of first, and last, and midst, and without end.

1799.

Thirty years afterwards I crossed the Alps by the
same Pass: and what had become of the forms and
powers to which I had been indebted for those emotions?
Many of them remained of course undestroyed and
indestructible.   But, though the road and torrent continued to run parallel to each other, their fellowship
was put an end to.   The stream had dwindled into
comparative insignificance, so much had Art interfered
with and taken the lead of Nature; and although the
utility of the new work, as facilitating the intercourse
of great nations, was readily acquiesced in, and the
workmanship, in some places, could not but excite
admiration, it was impossible to suppress regret for
what had vanished for ever.   The oratories heretofore
not unfrequently met with, on a road still somewhat
perilous, were gone; the simple and rude bridges swept
away; and instead of travellers proceeding, with leisure
to observe and feel, were pilgrims of fashion hurried
along in their carriages, not a few of them perhaps
discussing the merits of ' the last new Novel,' or poring
over their Guide-books, or fast asleep.   Similar remarks
might be applied to the mountainous country of Wales;
but there too, the plea of utility, especially as expe-
diting the communication between England and Ireland,
more than justifies the labours of the Engineer.   Not
so would it be with the Lake District.   A railroad is
already planned along the sea coast, and another from
Lancaster to Carlisle is in great forwardness: an intermediate one is therefore, to say the least of it, super-
fluous.   Once for all let me declare that it is not against
Railways but against the abuse of them that I am
contending.

How far I am from undervaluing the benefit to be

expected from railways in their legitimate application will appear from the following lines published in 1837, and composed some years earlier.

STEAMBOATS AND RAILWAYS.

Motions and Means, on sea on land at war
With old poetic feeling, not for this
Shall ye, by poets even, be judged amiss!
Nor shall your presence, howsoe'er it mar
The loveliness of nature, prove a bar
To the mind's gaining that prophetic sense
Of future good, that point of vision, whence
May be discovered what in soul ye are;
In spite of all that Beauty must disown
In your harsh features, nature doth embrace
Her lawful offspring in man's Art; and Time,
Pleased with your triumphs o'er his brother Space,
Accepts from your bold hand the proffered crown
Of hope, and welcomes you with cheer sublime.

I have now done with the subject. The time of life at which I have arrived may, I trust, if nothing else will, guard me from the imputation of having written from any selfish interests, or from fear of disturbance which a railway might cause to myself. If gratitude for what repose and quiet in a district hitherto, for the most part, not disfigured but beautified by human hands, have done for me through the course of a long life, and hope that others might hereafter be benefited in the same manner and in the same country, *be* selfishness, then, indeed, but not otherwise, I plead guilty to the charge. Nor have I opposed this undertaking on account of the inhabitants of the district *merely*, but, as hath been intimated, for the sake of every one, however humble his condition, who coming hither shall bring with him an eye to perceive, and a heart to feel and worthily enjoy. And as for holiday pastimes, if a scene is to be chosen suitable to them for persons thronging from a distance, it may be found elsewhere at less cost of every kind. But, in fact, we have too much hurrying about in these islands; much for idle pleasure, and more from over activity in the pursuit of wealth, without regard to the good or happiness of others.

Proud were ye, Mountains, when, in times of old,
Your patriot sons, to stem invasive war,
Intrenched your brows; ye gloried in each scar:
Now, for your shame, a Power, the Thirst of Gold,
That rules o'er Britain like a baneful star,
Wills that your peace, your beauty, shall be sold,
And clear way made for her triumphal car
Through the beloved retreats your arms enfold!
Heard ye that Whistle? As her long-linked Train
Swept onwards, did the vision cross your view?
Yes, ye were startled;—and, in balance true,
Weighing the mischief with the promised gain,
Mountains, and Vales, and Floods, I call on you
To share the passion of a just disdain.

WILLIAM WORDSWORTH.

POCKLINGTON'S OR VICAR'S ISLAND

GRASMERE

NOTES

THE illustration of Grasmere here given is reproduced from the frontispiece of West's *Guide to the Lakes* (4th ed., 1789).

Pages 1–20. DIRECTIONS AND INFORMATION FOR THE TOURIST (ed. 5, pp. i–xxiv). This section is an enlarged version of pp. 137–56 of ed. 3. Feeling, however, that it was not an integral part of the book, but 'a humble and tedious task' destined merely to fulfil the functions of an ordinary guide-book, Wordsworth placed it as a practical introduction to the main body of the volume, which as a whole is addressed not to the tourist, but to 'the minds of persons of taste'. Yet it is not without passages of characteristic beauty, such as the description of Windermere (p. 5), Gowbarrow Park (p. 16), and Red Tarn (p. 17).

A detailed collation of the different forms in which this section appears in edd. 1, 3 and 4, and 5 would hardly repay the labour involved ; for the lakes are described in each case in a somewhat different order, and many minor changes of reading were introduced, due in part to the fact that the first edition was principally concerned with calling attention to the scenes portrayed in the sketches of Mr. Wilkinson. But in the first edition there are one or two descriptive passages which are not to be found later, and are well worth preservation. Thus, after mention of Ambleside (p. 6 ; ed. 1, p. 39), is the following : —

'Within a quarter of a mile of Ambleside is a scene called the Nook, which deserves to be explored. It is to be found in Scandle Gill, the channel of the first Brook that comes down Scandle Fell to the north of Ambleside. I need not describe the scene ; its principal feature is a Bridge thrown over the Torrent. From this Bridge I wish it were in my power to recommend it to the Traveller to proceed northwards, along the slope of the hillside, till he reaches the Park of Rydale ; but this would be a trespass ; for there is no path, and high and envious stone walls interpose. We must therefore give up the best approach to some of the most glorious scenes in the world ; this may be yet said, though not without painful regret for the havoc which has been made among them. Some hundreds of oaks are gone,

> Whose boughs were mossed with age,
> And high tops bald with dry antiquity,

a majestic Forest covering a mountain side ! into the recesses of which penetrated like a vision, Landscapes of river, broad waters, vallies, rocks and mountains :—The Lake of Rydale on the North-west, with its Islands and rocky steeps, circular and deeply embosomed ; and to the South the long Valley of Ambleside and the gleaming Lake of Windermere. The noblest of these trees have been sacrificed ; but the side of the hill, though thinned, is not wholly laid bare ; and the Herons and Rooks that hover round this choice retreat have yet a remnant of their ancient roosting-place. The unfrequented spots of which I have been speaking may be visited, with permission from the Mansion, after the Waterfall has been seen.

' Of places at a distance from Ambleside, but commodiously visited from that Village, Coniston may be first mentioned ; though this Lake, as I said before, will thus be approached to great disadvantage.—Next comes Great Langdale, a Vale which should on no account be missed by him who has a true enjoyment of grand separate Forms composing a sublime Unity, austere but reconciled and rendered attractive to the affections by the deep serenity that is spread over everything. There is no good carriage road through this Vale ; nor ought that to be regretted ; for it would impair its solemnity : but the road is tolerable for about the distance of three miles from Ambleside, namely along the Vale of Brathay, and above the western banks of Loughrigg Tarn, and still further, to the entrance of Langdale itself ; but the small and peaceful Valley of Loughrigg is seen to much greater advantage from the eastern side. When therefore you have quitted the River Brathay, enquire at the first house for the foot road, which will conduct you round the lower extremity of the Tarn, and so on to its head, where, at a little distance from the Tarn, the path again leads to the publick road and about a mile further conducts you to Langdale Chapel.—A little way beyond this sequestered and simple place of worship is a narrow passage on the right leading into a slate-quarry which has been finely excavated. Pursuing this road a few hundred yards further, you come in view of the noblest reach of this Vale, which I shall not

RYDAL WATER

WINANDERMERE

attempt to describe. Under the Precipice adjoining to the Pikes lies invisibly Stickle Tarn, and thence descends a conspicuous Torrent down the breast of the Mountain. Near this Torrent is Dungeon Gill Force, which cannot be found without a guide, who may be taken up at one of the Cottages at the foot of the Mountain.

> Into the chasm a mighty block
> Hath fallen, and made a bridge of rock ;
> The gulph is deep below,
> And in a bason black and small
> Receives a lofty waterfall [1].

At the head of Langdale is a passage over to the Borrowdale ; but this ought on no account to be taken by a person who has not seen the main features of the country from their best approaches.'

So, after mention of Lowes-water (p. 13 ; ed. 1, p. 42), Wordsworth remarks :—

' I am not sure that the circuit of this Lake can be made on horseback ; but every path and field in the neighbourhood would well repay the active exertions of the Pedestrian. Nor will the most hasty Visitant fail to notice with pleasure, that community of attractive and substantial houses which are dispersed over the fertile inclosures at the foot of those rugged Mountains, and form a most impressive contrast with the humble and rude dwellings which are usually found at the head of these far-winding Dales. It must be mentioned also, that there is scarcely anything finer than the view from a boat in the centre of Crummock-water. The scene is deep, and solemn, and lonely ; and in no other spot is the majesty of the Mountains so irresistibly felt as an omnipresence, or so passively submitted to as a spirit incumbent upon the imagination. Near the head of Crummock-water, on the right, is Scale Force, a Waterfall worthy of being visited, both for its own sake, and for the sublime View across the Lake, looking back in your ascent towards the Chasm. The Fall is perpendicular from an immense height, a slender stream faintly illuminating a gloomy fissure. This spot is never seen to more advantage than when it happens, that, while you are looking up through the Chasm towards the summit of the lofty Waterfall, large fleecy clouds, of dazzling brightness, suddenly ascend into view, and disappear silently upon the wind.'

The illustration of Rydal, facing p. 168, is reproduced from Robinson's *Guide to the Lakes* (1819).

[1] *The Idle Shepherd Boys*, ll. 51-5.

Pages 1–4 *desunt* in edd. 3, 4. ' The third approach '
(*v.* p. 2) will be found described in Gray's *Journal in the
Lakes* (v. *Works of Gray*, ed. Gosse, i. 275–81).

P. 5. WINDERMERE. 1. 23. *The Islands.* In ed. 4 is the
following footnote, which was omitted in ed. 5 :—' This lake
has seventeen islands. Among those that lie near the largest,
formerly called " Great Holm", may be noticed " Lady
Holm ", so called from the Virgin who had formerly a Chapel
or Oratory there. On the road from Kendal to the Great-
boat, might lately, and perhaps may still be seen, the ruins
of the Holy Cross ; a place where the pilgrims to this beautifully situated shrine must have been in the habit of offering
up their devotions.—Two other of these islands are named
from the lily of the valley, which grows there in profusion.'

The illustration here given of Windermere from the Ferry
is taken from *A Series of Sixty Small Prints*, etched by
William Green of Ambleside (1814).

P. 7. The description of Blea Tarn, with the quotation
from *The Excursion*, ii. 327–48, was added in ed. 5.

P. 8, l. 27. *Black Comb*: *v.* Wordsworth's poem *View from the
Top of Black Comb* (written 1813, pub. 1815), which describes
the view in detail. Colonel Mudge (1762–1820) was a major-
general in the Royal Artillery, a distinguished mathematician
and surveyor ; he was elected Fellow of the Royal Society in
1798. In *Lines written with a slate pencil on a stone, on the side
of the mountain of Black Comb* (also written in 1813), Wordsworth thus described him :—

> On the summit whither thou art bound
> A geographic Labourer pitched his tent,
> With books supplied and instruments of art,
> To measure height and distance ; lonely task,
> Week after week pursued !—to him was given
> Full many a glimpse (but sparingly bestowed
> On timid man) of Nature's processes
> Upon the exalted hills.

' Mary and I,' said Wordsworth to Miss Fenwick, ' lived
some time under its shadow.'

P. 9, l. 7. *Chas. Farish, B.D.* (1766–1824), was a Fellow of
Queens' College, Cambridge, and later, Lecturer at St. Cuth-
bert's, Carlisle. Wordsworth spoke of him, in a note on
Guilt and Sorrow, as ' my schoolfellow and friend '. His
poems, among them *The Minstrels of Winandermere*, were
not published till 1811, hence the quotation is first found in
ed. 3 of the Guide.

WINDERMERE FROM THE FERRY

ULLESWATER

P. 11, l. 24. *the bridge that divides the Lake.* Since the Lake
was turned into a reservoir to supply Manchester with water,
the bridge has been removed and the Lake widened in the
centre so as completely to alter its contour. A view is here
given (p. 172) (from Robinson's *Guide to the Lakes*, 1819), which
suggests something of its appearance in Wordsworth's day.

P. 17, l. 11. *a silent Tarn in the recesses of Helvellyn* : i. e.
Red Tarn. Cf. *Fidelity*, 19, 20 :—

> A lofty precipice in front,
> A silent tarn below.

The story here told by Wordsworth was the subject of the
poem, as also of a poem by Sir Walter Scott, entitled
Helvellyn, and written in the same year, 1805. Scott had
visited Wordsworth at Grasmere in the October of this year,
and with him and Humphrey Davy had ascended Helvellyn.

P. 19, l. 9. *In Martindale.* Before these words ed. 3 reads:—
' This stream flows down Martindale, a valley deficient in
richness, but interesting from its seclusion. In vales of this
character the general want of wood gives a peculiar interest
to the scattered cottages, embowered in sycamores ; and few of
the Mountain Chapels are more striking than this of Martindale, standing as it does in the centre of the valley, with
one dark yew-tree, and enclosed by "a bare ring of mossy
wall". The name of Boardale, a deep, bare, and houseless
valley, which communicates with Martindale, shows that the
wild swine were once numerous in that nook ; and Martindale forest is yet one of the few spots in England ranged
over by red deer. These are the descendants of the aboriginal herds.' In edd. 4 and 5 this passage was discarded,
as some of it was utilized in the description of the *Excursion
on the Banks of Ullswater*, v, pp. 123–5.

l. 28. *Visitants, for the most part, see little of the beauty,*
&c. . . . P. 20, l. 3, *pedestrian* added in ed. 5. The note on
p. 20 was added in ed. 3.

DESCRIPTION OF THE SCENERY OF THE LAKES
SECTION FIRST

P. 21, l. 1. *At Lucerne . . . is shown* edd. 3–5 : At L. . . .
there existed some years ago and perhaps does still exist
ed. 1 : At L. . . . there existed some years ago ed. 2.
Wordsworth had visited Switzerland when on a walking tour
with his college friend Robert Jones in 1790 ; his next visit

was not till 1820, with his wife and sister. This accounts for the alteration in the text of the third edition, as well as for the addition of illustrative remarks upon the Scenery of the Alps, which is noticed on its title-page.

l. 17. *Something of this kind, &c.* This paragraph took a very different form in the first edition, when the text was designed to accompany Wilkinson's drawings. It ran thus :—

'Something of this kind (as far as can be performed by words, which must needs be most inadequately) will be attempted in the following introductory pages, with reference to the country which has furnished the subjects of the drawings now offered to the public, adding to a verbal representation of its permanent features such appearances as are transitory from their dependence upon accidents of season and weather. This, if tolerably executed, will in some instances communicate to the traveller, who has already seen the objects, new information ; and will assist him to give to his recollections a more orderly arrangement than his own opportunities of observing may have permitted him to do ; while it will be still more useful to the future traveller by directing his attention at once to distinctions in things which, without such previous aid, a length of time only could enable him to discover. And, as must be obvious, this general introduction will combine with the etchings certain notices of things which, though they may not lie within the province of the pencil, cannot but tend to render its productions more interesting ; especially in a case like the present, where a work wishes to recommend itself by a twofold claim, viz. by furnishing pleasing sketches, and at the same time accurate portraits of those scenes from which they are taken.'

P. 22, l. 14. *To begin, then, with the main outlines* : for 'outlines' ed. 1 has 'demarkation'.

l. 25. *a number of valleys, not fewer than eight* : in edd. 1 and 2 'nine'. The footnote on 'Langdale' was added in ed. 3.

P. 23, l. 13. *peculiar features* edd. 3–5 : features which, in the more minute details attached to the several parts of this work, will hereafter be described edd. 1 and 2.

ll. 14–17. *Its stream . . . Ravenglass* added in ed. 3.

l. 20. *neat dwellings scattered upon a plain* edd. 3–5 : neat scattered dwellings, a plain edd. 1 and 2.

l. 30. *The stream that issues from Wast-water . . .* P. 24, l. 9 *Cockermouth Castle* added in ed. 3 : The several vales of Ennerdale and Buttermere, with their lakes, next present themselves, and lastly the vale of Borrowdale edd. 1 and 2.

WYTHBURN WATER

GATESGARTHDALE

P. 24, ll. 33-4. *north of England.* After these words ed. 1 reads :—

'But it must be observed that the visits of travellers are for the most part confined to the Vales of Coniston, Winandermere, with the intermediate country between Ambleside and Keswick, the Vale of Keswick itself, Buttermere, and Ulswater, which are the most easy of access, and indeed from their several characters most likely to repay general curiosity ; though each of the other more retired vales, as will appear when we enter into detail in the several numbers of this publication, has its own appropriate beauties—all exquisite in their kind.

'This Introduction will be confined as much as possible to general remarks. And first, returning to the illustrative figure which has been employed,'

P. 25, l. 7. *and sublimity* added in ed. 3.

P. 26, ll. 12-13. *a kindred variety* edd. 3-5 : the same variety edd. 1 and 2.

ll. 18-19. *to which the reader's attention has been directed* ed. 5 : to which I have directed the reader's attention edd. 1-4.

l. 36. *What long tracts of desolate country intervene!* edd. 3-5. In edd. 1 and 2 this is expressed far more strongly : 'What long desolate and unimpressive tracts of country almost perpetually intervene !'

P. 27. ll. 8-9. *of the* MOUNTAINS. *Their* forms, &c. In ed. 1 Wordsworth writes : ' for the forms of these mountains I refer to the Etchings to which these pages are an introduction, and from which it will appear that their outlines,' &c.

l. 26. *not unfrequently* edd. 3-5 : occasionally edd. 1 and 2.

ll. 31-2. *In the ridge that divides Eskdale from Wasdale, granite is found ; but* added in ed. 4.

P. 28, ll. 29-30. *though in many places they are adorned by those plants, so beautiful when in flower* ed. 5 : . . . by the rich hues of those plants ed. 4 : though in some places they are richly adorned by them edd. 1-3.

P. 29, l. 27. *upon the steep rocks* edd. 3-5 : among the woody rocks edd. 1 and 2.

l. 28. *the deep summer-green* edd. 3-5 : the uniform summer-green edd. 1 and 2.

P. 30, ll. 22-3. *the monotony of snow* edd. 2-5 : all the monotony of snow ed. 1. The word probably dropped out through inadvertence. Further on, after ' snow-powdered twigs', ed. 1 gives an interesting though rather confused description :—' These hills, all distinguishable indeed from the summit downward, but none seen all the way down, so as to give the strongest sense of number with unity ; and these hills so variously situated to each other and to the view in general, so variously powdered, some only enough to give the herbage a brown tint, one intensely white and rich, lighting up all the others, and yet so placed as in the most inobtrusive manner to harmonize by contrast with a perfect naked, snowless bleak summit in the far distance on the left— the variety of site, of colour, of woodiness, of the situation of the woods, &c., &c., made it not merely number with unity, but intricacy combined that activity of feeling, which intricacy awakens, with the complacency and repose of perfect unity.'

P. 31, l. 25. *In such of the valleys as make* edd. 2-5 : As these vallies make ed. 1.

P. 32, l. 8. *Donnerdale* edd. 2-5 : Seathwaite ed. 1.

l. 15. *I shall now speak of the* LAKES edd. 2-5 : I shall now say a few words concerning ed. 1.

l. 31. *The visible scene,* &c. From *There was a boy,* &c., written in Germany, Nov. or Dec., 1798, and published in 1800. The lines are also to be found in *The Prelude,* v. 384-8. Coleridge noted that the last two lines were essentially characteristic of Wordsworth. ' Had I met them running wild in the deserts of Arabia, I should have instantly screamed out " Wordsworth ! " '

P. 33, ll. 16-17. *the largest of them are comparatively small* edd. 2-5 : the largest of them are small ed. 1.

ll. 31-5. *But, who ever travelled . . . interposition* edd. 2-5 : But who ever travelled along the banks of Loch Lomond, variegated as the lower part is with islands, without wishing for a speedier termination of the long vista of blank water, for an interposition ed. 1.

P. 34, l. 26-P. 37 (*end of quotation*). *As the comparatively small size of the Lakes,* &c. This fine passage was the result of much gradual addition and alteration. The only part of which traces are to be found in ed. 1 is ll. 10-21 of p. 36. In ed. 2 was added p. 34, l. 26—p. 36, l. 10, but this underwent some modifications of style in ed. 3. In ed. 4 was added at p. 36, l. 24, two lines of delicate observation :— ' half of it perhaps gleaming under the water, and the corresponding half of a lighter hue ' ; whilst in ed. 4, also (not ed. 5, as stated by Prof. Knight), was added the picture of the water-fowl, p. 36, l. 22—p. 37, l. 23.

P. 34, l. 36. *Using the word* deficiencies edd. 3–5 : It need scarcely be said that in using the word, &c. ed. 2.

P. 36, l. 4. *But, checking these intrusive calculations* edd. 3–5 : But the man of taste will say, it is an impertinent calculation, that leads to such unwelcome conclusions ed. 2.

ll. 18–20. *plots of water-lilies lifting up their large target-shaped leaves to the breeze* edd. 3–5 : water-lilies lifting up the orb of their large leaves to the breeze, if it be stirring ed. 1. Ed. 2 as 3, but with ' circular' for ' target-shaped '.

ll. 22–3. *the birds that enliven the waters.* Many passages in Wordsworth's poems illustrate the feeling here expressed for the birds of the Lake district. On the wild ducks which ' in spring-time hatch their young in the islands', compare *Miscellaneous Sonnets*, Part I, no. xv : *The Wild Duck's Nest.* ' I observed this beautiful nest,' wrote Wordsworth, ' on the largest island on Rydal Water.' On the sand-piper, compare *Lines left on a seat in a Yew-tree*, &c., 27, ' The stone-chat, or the glancing sand-piper', a line which in the 1815 ed. ran :—

> The stone-chat, or the sand-lark, restless bird,
> Piping along the margin of the lake.

For ' upon some jutting rock . . . the stately heron' compare *Farewell Lines*, ' High bliss,' &c., 13–16 :—

> So when the rain is over, the storm laid,
> A pair of herons oft-times have I seen,
> Upon a rocky islet, side by side,
> Drying their feathers in the sun, at ease.

Of few birds has Wordsworth written so much as of the swan. In *An Evening Walk* (1787–9, published 1793), he gives a description of them ' taken from the daily opportunities I had of observing their habits, not as confined to a gentleman's park, but in a state of nature. There were two pairs of them that divided the lake of Esthwaite and its in-and-out-flowing streams between them, never trespassing a single yard upon each other's separate domain. They were of the old magnificent species, bearing in beauty and majesty about the same relation to the Thames swan which that does to the goose. It was from the remembrance of those noble creatures I took, thirty years after, the picture of the swan which I have discarded from the poem of *Dion* (q. v.). While I was a schoolboy, the late Mr. Curwen introduced a little fleet of those birds, but of the inferior species, to the lake of Windermere. Their principal home was about his own island ; but they sailed about into remote parts of the lake, and, either from real or imagined injury done to the adjoining fields, they were got rid of at the request of the farmers and proprietors, but to the great regret of all who had become attached to them, from noticing their beauty and quiet habits' (I. F. note to *An Evening Walk*). A beautiful description of a pair of swans who settled on Grasmere lake at the same time as Wordsworth took up his own abode there is to be found in Book I of the *Recluse: Home at Grasmere*, just following the passage which is quoted on p. 37. In that passage a few differences of reading are noticeable from the version given here. For ll. 1–3 we read :—

> Behold how with a grace
> Of ceaseless motion, that might scarcely seem
> Inferior to angelical, they prolong

in l. 12 ' Upwards and downwards'; in l. 15 ' Ten times and more '; and in l. 21 :—

> Tempt the smooth water or the gleaming ice.

P. 38, ll. 2–9. *or other places of defence . . . Derwent-water. The islands of the last-mentioned lake are neither* edd. 4, 5. Wordsworth's increasing interest in matters ecclesiastical is illustrated by a comparison of this passage with its form in ed. 3 (1822), where we read simply :—' or other places of defence, or of monastic edifices. Those of Derwent-water are neither '. (Cf. note to p. 5.)

l. 8. *St. Herbert's Island* : cf. *Inscription for the spot where the Hermitage stood on St. Herbert's Island, Derwentwater* (Wordsworth, *Poems*). On *the floating island* v. Dorothy Wordsworth's poem, *Harmonious Powers with Nature work.*

l. 19. *The haunt of cormorants and sea-mew's clang.* A misquotation (probably intentional) from Milton, *Paradise Lost*, xi. 831 :—

> The haunt of Seales and Orcs, and Seamews clang.

ll. 20–1. *stern and wild character of the several scenes!* The rest of this paragraph (' It may be . . . natantes ') is not found in edd. 1–3, but was added in ed. 4.

P. 39, l. 15. *which Carver so beautifully describes.* Jonathan Carver (1732–80) was a distinguished American traveller whose books had much vogue at the time of their composition. The passage referred to by Wordsworth does not describe Erie or Ontario, but Lake Superior, of which Carver writes :—
' After I first entered it from Goddard's River on the west bay,

I coasted near twelve hundred miles of the north and east
shores of it, and observed that the greatest part of that
extensive track was bounded by rocks and uneven ground.
The water in general appeared to lie on a bed of rocks.
When it was calm, and the sun shone bright, I could sit in
my canoe, where the depth was upwards of six fathoms, and
plainly see huge piles of stone at the bottom, of different
shapes, some of which appeared as if they were hewn. The
water at this time was as pure and transparent as air ; and
my canoe seemed as if it hung suspended in that element.
It was impossible to look attentively through this limpid
medium at the rocks below, without finding, before many
minutes were elapsed, your head swim, and your eyes no
longer able to behold the dazzling scene.' (*Travels through
the Interior Parts of North America*, 1778, pp. 132-3.)

l. 22. *In the economy of Nature* . . . P. 40, l. 2 *fall of
rain* : *desunt* in edd. 1-3, first found in ed. 4.

P. 40, l. 9. *an unsightly tract of boggy ground* edd. 3-5 :
a tract of ground that has an unsightly appearance edd. 1, 2.

ll. 14-16. *of miniature lakes, Loughrigg Tarn* . . . *is the
most beautiful example.* Cf. *Epistle to Sir George Beaumont*
(1811), ll. 164-70 :—

> Thus gladdened from our own dear Vale we pass
> And soon approach Diana's Looking-glass !
> To Loughrigg-tarn, round, clear, and bright as heaven,
> Such name Italian fancy would have given,
> Ere on its banks the few grey cabins rose
> That yet disturb not its concealed repose
> More than the feeblest wind that idly blows.

Wordsworth appended the following note to his poem :--
' Loughrigg Tarn, alluded to in the foregoing Epistle, resembles, though much smaller in compass, the Lake Nemi, or
Speculum Dianae as it is often called, not only in its clear waters
and circular form, and the beauty immediately surrounding
it, but also as being overlooked by the eminence of Langdale
Pikes as Lake Nemi is by that of Monte Calvo. Since this
Epistle was written Loughrigg Tarn has lost much of its
beauty by the felling of many natural clumps of wood, relics
of the old forest, particularly upon the farm called "The
Oaks", from the abundance of that tree which grew there.'
Later he dictated to Miss Fenwick the following note :—
' This beautiful pool and the surrounding scene are minutely
described in my little book on the Lakes. Sir G. H. Beaumont,

in the earlier part of his life, was induced, by his love of
nature and the art of painting, to take up his abode at Old
Brathay, about three miles from this spot, so that he must
have seen it under many aspects ; and he was so much pleased
with it that he purchased the Tarn with a view to build, near
it, such a residence as is alluded to in this Epistle. Baronets
and knights were not so common in that day as now, and Sir
Michael le Fleming, not liking to have a rival in that kind of
distinction so near him, claimed a sort of lordship over the
territory, and showed dispositions little in unison with those
of Sir G. Beaumont, who was eminently a lover of peace.
The project of building was in consequence given up, Sir
George retaining possession of the Tarn.'

The illustration here given of Loughrigg Tarn is from
Green's *Series of Sixty Small Prints* (1814).

l. 34. *At all events* edd. 2–5 : In the first place ed. 1.

P. 41, l. 6. *where the sun is not shining upon it* edd. 2–5 :
desunt ed. 1.

ll. 8–19. *some defying conjecture . . . natural to such scenes*
ed. 3–5 : *desunt* ed. 1. The sense also of some repulsive
power strongly put forth—excited by the prospect of a
body of pure water, unattended with groves and other
cheerful images by which fresh water is usually accompanied,
and unable to give any furtherance to the meagre vegetation
around it—heighten the melancholy natural to such scenes
ed. 2.

l. 19. *Nor is . . . often* edd. 2–5 : . . . is seldom ed. 1.

ll. 26–7. *not content with this scanty allowance of society*
edd. 2–5 : not content with this ed. 1.

l. 33. *There, sometimes does a leaping fish.* From *Fidelity*,
ll. 25–31 ; cf. note to p. 17.

P. 42, ll. 4–15. *It will be observed . . . fresh water* edd. 3–5,
rewritten from a shorter form. ' Though the country is on
one side bounded by the sea, which combines beautifully, from
some elevated points of view, with the inland scenery ; yet
nowhere are found the grand estuaries which are common in
Scotland and Wales : the lakes are such in the strict and usual
sense of the word, being all of fresh water' ed. 1. In ed. 2,
'Though . . . scenery', as ed. 1 : ' yet the estuaries cannot
pretend to vie with', &c. as ed. 1. The footnote to page was
added in ed. 5.

ll. 24–5. *the rivers Derwent and Duddon.* Wordsworth's
early childhood was passed by the Derwent. Cf. for a poetical
description of it, *Prelude*, i. 269-300. On the Duddon he

LOUGHRIGG TARN

wrote his well-known series of sonnets, and spoke of it to Sir George Beaumont as ' my favourite river'.

P. 43, l. 7. *for shelter* edd. 2-5 : for household accommodation and shelter ed. 1.

ll. 8-10. *and hence . . . feelings* edd. 2-5 : and hence the retirement and seclusion by which these cottages are endeared to the eye of the man of sensibility ed. 1.

ll. 11-15. *birch . . . thorn . . . hollies . . . yews among the rocks* : cf. the description of Emma's dell in *It was an April morning*, ll. 30-3 :—

> Green leaves were here;
> But 'twas the foliage of the rocks—the birch,
> The yew, the holly, and the bright green thorn,
> With hanging islands of resplendent furze.

l. 12. *and here and there Wych-elm* ed. 5 : and here and there a species of elm edd. 2-4 : and here and there (though very rarely) a species of elm ed. 1.

ll. 17-19. *where native Scotch firs . . . to this day* edd. 4, 5 : where native Scotch firs (as in the Northern parts of Scotland to this day) must have grown in great profusion edd. 1-3.

ll. 19-21. *But not one of these old inhabitants has existed, perhaps, for some hundreds of years* edd. 3-5 : . . . remains or perhaps has done for . . . edd. 1, 2.

ll. 22-3. *the country formerly had* edd. 2-5 : which the country formerly had ed. 1.

ll. 23-4. *that have been protected* edd. 3-5 : which remain and which have been protected ed. 1 : that remain and have, &c. ed. 2.

Footnote 1 of this page was added in ed. 5, footnote 2 in ed. 4.

l. 25. *hollies.* Wordsworth had always a special feeling for the holly native to the Lake District. Writing to Sir George Beaumont in November, 1806, he commented upon its absence from the Coleorton garden. ' The holly I looked for in Lady B.'s ground, and could not find. For its own beauty, and for the sake of the hills and crags of the North, let it be scattered here in profusion. It is of slow growth, no doubt, but not so slow as is generally supposed ; and then it does grow, and somebody, we hope, will enjoy it. Among the barbarisers of our beautiful Lake region, of those who bring and those who take away, there are few whom I have execrated more than an extirpator of this beautiful shrub, or rather tree—the holly.' A passage follows of interest, further illustrating Wordsworth's natural taste. ' I should not plant many forest trees . . . by the side of those which are already at their full growth ; when I planted at all there, I should rather choose thickets of underwood, hazels, wild roses, honeysuckle, hollies, thorns, and trailing plants, such as traveller's joy, &c. My reason, in addition to the beauty of these, is that they would never be compared with the grown-up trees, whereas young trees of the same kind will, and must, appear insignificant.'

P. 44, l. 10–13. *sycamore . . . the favourite of the cottagers*; *. . . with the fir.* Cf. *Excursion*, vii. 612–9 :—

> Yon household fir,
> A guardian planted to fence off the blast,
> But towering high the roof above, as if
> Its humble destination were forgot—
> That sycamore, which annually holds
> Within its shade, as in a stately tent
> On all sides open to the fanning breeze,
> A grave assemblage.

l. 25. *matchless store of ancient trees* edd. 3–5 : store of the grandest trees ed. 1 : matchless store of the grandest trees ed. 2.

l. 27. *vegetable ornaments*, edd. 3–5 : vegetable ornaments which nature has here provided ed. 1 : provided by nature ed. 2. All the poetry of this passage was added in ed. 3 to a somewhat bare catalogue of plants, in edd. 1 and 2 merely enumerated thus :—' The juniper, bilberry, and the broom plant, with which the hills and woods abound, the Dutch myrtle in moist places, and the endless variety,' &c.

l. 33–6. *the broom . . . interveins the steep copses with its golden blossoms* : cf. *To Joanna*, ll. 38–50 :—

> 'Twas that delightful season when the broom,
> Full-flowered, and visible on every steep,
> Along the copses runs in veins of gold.
> . . . . such delight I found
> To note in shrub and tree, in stone and flower,
> That intermixture of delicious hues
> Along so vast a surface, all at once,
> In one impression, by connecting force
> Of their own beauty, imaged in the heart.

P. 46, l. 32. *It has been said . . .* P. 50 (*end of section* 1) added in ed. 4.

P. 47, ll. 4–5. *Buchanan with his beautiful Ode to the first of May.* George Buchanan (1506–1582), the famous Scottish humanist and reformer, was the first Latin scholar of a time when Latin was the universal language. He was esteemed in his own day ' as easily the first poet of his age '. Later,

Dr. Johnson referred to him as ' a great poetical genius', and
Wordsworth elsewhere spoke of this poem, the *Calen lae Maiae*,
as ' equal in sentiment, if not in elegance, to anything in
Horace' (*Memoirs of Wordsworth*, ii. 469). The lines of the
Ode which are here referred to run thus :—

> Cum blanda veris temperies novo
> Illuxit orbi, primaque secula
>   Fulsere flaventi metallo
>   Sponte sua sine lege iusta :
> Talis per omnes continuus tenor
> Annos tepenti rura Favonio
>   Mulcebat, et nullis feraces
>   Seminibus recreabat agros.
> Talis beatis incubat insulis
> Felicis aurae perpetuus tepor,
>   Et nesciis campis senectae
>   Difficilis querulique morbi.
> Talis silentum per tacitum nemus
> Levi susurrat murmure spiritus,
>   Lethenque iuxta obliviosam
>   Funereas agitat cupressos.
> Forsan supremis cum Deus ignibus
> Piabit orbem, laetaque secula
>   Mundo reducet, talis aura
>   Aethereos animos fovebit.

Of these Dr. Hume Brown (*Life of George Buchanan*, p. 179)
supplies the following translation :—

> When, still rejoicing in her birth,
> Spring brightened all the new-made earth
> And in that happy golden age
> Men knew no lawless passion's rage,
> Thy train of joys embraced the year ;
> Soft breezes wooed the untilled field
> Its blessings all unforced to yield.
>   Even in such mildest atmosphere
> For ever bask those happy isles,
> Those blessèd plains, that never know
> Life's slow decay, or poisoned flow.
>   Thus 'mid the still abodes of death
> Should steal the soft air's softest breath,
> And gently stir the solemn wood
> That glooms o'er Lethe's dreamless flood.
>   And, haply when made pure of stain
> By cleansing fire, the earth renewed
> Shall know her ancient joys again,
> Even such mild air shall o'er her brood !

P. 48, ll. 23–4. *Milton . . . has given a* clouded *moon to*
Paradise itself. Cf. *Paradise Lost,* iv. 605–9 :—

                              Hesperus that led
     The starrie Host, rode brightest, till the Moon
     Rising in clouded Majestie, at length
     Apparent Queen unvail'd her peerless light,
     And o're the dark her Silver Mantle threw.

ll. 29–30. *the Abyssinian recess of Rasselas.* ' A spacious
valley in the kingdom of Amhara, surrounded on every side by
mountains, of which the summits overhang the middle part.
The only passage by which it could be entered, was a cavern
that passed under a rock' (Johnson's *Rasselas,* pp. 1, 2).

The happy valley of Rasselas had other characteristics
which Wordsworth would notice as similar to the vale that
he loved. 'From the mountains on every side, rivulets
descended that filled all the valley with verdure and fertility,
and formed a lake in the middle inhabited by fish of every
species, and frequented by every fowl whom nature has
taught to dip the wing in water. This lake discharged its
superfluities by a stream. . . . The sides of the mountains
were covered with trees, the banks of the brooks were
diversified with flowers.'

The peculiar beauty of the stars in a mountainous district
was often remarked by Wordsworth. As a note to his
Prefatory Lines, If thou indeed derive thy light from Heaven,
&c. (q. v.), he wrote : ' I will take occasion to observe upon
the beauty of that situation (i. e. Rydal Mount), as being
backed and flanked by lofty fells, which bring the heavenly
bodies to touch, as it were, the earth upon the mountain-
tops, while the prospect in front lies open to a length of
level valley, the extended lake and a terminating ridge of
low hills ; so that it gives an opportunity to the inhabitants
of the place of noticing the stars in both the positions here
alluded to, namely, on the tops of the mountains, and as
winter lamps at a distance among the leafless trees.'

Hesperus in particular is viewed with peculiar advantage
from the east side of the valley, on which stand both Dove
Cottage and Rydal Mount, in that the hills upon the west
shut out the evening sun. Cf. *It is no Spirit,* ll. 4–8 :—

     'Tis Hesperus—there he stands with glittering crown,
     First admonition that the sun is down !
     For yet it is broad daylight : clouds pass by ;
     A few are near him still—and now the sky,
     He hath it to himself—'tis all his own.

on which Wordsworth remarks (I. F. note), ' I remember the instant my sister, Sarah Hutchinson, called me to the window of our cottage, saying, " Look, how beautiful is yon star ! *It has the sky all to itself!* " '

P. 50, l. 3. *Dr. Brown, the author of this fragment.* John Brown, D.D. (1715-66), the friend of Warburton, was a voluminous writer whose most famous works are an *Essay on Satire*, occasioned by the death of Mr. Pope (1745), published in Dodsley's *Collection of Poems* (1763), and *An Estimate of the Manners and Principles of the Times* (1757). This was so popular as to attain its seventh edition in the year following its publication, and is alluded to by Cowper in the lines : —

> The inestimable Estimate of Brown
> Rose like a paper kite and charmed the town.
>
> (*Table Talk*, 384-5.)

Dr. Brown's letter to a Friend (*v.* p. 69) was addressed to Lord Lyttelton, and first published in 1770 (it was not, therefore, as Wordsworth states, published by the author), and the fragment here quoted first appeared in 1776 in *The Dedication to Mr. Romney* of Cumberland's *Ode to the Sun* (v. Introduction, p. xiv). Wordsworth probably became acquainted with it in West's *Guide to the Lakes*, where it is quoted in full.

SECTION SECOND

P. 51, l. 1. *Hitherto* edd. 4, 5 : Thus far edd. 1-3.

ll. 12-14. *the shapes of the valleys . . . substance of the intervening mountains* edd. 2-5 : the description which I have given of the substance and form of these mountains, the shape of the vallies and their position with respect to each other ed. 1.

ll. 15-16. *the valleys with lakes and rivers; the coves and sides* edd. 2-5 : the vallies with lakes and rivers, the sides and coves ed. 1.

ll. 19-20. *the point upon which he stood* edd. 3-5 : the point upon which he before stood edd. 1, 2.

P. 52, l. 2. *voice* edd. 2-5 : noise ed. 1.

l. 7. *an animated writer*). West, the author of *Antiquities of Furness* and that *Guide to the Lakes* which had most vogue in Wordsworth's day; it appeared first in 1778, reached a fourth edition in 1789, and a tenth in 1813.

ll. 28-9. *mountains, except for military purposes, or in subservience to* edd. 2-5 : mountains which were not subservient to ed. 1.

l. 35. *A few, though distinct, traces* edd. 2-5 : A few traces ed. 1.

l. 36–P. 53, l. 1.   *Dunmallet and a few circles* edd. 3–5 :
Dunmallet, and   two   or   three circles ed. 2 : Dunmallet
(erected probably to secure a quiet transfer of the ore from
the mines), and two or three circles ed. 1.

    P. 53, l. 2.   *the only vestiges* edd. 2–5 : the only visible
vestiges ed. 1.

    Footnote added in ed. 3.   The *friend of the Author* (l. 5) is
' Thomas Wilkinson, a Quaker by religious profession. . . .
He had inherited a small estate, and built a house upon it
near Yanwath, upon the banks of the Emont. . . . Through
his connexion with the family in which Edmund Burke was
educated, he became acquainted with that great man, who
used to receive him with great kindness and consideration ;
and many times have I heard Wilkinson speak of those
interesting interviews.   He was honoured also by the friend-
ships of Elizabeth Smith, and of Thomas Clarkson and his
excellent wife, and was much esteemed by Lord and Lady
Lonsdale, and every member of that family.   The latter
part of the innocent and good man's life was melancholy.
He became blind, and also poor by becoming surety for some
of his relations.   He was a bachelor.   He bore, as I have
often witnessed, his calamities with unfailing resignation '
(I. F. note).   It is to him that Wordsworth addressed the
well-known poem, *To the Spade of a Friend.*

    The insertion of this note in ed. 3 was probably due to an
expedition made by Wordsworth in Jan. 1821 to Appleby.
' In returning,' he writes to Sir George Beaumont on Jan. 6,
1821, ' I was obliged to make a circuit which showed me for the
first time several miles of the course of that beautiful stream
the Eden, from the bridge near Temple Lomerby down to
Kirkoswald.   Part of this tract of country I had indeed seen
before, but not from the same points of view.   It is a charming region, particularly at the spot where the Eden and
Emont join.   The rivers appeared exquisitely brilliant, gliding
under rocks and through green meadows, with woods and
sloping cultivated grounds, and pensive russet moors interspersed, and along the circuit of the horizon, lofty hills and
mountains clothed, rather than concealed, in fleecy clouds and
resplendent vapours.

    ' My road brought me suddenly and unexpectedly upon that
ancient monument, called by the country people Long Meg
and her Daughters.   Everybody has heard of it, and so had
I from my early childhood, but had never seen it before.
Next to Stonehenge, it is beyond dispute the most noble relic

of the kind that this or probably any other country contains. Long Meg is a single block of unhewn stone, eighteen feet high, at a small distance from a vast circle of other stones, some of them of huge size, though curtailed of their stature by their own incessant pressure upon it.'

The sonnet quoted in the note was first published in the *Guide to the Lakes*, the text varying slightly from the form in which Wordsworth left it in his Collected Poems. There we read in l. 4 ' family ' for ' sisterhood'; in l. 5 : —

Speak Thou, whose massy strength and stature scorn ;

and ll. 11-14 :—

At whose behest uprose on British ground
That Sisterhood, in hieroglyphic round
Forth-shadowing, some have deemed, the infinite
The inviolable God, that tames the proud !

Another Druid circle, more famous in English poetry, is that on the Keswick-Penrith road, about one and a half miles from Keswick, visited by Keats in 1818 and referred to in *Hyperion*, ii. 34-8 : —

A dismal cirque
Of Druid stones, upon a forlorn moor,
When the chill rain begins at shut of eve
In dull November and their chancel vault,
The heaven itself, is blinded throughout night.

ll. 13-16. *Stonehenge . . . cathedrals* edd. 4, 5 : Stones of Shap, or Long Meg and her Daughters, near the banks of the Eden, that a rural chapel bears to our noble cathedrals ed. 3.

l. 20. *destroyed also* edd. 4. 5. Ed. 3 adds the following : — ' It is thus described in the History of Westmorland : —" Towards the south end of the village of Shap, near the turnpike road, on the east side thereof, there is a remarkable monument of antiquity ; which is an area upwards of half a mile in length, and between twenty and thirty yards broad, encompassed with large stones (with which that country abounds), many of them three or four yards in diameter, at eight, ten, or twelve yards distance, which are of such immense weight that no carriage now in use could support them. Undoubtedly this hath been a place of Druid worship, which they always performed in the open air, within this kind of enclosure, shaded with wood, as this place of old time appears to have been, although there is now scarce tree to be seen (*Shapthorn* only excepted, planted on the

top of the hill for the direction of travellers). At the high
end of this place of worship there is a circle of the like stones
about eighteen feet in diameter, which was their *sanctum
sanctorum* (as it were), and place of sacrifice. The stone
is a kind of granite, and when broken appears beautifully
variegated with bright shining spots, like spar. The country
people have blasted and carried away some of these stones,
for the foundation-stones of buildings. In other places some
have cut these stones (but with difficulty), for mill-stones.
When polished they would make beautiful chimney-pieces."
Some contend that this is a Danish monument.'

P. 54, ll. 4–5. *seem at first to have confined* edd. 2–5 : seem
to have confined ed. 1.

ll. 9–10. *choked up as they must have been* edd. 2–5 :·
choked up as they would be ed. 1.

l. 19. (*and to such* edd. 3–5 : (and observe it is to these
edd. 1, 2.

l. 31. *long ago a residence of the Flemings* edd. 2–5 : the
original residence of the Flemings ed. 1.

P. 55, ll. 1–2. *though it also was fashioned, not a little, by its
neighbourhood to a hostile kingdom* edd. 3–5 : though it was
fashioned not a little, with the rest of this country, by its
neighbourhood to a hostile kingdom edd. 1, 2.

P. 57, ll. 4–5. *a population, mainly of Danish or Norse
origin, as the dialect indicates, crept on* edd. 2–5 : population
creeps on ed. 1.

l. 11. *planted, at length* edd. 3–5 : scattered, at length
edd. 1, 2.

ll. 18–19. *dales, from the word* deylen, *to distribute* edd. 2–5:
dales, probably from the Belgic word *deylen* (to distribute) ed. 1.

ll. 27–9. *intersected, as they are, almost to the summit,
with stone walls. When first erected, these stone fences* edd. 4, 5 :
intersected, as they are, almost to the summit with stone walls,
of which the fences are always formed. When first erected,
they ed. 3 : intersected, as they are, almost to their summit,
&c. (as ed. 3) edd. 1, 2.

P. 58, ll. 12–13. *number of ash-trees planted* edd. 3–5 :
number of ash-trees which have been planted edd. 1, 2.

ll. 33–4. *must rapidly have diminished* edd. 3–5 : would
rapidly diminish, edd. 1, 2.

P. 59, ll. 19–20. *would fall into decay, and the places of many
be supplied* edd. 3–5 : would many of them fall into decay,
and wholly disappear, while the place of others was supplied
edd. 1, 2.

COTTAGE AT BUTTERMERE

l. 25. *sixty years* edd. 3–5 : fifty years ed. 2 : forty years ed. 1.

P. 60, ll. 5–6. *Every family spun from its own flock the wool*, &c. Cf. also p. 90, and *Michael*, ll. 80–5.

l. 24. *the native forest* edd. 2–5 : the native forests ed. 1.

l. 29. *native woods* edd. 3–5 : native forest edd. 1, 2.

P. 61, l. 4. *steeper* edd. 2–5 : steepest ed. 1.

l. 8. *The reader's attention has been directed* edd. 3–5 : I have already directed the reader's attention edd. 1, 2.

l. 32. *Cluster'd like stars*, &c. : from Wordsworth's description of Grasmere in the *Recluse : Home at Grasmere*, a MS. poem first published in 1888.

P. 62, l. 4. *the Dwelling or Fire-house, as it is ordinarily called* edd. 4, 5 : the dwelling-house edd. 1–3.

ll. 12–13. *they have received without incongruity additions* edd. 4, 5 : they have received additions edd. 1–3.

ll. 16–19. *these humble dwellings remind the contemplative spectator of a production of Nature, and may . . . rather be said to have grown than to have been erected*, &c. So of a cottage in *Excursion*, vi. 1143–6 :—

> Ye might think
> That it had sprung self-raised from earth, or grown
> Out of the living rock, to be adorned
> By nature only :

The illustration here given of a characteristic Lake country cottage is taken from *Picturesque Sketches of Rustic Scenery* (1815).

ll. 32–3. *the singular beauty of the chimneys.* Cf. *Wordsworthiana : Reminiscences of Wordsworth*, by H. B. Rawnsley : 'Wudsworth was a great un for chimleys, had summut to say in the making of a deal of 'em hereabout. There was 'most all the chimleys Rydal way built after his mind. I 'member he and the Doctor (Mr. Arnold) had great arguments about the chimleys time we was building Foxhow, and Wudsworth sed he liked a bit o' colour in 'em. And that the chimley coigns sud be natural headed and natural bedded, a little red and a little yallar. For there is a bit of colour in the quarry stone up Easedale way. And he'ed a great fancy an 'aw for chimleys square up hauf way, and round the t'other. And so we built 'em that how.'

P. 63, ll. 9–10. *ascending from it through the still air* edd. 4, 5 : through the still air ascending from it edd. 1–3.

ll. 10–11. *These dwellings, mostly built, as has been said, of rough unhewn stone, are roofed with slates* edd. 3–5 : These

188 NOTES

dwellings, as has been said, are built of rough unhewn stone ; and they are roofed with slates edd. 1, 2.

ll. 13–14. *and are, therefore, rough and uneven in their surface, so that both* edd. 2–5 : and the slates are therefore rough and uneven in their surfaces. Both ed. 1.

l. 19. *clothed in part with a vegetable garb* ed. 5 : clothed with this vegetable garb edd. 2–4 : by this vegetable garb with which they are clothed ed. 1.

l. 26. *Add the little garden.* The picture of the cottage garden in *Excursion*, vi, resumes many of the qualities here enumerated :—

> Brought from the woods the honeysuckle twines
> Around the porch, and seems, in that trim place,
> A plant no longer wild ; the cultured rose
> There blossoms, strong in health, and will be soon
> Roof-high ; the wild pink crowns the garden wall,
> And with the flowers are intermingled stones
> Sparry and bright, rough scatterings of the hills.
> . . . . yet hath she,
> Within the garden, like the rest, a bed
> For her own flowers and favourite herbs, a space,
> By sacred charter, holden for her use.
> —These, and whatever else the garden bears
> Of fruit and flower, permission asked or not,
> I freely gather ; and my leisure draws
> A not unfrequent pastime from the hum
> Of bees around their range of sheltered hives
> Busy in that enclosure ; while the rill,
> That sparkling thrids the rocks, attunes his voice
> To the pure course of human life which there
> Flows on in solitude.

(*Excursion*, vi. 1149–55, 1161–72.)

Cf. also the description of Margaret's cottage (*Excursion*, ii. 713–29) with the ' honeysuckle, crowding round the porch ', the ' daisy flowers and thrift', and the ' carnations, once prized for their surpassing beauty '.

ll. 21–2. *will lead him on into* edd. 3–5 : will introduce him, nay will lead him on into edd. 1, 2.

l. 26. *bridges.* The view of Grisedale Bridge, with Place Fell behind it, here given, is taken from Green's *Series of Sixty Small Prints* (1814).

P. 64, l. 4. *sixty years* edd. 3–5 : fifty years ed. 2 : forty years ed. 1.

P. 65, l. 12. *The architecture of the churches . . .* P. 66, l. 10 *these objects*, &c. edd. 2–5 : The lowliness and simple elegance

GRIZEDALE BRIDGE

of these churches and chapels, a well-proportioned oblong
with a porch, in some instances a steeple tower, and in others
nothing more than a small belfry in which one or two bells
hang visibly—these are objects which, &c. ed. 1.
Footnote 1 was added in ed. 4 ; footnote 2 in ed. 3.

P. 67, l. 8. *majestic timber* edd. 4, 5 : In addition to such
objects as have been hitherto described, it may be mentioned
that, as we descend towards the open part of the Vales,
we meet with the remains of ancient Parks, and with old
Mansions of more stately architecture ; and it may be observed that to these circumstances the country owes whatever
ornament it retains of majestic and full-grown timber, as the
remains of the park of the ancient family of the **Ratcliffs**
at Derwent-water, Gowbray-park, and the venerable woods of
Rydal edd. 1–3.

ll. 9–11. *scattered, also, houses of a middle rank between
the pastoral cottage and the old hall residence of the knight or
esquire* edd. 4, 5 : scattered, with more spacious domains
attached to them, houses of a middle rank, between the
pastoral cottage and the old hall-residence of the more
wealthy *Estatesman* edd. 2, 3 : also are scattered houses . . .
hall-residences of the more wealthy estatesman with more
spacious domains attached to them ed. 1.

ll. 11–21. *Such houses . . . unavoidably commands* added
in edd. 4, 5.

l. 25. *sixty* edd. 3–5 : fifty ed. 2 : forty ed. 1.

ll. 26–7. *perfect Republic of Shepherds and Agriculturists.*
On the natural republicanism of the Lake country in Wordsworth's youth, cf. *Prelude*, ix. 215–22.

l. 30. *neighbour* : footnote added in ed. 3.

SECTION THIRD

P. 69, l. 1. *as hath been said* edd. 3–5 : as I have said
edd. 1, 2.

l. 2. *the last sixty years* edd. 3–5 : these last fifty years
ed. 2 : these last forty years ed. 1.

ll. 2–3. *A practice, denominated Ornamental Gardening*
edd. 4, 5 : a practice, by a strange abuse of terms, denominated Ornamental Gardening edd. 2, 3 : a practice which by
a strange abuse of terms has been denominated Ornamental
Gardening ed. 1.

l. 28. *Every reader* . . . P. 70, l. 3 *Grasmere* edd. 2–5 :
The Vale of Grasmere is thus happily discriminated at the

close of his description ed. 1. Cf. Gray's *Journal in the Lakes* (ed. Gosse), i. 266.

P. 70, ll. 10–12. *the Poet . . . take place* edd. 2–5 : the Poet's mind that he had no forebodings of what was so soon to take place ed. 1.

ll. 13–15. *indicating how much the charm of what* was *depended upon what was* not, *would of themselves have preserved* edd. 2–5 : at once the dictate of a sympathetic heart, a pure imagination, and a genuine taste, would almost of themselves have preserved ed. 1.

l. 16. *from trespass* edd. 2–5: from trespass or intrusion ed. 1.

ll. 19–21. *celebrated ; visitors flocked hither from all parts of England ; the fancies of some were smitten so deeply* edd. 2–5 : celebrated ; the mania of ornamental gardening and prospect hunting had spread wide ; visitors flocked hither from all parts of the Island ; the fancies of some of these were so strongly smitten ed. 1.

ll. 21–4. *and the Islands . . . seized upon* added in ed. 2.

l. 24. *and were instantly defaced by the intrusion* edd. 2–5 : and numerous violations soon ensued ed. 1.

P. 70, l. 25–P. 72, l. 23. *The venerable wood . . . plantations in general* edd. 2–5. Not in ed. 1.

P. 70, l. 26. *St. Herbert's Hermitage* : cf. p. 38, and note.

l. 34. *the place of which was* edd. 3–5 : the place of which is ed. 2.

P. 71, l. 4. *they stood* edd. 3–5 : they had stood ed. 2.

ll. 7–8. *an astronomer's observatory* edd. 3–5 : an observatory ed. 2.

P. 72, l. 23. *plantations* (footnote) ed. 5 : plantations (no footnote) edd. 2–4.

ll. 24–8. *But, in truth, no one can now travel through the more frequented tracts, without being offended, at almost every turn, by an introduction of discordant objects, disturbing that peaceful harmony of form and colour* edd. 2–5 : This beautiful country has, in a great variety of instances, suffered from the spirit of tasteless and capricious innovation. No one can now travel through the more frequented tracts, without finding, at almost every turn, the venerable and pure simplicity of nature vitiated by some act of inconsiderate and impertinent art ; without being offended by an introduction of discordant objects, disturbing everywhere that peaceful harmony of form and colour ed. 1.

l. 30. *of this kind* edd. 2–5 : of this kind in matters of taste ed. 1.

ll. 30–1. *originate, doubtless, in* edd. 2–5: originate in ed. 1.

l. 32. *which it receives* edd. 2–5 : which we receive ed. 1.

The bad taste of the ornamental gardening upon the islands of Windermere had already been attacked by Hutchinson (1774), and by West. But that public opinion was in part at least upon the side of the 'improver' of Nature is shown by the fact that the editor of West's Guide (ed. 4) adds a note defending their ingenious changes against West and Hutchinson ' as a considerable accession to the beauties of the lake '. And West himself urged the erection of obelisks and octagonal summer-houses upon the hills, so that they should be ' seen at great distance, and much in sight of the principal roads. . . . But a series of columns constituting a temple, or supporting arches, pediments, &c., would have by much the best effect, provided they were properly large, for the ordinary points of view. Through the openings of these columns, the sky would give them a striking appearance ; but in an evening, if the sun be set behind them, no spectacle of the kind could be imagined more grand and attractive, or more accordant with the sublimity of the surrounding mountains ' (!).

P. 73, ll. 1–2. *objects that are divided from each other by strong lines of* edd. 2–5 : objects between which there exists eternally a strong ed. 1.

l. 3. *the delight* edd. 2–5 : the pleasure ed. 1.

ll. 4–10. *But I would beg . . . their desires* edd. 2–5 : But I would beg of those who, under the control of this craving for distinct ideas, are hastily setting about the production of food by which it may be gratified, to temper their impatience, to look carefully about them, to observe and to watch ; and they will find gradually growing within them a sense by which they will be enabled to perceive in a country so lavishly gifted by nature an ever-renewing variety of forms which will be marked out with a precision that will satisfy their desires ed. 1.

ll. 11. *will be formed opposite to this, arising* edd. 2–5 : will be forming in the mind the opposite of this, viz. a habit arising ed. 1.

ll. 11–13. *the perception of the fine gradations by which in Nature one thing passes away into another.* This was a fundamental principle with Wordsworth. So in his *Essay supplementary to Preface* (1815) he had written, ' In nature everything is distinct, yet nothing defined into absolute independent singleness ' ; and his objection to the larch plantation, on

which he enlarges on pp. 82-8, is based upon the same principle.
Cf. also *To Joanna*, 45–50 :—

> such delight I found
> To note in shrub and tree, in stone and flower,
> That intermixture of delicious hues,
> Along so vast a surface, all at once,
> In one impression, by connecting force
> Of their own beauty, imaged in the heart.

l. 15. *only to be revived elsewhere* edd. 2–5 : only to be renewed in another ed. 1.

ll. 16–18. *The hill of Dunmallet, at the foot of Ullswater, was once divided into different portions by avenues of fir-trees* edd. 2–5 : My meaning will at once be obvious to those who remember the hill of Dunmallet at the foot of Ulswater, divided into different portions, as it once was, by avenues of fir-trees ed. 1.

ll. 20–2. *contrast this quaint appearance with the image of the same hill overgrown with self-planted wood* edd. 2–5 : Who can recal to mind the delight with which they might as children have looked at this quaint appearance ; and are enabled to contrast that remembrance with the pleasure which the more practiced eye of mature age would create for itself from the image of the same hill over-grown with self-planted wood ed. 1.

ll. 32–3. *The disfigurement which this country has undergone has not, however* edd. 3–5 : I cannot, however, omit observing that the disfigurement which this country has undergone, has not edd. 1, 2.

P. 74, ll. 2–3. *a warping of the natural mind occasioned by a consciousness* edd. 2–5 : a constraint or warping of the natural mind arising out of a sense ed. 1.

l. 8. *Persons, who* edd. 3–5 : men, who edd. 1, 2.

ll. 17–18. *rising as they do from* edd. 2–5 : starting as they do on ed. 1.

ll. 20–2. *No man is to be . . . I would show* edd. 2–5 : I do not condemn in any man a desire that his residence and possessions should draw upon them the approbation of the judicious ; nor do I censure attempts to decorate them for that purpose. I rather applaud both the one and the other ; and would shew ed. 1.

l. 36. *Expense to be avoided . . . P. 75, l. 1 may prevent* edd. 2–5 : But should expense to be avoided . . . prevent ed. 1.

P. 75, ll. 4–5. *the thirst for* edd. 2–5 : the craving for ed. 1.

l. 16. *Into that forest farre* : v. Spenser, *Faerie Queene*, ii. 5. 39–40 ; edd. 4, 5 misprint 'puny' for 'pumy' (l. 23).

l. 35-P. 76, l. 1. *Houses or mansions suited to a mountain-ous region, should be* edd. 2-5 : I have been treating of the erection of houses or mansions suited to a grand and beautiful region ; and I have laid it down as a position that they should be ed. 1.

P. 76, ll. 5-6. *as manifested in* edd. 2-5 : as it is exhibited in ed. 1.

ll. 17-18. *the view. It is* edd. 2-5 : the view ; nor are the grand features of nature to be absorbed by the puny efforts of human art. It is ed. 1.

l. 34. *Child of loud-throated war,* &c. The quotation was added in ed. 2. It is from *Address to Kilchurn Castle, upon Loch Awe*, begun in 1803 and finished ' long after ' (published 1827). The poem expresses in the main the same conception as Wordsworth here presents in prose, and uses at times the same phraseology. Thus in the poem the Castle is addressed as the *Vicegerent* of Nature who rules

> Over the pomp and beauty of a scene
> Whose *mountains, torrents, lake,* and woods unite
> To pay thee homage :

But it should be compared as a whole, as an interesting example of the relation of Wordsworth's poetry and prose.

P. 77, ll. 1-7. *To such honours . . . or flat country* edd. 2-5 : These honours render it worthy of its situation ; and to which of these honours can a modern edifice pretend ? Obtruding itself in rivalry with the grandeur of Nature, it only displays the presumption and caprice of its individual founder, or the class to which he belongs. But, in a flat or merely undulating country ed. 1.

P. 78, ll. 16-17. *a safe direction* edd. 2-5 : a safe general direction ed. 1.

P. 79, ll. 4-7. *the objects . . . iron tinge* edd. 2-5 : the objects of which the picture is composed. Where, however, the cold blue tint of the rocks is animated by hues of the iron tinge ed. 1.

ll. 11-15. *The pure blue gravel . . . the builder* edd. 2-5 : But, should the mason object to this, as they will do, and insist upon the mortar being tempered by blue gravel from the bed of the river, and say that the house must be rough-cast, otherwise it cannot be kept dry, then the builder ed. 1.

ll. 22-8. *That white should be . . . produces moral associations* edd. 2-5 : I will therefore say a few words upon this subject ; because many persons, not deficient in taste, are

admirers of this colour for rural residences. The reasons
are manifold ; first, as is obvious, the air of cleanliness and
neatness which is thus given not only to an individual house,
but, where the practice is general, to the whole face of the
country ; which moral associations are ed. 1.

l. 29.   *all others* edd. 3–5 : every other relating to such
objects edd. 1, 2.

COLOURING OF BUILDINGS. On Wordsworth's feeling
for warmth of colour in buildings cf. passage about the colour
of chimneys quoted on p. 187.

P. 80, ll. 11–12.   *with a wilful sacrifice of some higher enjoyments* edd. 2–5 : in the sleep of some of the higher faculties
of the mind ed. 1.

l. 22.   *with the gloom of monastic life* edd. 2–5 : with the
feeling of gloom associated with monastic life ed. 1.

ll. 25–7.   *The objections to white . . . are insurmountable.*
For this same objection to patches of white in a landscape cf.
Wordsworth's *Inscription written with a slate pencil upon a
stone, the largest of a heap lying near a deserted quarry, upon
one of the islands at Rydal,* ll. 25–35 : —

> If thou art one
> On fire with thy impatience to become
> An inmate of these mountains,—if, disturbed
> By beautiful conceptions, thou hast hewn
> Out of the quiet rock the elements
> Of thy trim Mansion destined soon to blaze
> In snow-white splendour,—think again ; and . . . leave
> Thy fragments to the bramble and the rose ;
> There let the venal slow-worm sun himself,
> And let the redbreast hop from stone to stone.

l. 30.   *Gilpin.* William Gilpin (1724–1804), whose *Observations, relative to picturesque beauty, in several parts of England,
particularly to the Mountains and Lakes of Cumberland and Westmoreland,* is here referred to, is among the most interesting and
important of Wordsworth's predecessors in topographical
writing.   A native of Cumberland, he went to school at
Carlisle and St. Bees, and 1740 proceeded to Queen's College,
Oxford, where he spent six or seven years under a system of
teaching ' no better than solemn trifling '.   He took orders,
and became a schoolmaster at Cheam in Surrey, where he
remained for thirty years ; and was famous as an educational
reformer who objected to corporal punishment, encouraged love
of gardening and habits of business, and thought it more use to

the boys to 'study their own language with accuracy than a dead one'. In his summer holidays Gilpin undertook a series of sketching tours : in 1769 and 1773 to Cambridge, Norfolk, and Suffolk ; in 1770 and 1772 to the Wye and South Wales ; in 1776 to Cumberland, Westmorland, and the Highlands. The later publication of books descriptive of his tours brought him a wide reputation, and several of them were translated into both French and German. The first of them to appear, *Observations on the River Wye*, &c., was said to create 'a new class of travels'. In 1777 he was presented to a living in the New Forest, which was his home for the rest of his life. [*Information from the Dict. Nat. Biog.*]

P. 81. Footnote added in ed. 5.

P. 82, ll. 5–6. *management of the grounds and plantations.* The most interesting commentary upon this part of the *Guide* is the letter written by Wordsworth to Sir George Beaumont as to the building and gardening and laying out of grounds at Coleorton. It will be found at pp. 139–45 of this volume.

l. 31. *other deciduous trees* edd. 2–5 : other native deciduous trees ed. 1.

l. 34. *liable to injury* ed. 2–5 : liable to the injuries which I have mentioned ed. 1.

ll. 35–6. *But the circumstances . . . taste* edd. 3–5 : But there are many whose circumstances permit them, and whose taste edd. 1, 2.

P. 83, ll. 16–17. *Before I proceed . . . not satisfied* edd. 3–5 : Before I proceed with this subject, I will prepare my way with a remark of general application, by reminding those who are not satisfied edd. 1, 2.

ll. 21–2. *emphatically acknowledged* edd. 2–5 : emphatically and conspicuously acknowledged ed. 1.

l. 27. *Having adverted to the feelings* edd. 3–5: But to return :—having adverted to the considerations edd. 1, 2.

P. 84, l. 10. *such as are natives of the country* ed. 2–5 : such as are natives of the country, oak, ash, birch, mountain ash, &c., &c. ed. 1.

ll. 15–21. *The Scotch fir . . . both these trees* edd. 4, 5 : Sycamore and the Scotch fir (which, when it has room to spread out its arms, is a noble tree) may be placed with advantage near the house ; for, from their massiveness, they edd. 1–3.

It is worth noting that the fir and sycamore, here recommended by Wordsworth, are the trees most often found near the cottages. Cf. p. 63 and note.

P. 85, ll. 6–7. *the soil and situation upon which they fall are* edd. 3–5 : the soil upon which they fall is edd. 1, 2.

ll. 9–11. *animals (which Nature . . .), thrives* edd. 4, 5 : animals, thrives edd. 1–3.

ll. 34–5. *Contrast the liberty . . . with* edd. 2–5 : Contrast the liberty and law under which this is carried on, as a joint work of nature and time, with ed. 1.

P. 86, l. 3. *qualified for his task* edd. 2–5 : qualified to tread in the path of nature ed. 1.

l. 6. *this necessity* edd. 3–5 : this circumstance edd. 1, 2.

l. 9. *and appears* edd. 2–5 : and which appears ed. 1.

l. 20. *we shall look in vain . . . natural wood* edd. 2–5 : an absolute and insurmountable obstacle will prevent the realization of any of those appearances which we have described as the chief cause of the beauty of a natural wood ed. 1.

ll. 35–6. *wherever it . . . is produced* edd. 2–5 : it makes a speck and deformity in the landscape ed. 1.

P. 87, ll. 1–5. *in autumn . . . absolutely dead* edd. 2–5 : in winter appears absolutely dead. In this respect it is lamentably distinguished from every other tree of the forest ed. 1.

ll. 10–12. *The terminating spike . . . should ever* edd. 3–5 : The spike, in which it terminates, renders it impossible, when it is planted in numbers, that the several trees should ever edd. 1, 2.

P. 88, l. 3. *ornament merely* edd. 2–5 : ornament mainly ed. 1.

l. 8. *highest and most barren* edd. 2–5 : higher and more barren ed. 1.

ll. 18–19. *if my limits . . . overstepped* edd. 3–5 : if I had not already overstepped my limits edd. 1, 2.

ll. 24–5. *those found in* edd. 2–5 : those which form ed. 1.

P. 89, l. 5. *'Many hearts deplored,* &c. edd. 2–5 : ' Many hearts,' says a living Poet speaking of a noble wood which had been felled in an interesting situation ;—many hearts deplored ed. 1. The quotation is from the Sonnet, *Degenerate Douglas,* &c. (composed 1803).

P. 90, ll. 5–6. *The author has been induced . . . by a wish* edd. 4, 5 : I have been induced . . . by a wish ed. 3 : I have been induced . . . with a wish edd. 1, 2.

l. 28. *has been cut off* edd. 3–5 : has been wholly cut off ed. 2 : has been almost wholly cut off ed. 1. With this passage cf. *Excursion,* viii. 251–333.

P. 91, l. 13. *that proprietors and farmers being* edd. 3–5 : that farmers being edd. 1, 2.

ll. 22-3. *graces that grew out of them* edd. 2-5: graces which grew out of them and around them ed. 1.

ll. 23-4. *tenure under which the estates are held* edd. 2-5: tenure of these estates ed. 1.

ll. 28-9. *the country on the margin of the Lakes* edd. 2-5; the country of the Lakes ed. 1.

P. 92, l. 7. *heart to enjoy* edd. 2-5. Ed. 1 adds: ' The Writer may now express a hope that the end, which was proposed in the commencement of this Introduction, has not been wholly unattained, and that there is no impropriety in connecting these latter remarks with the Etchings now offered to the public. For it is certain that, if the evil complained of should continue to spread, these Vales, notwithstanding their lakes, rivers, torrents and surrounding rocks and mountains, will lose their chief recommendation for the eye of the painter and the man of imagination and feeling. And, upon the present occasion, the Artist is bound to acknowledge that, if the fruit of his labours have any value, it is owing entirely to the models which he has had before him, in a country which retained till lately an appearance unimpaired of Man and Nature animated, as it were, by one spirit for the production of beauty, grace and grandeur.' (The End.)

MISCELLANEOUS OBSERVATIONS.

P. 93. *Miscellaneous Observations* edd. 3-5; no heading in ed. 2. Section I. Of the best time for visiting the Lakes ed. 1.

ll. 1-3. *Mr. West... the interval* edd. 3-5: A few words may not improperly be annexed, with an especial view to promote the enjoyment of the Tourist. And first, in respect to the time when this country can be seen to most advantage. Mr. West, in his well-known Guide to the Lakes, recommends the interval ed. 2: In the Introduction to this work a survey has been given of the face of the country, in which our English Lakes are situated, which will not perhaps prove unserviceable even to Natives and Residents, however well acquainted with its appearance: as it will probably direct their attention to some objects which they have overlooked, and will exhibit others under relations of which they have been unconscious. I will now address myself more particularly to the Stranger and the Traveller; and, without attempting to give a formal tour through the country, and without binding myself servilely to accompany the Etchings, I will attach to the work such directions, descriptions and remarks, as I hope will confer an additional interest upon the Views, and will also be of use to a person preparing for a first visit to these scenes, and during his progress through them. To begin then with the time which he ought to choose :— Mr. West recommends the interval ed. 1.

ll. 5–6. *being a time . . . resort hither* edd. 3–5 : being a season of vacation and leisure, it is almost exclusively in these that strangers visit the country ed. 2 : being a season of vacation and leisure, are those which are generally selected ed. 1.

l. 7. *But that season* edd. 2–5 : but they are ed. 1.

ll. 7–8. *the colouring . . . unvaried a green* edd. 3–5 : there is a want of variety in the colouring of the mountains and woods, which, unless where they are diversified by rocks, are of a monotonous green ed. 2 : for the disadvantages belonging to them are many and great. The principal are, the monotonous green of the Mountains and of the Woods ed. 1.

ll. 10–12. *and, as a large . . . there also* edd. 2–5 : and the embrowned colour of the grass in the Vallies ed. 1.

l. 12. *The meadows, however, are* edd. 2–5 : This, however, is ed. 1.

l. 15. *A stronger objection* edd. 2–5 : An objection which will be more strongly felt ed. 1.

l. 18. *of those deluges* edd. 2–5 : of the wet season between the Tropics, or of those deluges ed. 1.

l. 20. *supply of the Nile. The months* edd. 2–5 : supply of the Nile. Hence, as a very large majority of strangers visit the Lakes at this season, the country labours under the ill repute of being scarcely ever free from rain. The months ed. 1.

l. 27. *Nevertheless, to the sincere* edd. 2–5 : Nevertheless the beauty of this country in Autumn so far surpasses that of Midsummer, that to the sincere ed. 1.

P. 94, l. 11. *an admirable compass* edd. 2–5 ; an admirable and affecting compass ed. 1.

l. 12. *harmony in colour* edd. 3–5 : harmony in form and colour edd. 1, 2.

ll. 25–7. *the space between . . . may be pointed out as* edd. 4, 5 : I would recommend the space between . . . as edd. 1–4.

ll. 35–6. *copses are interveined* edd. 2–5 : copses are variegated ed. 1. Cf. *To Joanna*, 38–40.

P. 95, l. 2. *the spring-flowers* edd. 2–5 : the earlier spring-flowers ed. 1.

ll. 9-13. *the birds of prey . . . the cause why, in the narrow valleys, there are no skylarks.* It is interesting to notice that Gray, in his *Journal in the Lakes* (ed. Gosse, i. 268), makes the same observation. On leaving Kendal he writes :—
' Oct. 9.—All corn off the ground ; skylarks singing aloud (by the way I saw not one at Keswick, perhaps because the place abounds in birds of prey).' In ed. 1 Wordsworth had omitted the word ' probably'.

ll. 16-17. *It is not often that the nightingale resorts to these vales* edd. 2-5 : Neither are nightingales here to be heard ed. 1. This significant change suggests that between 1810 and 1820, Wordsworth had heard the nightingale at Grasmere ; but, as Mr. Warde Fowler has pointed out to me, all the authority of naturalists is against him. In *The Birds of Lancashire* (F. S. Mitchell, 1892), the nightingale is not included in the list of birds, though in the introduction it is mentioned as a possible occasional visitor ; in Macpherson's *Fauna of Lakeland*, the standard authority, the nightingale is not even mentioned. It is usual to say that the bird is not found north or west of a line drawn between the mouth of the Humber and Start Point in S. Devon. It is noteworthy that Wordsworth's poem to the Nightingale was written at Coleorton.

ll. 22-3. *have the compass . . . accordingly* edd. 2-5 : have much more power over the heart and the imagination than in other places ed. 1.

ll. 23-5. *an imaginative influence of the voice of the cuckoo, when that voice has taken possession of a deep mountain valley* : cf. Wordsworth's poem, *Yes, it was the mountain echo . . .* which the poet annotated : ' The Echo came from Nabscar, when I was walking on the opposite side of Rydal Mere. I will here mention, for my dear sister's sake, that while she was sitting alone one day, high up on this part of Loughrigg Fell, she was so affected by the voice of the cuckoo, heard from the crags at some distance, that she could not suppress a wish to have a stone inscribed with her name among the rocks from which the sound proceeded.'

ll. 27-8. *Nor must . . . omitted* edd. 2-5 : Nor must I omit ed. 1.

l. 31. *The herbage . . . as it springs* edd. 2-5 : The springing herbage ed. 1.

P. 96, l. 2. *These sportive creatures, as* edd. 2-5 : which, as ed. 1.

l. 6. *rocks and lawns, upon which* edd. 2-5 : lawns and rocks, upon and among which ed. 1.

ll. 7-10. *And last ... smaller inns* edd. 2-5 : But, what is of most consequence, the Traveller at this season would be almost sure of having fine weather.   The opinion which I have given concerning the comparative advantages of the different times for visiting these Lakes, is founded upon a long acquaintance with the country, and an intimate knowledge of its appearance at all seasons ed. 1.

ll. 10-12. *those who may be inclined ... able to do so* edd. 2-5 : those, who may be satisfied with the reasons, by which this opinion is supported, will be able to profit from what has been said ed. 1.

l. 17. *liable to many objections* edd. 2-5: liable to the objections which have been mentioned ed. 1.

it often happens edd. 3-5 : it not unfrequently happens edd. 1, 2.

ll. 20-1. *their utmost sublimity* edd. 2-5 : their height of sublimity ed. 1.

ll. 27-8. *Insensible must he be who would not* edd. 2-5 : and he would ed. 1.

ll. 32-5. *At such a time ... hot days* edd. 2-5 : At such a time the monotony of midsummer colouring and the want of variety caused by this, and by the glaring atmosphere of long cloudless and hot days, is wholly removed ed. 1.

l. 36. *Thus far concerning ... P. 100, l. 33 those of Switzerland* not in ed. 1.   Wordsworth, it will be remembered, visited Switzerland in 1820.

Thus far concerning ... P. 97, l. 1 seasons ed. 5 : Thus far respecting the most eligible season edd. 2-4.

P. 97, ll. 5-6. *it follows, that it will* edd. 3-5 : it follows from the nature of things that it will ed. 2.

P. 98, ll. 3-15. *A stranger ... should be taken* edd. 3-5 : desunt ed. 2.

l. 19. *a few words* edd. 3-5 : a concluding word ed. 2.

l. 33. *apparent ... agitated* edd. 3-5 : apparent where even it is unagitated ed. 2.   On the comparison between the waterfalls of the English Lakes and Switzerland, cf. also Wordsworth's note on *The Forsaken*, where he says :—' The natural imagery of these views was supplied by frequent, I might say intense, observation of the Rydal Torrent.   What an animating contrast is the ever-changing of that, and indeed of every one of our mountain brooks, to the monotonous tone and unmitigated fury of such streams among the Alps as are fed all the summer long by glaciers and melting snows ! '

P. 99, l. 15. *While the coarse rushes, &c.*: quoted from the

Ode, *Pass of Kirkstone*, given in full on pp. 129–31. With the paragraph which follows, cf. Wordsworth's poem *The Simplon Pass*.

P. 100, ll. 9–15. *In other instances . . . observed that* added in ed. 4. For the beautiful phrase ' breath of the precipitous water', *v.* the I. F. note to *Lines written in Early Spring*, describing a waterfall at Alfoxden :—' Across the pool below had fallen a tree, from which rose perpendicular boughs in search of the light intercepted by the deep shade above . . . from the under side of this natural sylvan bridge depended long and beautiful tresses of ivy, which waved gently in the breeze that might poetically be called the breath of the waterfall.'

ll. 21–4. *The beauty . . . peculiar manner* edd. 3–5 : Peculiarly also is the beauty of such a scene, where there is naturally so much agitation, heightened ed. 2.

ll. 28–9. *A happy proportion* edd. 3–5 : I will conclude with observing that a happy proportion ed. 2.

l. 33. *those of Switzerland.* Ed. 2 ends here.

P. 102, ll. 6–8. *a certain point of elevation . . . the sense* ed. 5 : a certain point, the sense edd. 3, 4. This addition to ed. 5 affords an interesting example of Wordsworth's desire for accuracy. In a letter to G. H. Gordon, Esq., dated Dec. 15, 1828, he had written :—' In the book on the Lakes, which I have not at hand, is a passage rather too vaguely expressed, where I content myself with saying, that after a certain point of elevation the effect of mountains depends much more upon their form than upon their absolute height. This point, which ought to have been defined, is the one to which fleecy clouds (not their watery vapours) are accustomed to descend.'

l. 13. *magnifying and softening powers* edd. 4, 5 : magnifying powers ed. 3.

ll. 22–4. *do indeed agreeably unite . . . or make* edd. 4, 5 : do indeed make ed. 3.

P. 104, l. 33. *In fact the sunshine . . . P. 106, l. 8 Lowther, and Rydal do at this day* added in ed. 4. Prof. Knight notes that the quotation from Lucretius occurs in *de Rerum Naturae*, v. 1370–8.

P. 105, l. 22. *hoariness of hue*: cf. *Hamlet*, iv. 7. 166–8 :—

> There is a willow grows aslant a brook,
> That shows his hoar leaves in the glassy stream.

P. 106, l. 17. *agitation from the winds.* The footnote, with the quotation from Landor, *Idyllia Heroica Decem*, was added in ed. 4.

P. 108, l. 23. *Lyulph's Tower*: cf. Wordsworth's poem *The Somnambulist*.

P. 112. *EXCURSIONS, &c.*, heading added in ed. 4.

P. 114, l. 22. *celestial liquid* edd. 4, 5 : celestial beverage ed. 3.

P. 116, ll. 21-4. *Afterwards . . . pass away* ed. 3 : Afterwards we had the storm, which exhibited the grandeur of the earth and heavens commingled ; yet without terror. We knew that it would pass away edd. 1, 2.

l. 28. *Scawfell and Helvellyn . . .* P. 128, l. 30 *midnight* added in ed. 4.

P. 117, l. 1. *To* —— ; written 1816, and first published 1820. The lady was Miss Blackett, then residing with Mr. Montague Burgoyne at Fox Ghyll. The reading 'coral' in l. 27 is a change made by Wordsworth for the original 'choral'.

P. 118, l. 9. *points of view* ed. 5 : a point of view ed. 4.

This account of an excursion to Ullswater is a revised form of Dorothy Wordsworth's Journal, Nov. 7-13, 1805. The two versions may be compared throughout with great interest. The Journal opens thus :—

'*Wednesday, Nov. 7.* On a damp and gloomy morning we set forward, William on foot, and I upon the pony, with William's greatcoat slung over the saddle crutch, and a wallet containing our bundle of "needments". As we went along the mist gathered upon the valleys, and it even rained all the way to the head of Patterdale ; but there was never a drop upon my habit larger than the smallest pearls upon a lady's ring. The trees of the larger island upon Rydale Lake were of the most gorgeous colours ; the whole island reflected in the water, as I remember once in particular to have seen it with dear Coleridge, when either he or William observed that the rocky shore, spotted and streaked with purplish brown heath, and its image in the water, together were like an immense caterpillar, such as, when we were children, we used to call *Woolly Boys*, from their hairy coats. . . . As the mist thickened, our enjoyments increased, and my hopes grew bolder ; and when we were at the top of Kirkstone (though we could not see fifty yards before us) we were as happy travellers as ever paced side by side on a holiday ramble. At such a time and in such a place every scattered stone the size of one's head becomes a companion,' &c., &c.

The illustration here given of Ullswater Head is taken from Green's *Series of Sixty Small Prints* (1814).

ULLESWATER HEAD

P. 120, ll. 8-9. *the only part of the country where goats
are now found.* In 1835 Wordsworth was obliged to append a
note to the passage : ' A.D. 1805. These also have disappeared.'
But they were familiar to the Wanderer in the *Excursion*
as still inhabiting the mountains. Cp. *Excursion,* iv. 499.

P. 121, ll. 20-1. *white dog, lying in the moonshine* : a picture
which evidently suggested to Wordsworth his description
(written two years afterwards, 1807) of the White Doe in the
garden at Rylstone (cf. *White Doe of Rylstone,* 938–1010).
Wordsworth's reference to the scene as ' Ossianic ' is strange
and unexpected. ' The torrents . . . they were there ' has no
counterpart in the *Journal.* The quotation is from *Excursion,*
ii. 871 : ' I saw not, but I felt that it was there.'

P. 122, l. 5. *the iron tone of the raven's voice* : cf. *Excursion,*
iv. 1177-81 :—

> Within the circuit of this fabric huge
> One voice—the solitary raven, flying
> Athwart the concave of the dark blue dome, . . .
> An *iron knell.*

P. 128, l. 30. *The following verses,* &c. . . . P. 131, end: added
in ed. 5. *The Pass of Kirkstone* was written in 1817, and first
published in 1820. ' Thoughts and feelings of many walks
in all weathers, by day and night, over this Pass, alone and
with beloved friends ' (I. F. note). In ed. 5 is an unfortunate
misprint in l. 19 of the Ode, ' raised ' for ' razed '.

INDEX

212 INDEX